THE YOUNG AMERICAN POETS

Congratulations on an excellent Poetry Book of your own! I hope you will continue to develop your interest and ability in Poetry.

Regina Denton

THE YOUNG AMERICAN POETS

A BIG TABLE BOOK

Edited By Paul Carroll

Introduction By James Dickey

Big Table Publishing Company
Chicago

Library of Congress Catalog Card Number: 68-18505

ISBN 0-695-89873-6 paper binding

ISBN 0-695-89874-4 cloth binding

First printing June, 1968
Second printing October, 1968
Third printing June, 1969
Fourth printing June, 1970

CONTENTS

6   *Contents*

THE SON, THE CAVE, AND THE BURNING BUSH

By James Dickey

"Young poet" is a term that enjoys a particular favor. Everyone who cares about poetry hopes that each young or new poet to appear on the scene may be the one to bring forth the whole magnificent potential of poetry and lay it on the page, and thus realize the promise that poetry makes in age after age but seldom succeeds in keeping. This is the promise to bring the reader to the place where the flame breaks forth from the pit and the gods speak from the burning bush, lifting human words from their mereness, out of the range of teachable amenities and into the realm of salvation, redemption and rebirth. Such is the promise of the 54 young American poets collected in this anthology.

For a middleaged poet like myself this promise takes on a particularly acute anguish of hope. In fact, the potential of the poems represented here is more exciting to an older poet than it is, possibly, for anyone but the young poets themselves. The aging process almost always brings to the poet the secret conviction that he has settled for far too little, that he has paid too much attention to the "limitations" that his contemporaries have assured him he has, as well as to literary tradition and the past. He believes that either he has given unnecessary attention to these things or that he has not learned to get the most out of them. The nearer he gets to his end the more he yearns for the cave: for a wild, shaggy, all-out, all-involving way of speaking where language and he (or, now, someone: some new poet) engage each other at primitive levels, on ground where the issues are not those of literary fashion but are quite literally those of life and death. All his lifelong struggle with "craft" seems a tragic and ludicrous waste of time; and he looks on the productions of the whole history of literature—indeed, of all human communication and expression—as so much self-indulgent and irrelevant chatter in the unspeaking and accusing face of what *could* be said, if someone had the luck, the vision and the guts.

It is a sad dream; but one that gathers force. The young or new poet, like the son real or imagined, holds out the prospect of hope, of that kind of engagement with language that older poets feel they have—with the best will in the world, with much toil and conscientiousness—betrayed. Teaching the "craft of verse" for years, as many of our older and middle generation of American poets have done, only increases the irrational longing for the unwritten and perhaps unwritable poem. Anyone who cares for poetry enough to write and teach it all his life wants it to be capable of more than he has ever been able to make poetry do: more than has ever been dreamed of in the seminar's philosophy. What he wants to hear is nothing less than the poetry of the burning bush. If he lives long enough, the poet comes to believe in the rarest of possibilities that, once seen, no longer seems rare but simply a miracle—something like the cave man's identification of the red deer on the wall of the cave with the one miles away on the plain. The older poet looks for signs beyond those that have been given, and certainly beyond those that he has been able to give. He looks to the new poets.

And so, when a writer of my age picks up an anthology like this, it is with the feeling: "Maybe it is here." Most of these poets are young, and all of them are comparatively new, insofar as academic or beer-hall discussion, anthologies, publication and reputation are concerned. But it seems to me that almost all of them have the kind of vitality, linguistic and physical, that is as exciting as anything in poetry can be, save the Poetry of the Impossible: the burning bush itself.

The enormous variety of these 54 poets is not *just* variety. It is a kind of variety with significance: for the conformity of sensibility that has overlain and undermined poetry in the English language since Pound and Eliot is gone. The withdrawnness and the literarily connoisseurish stance—the poet waiting in the crafty lair of his sensibility poring over books for his ideas—is not much in evidence here among these young poets. Their poems are not merely reworkings of known and established forms; they are personal explorations for which, most of the time, there is no precedent. For this reason a good many of them may seem somewhat rough-edged or ragged and even on occasion naive: the smoothness of the poem in which all the chinks have been carefully filled in is notably absent. But at the stage of things where we now are in American poetry, too much smoothness is suspect, and the carpentered poem is slowly becoming synonymous with the predictable and inconsequential one. The techniques of these poets vary a good deal, as they should, but what ought to be noted is that there is a new and refreshing concentration on content as well: here, the "what" matters as much as the "how," and in some cases more. Turning the pages of this book, one muses and drops back into the kind of revery that may produce everything or nothing. Could the voice that spoke to Moses have benefitted from a course in Modern Rhetoric? And what if Dylan Thomas had gone to school in a writers' workshop in an American university to learn how to write poetry?

And yet technique matters, even so. God uses it, for a buffalo is not a leopard; as my grandmother used to say, "He is made different." God and the angels use technique, only it is better than ours, and operates on better materials. The divine technique is both consummate technique that no one has ever heard of, and beyond all considerations of technique. All roads are long, as Allen Tate says, and in the end they lead to the problem of form. The poets in this book are working on, around and through the problem of form; and it should be obvious from a look through these pages—a flipping, even—that some of them appear to have wandered into old or dead-end streets. For example, there are some attempts here at the kind of calculated boldness that one associates with the experimentalism of the 1920s. On the other hand, a few of them have tried to write rather complacent formal exercises in rhyme and regular meter that show into what a mortuary a misunderstood classicism can lead poems. And it is of course possible that the huge and ghostly figures of Eliot and Pound may hover around many of these poems in ways that the poets would be the last to suspect (and not as entirely baleful influences, either, for one must not forget the very real value of their examples). But the important thing to note is that the writers in this anthology are attempting in a new way to speak with as much real boldness as they can summon of passion and involvement, rather than in the distant and learnedly disdainful tone of Eliot or with the manic scholarliness of Pound.

Most of these poets do not seem to be as informed or well-read as some of the best poets who immediately preceded them. Not one of them has the sheer amount of information that Randall Jarrell had when he began writing, nor the grasp of European history that Robert Lowell had, nor the knowledge of prosody with which Karl Shapiro or John Berryman began, nor Auden's spectacular ability to generalize. Auden and Jarrell, like the fox of the Russian fable, know many things; but each of these poets, like the hedgehog of the same fable, feel that he knows one *big* thing: what it is to *be*, in a particular skin and at a particular time and place; and what it is like to respond with directness and passion, beyond or to the side of established literary precedent. Sometimes this happens with an earthiness and vulgarity that probably would have caused Mr. Eliot to shudder. But the too-close world of sweat and sperm and yelling and drunkenness, the precarious realm of betrayal and that of true and deep encounters between human beings is always with us, is always possible, with or without archetypal significations and symbolical precedents, and that is where most of these poets are living and writing.

I have no wish to talk about "schools" or movements, real or fancied. It is enough for me that this anthology gives a various and exciting voice to a poetic generation that insists on its full right to its human responses, as well as on its right to make mistakes, and above all on its right to fly in the face of the graduate-school's well-documented notion of what is "proper" and of what is commonly designated "literature." These poems seem to me to be evidence that imposed styles are not, finally, the shapers of the sensibilities of men. Such styles may appear to be so for a while, and sometimes for a long while. But in the end the animal responsiveness of individuals breaks through. This is what saves poetry from itself and from its practitioners and theorists; this is what creates change and makes of poetry a fluid and volatile condition where anything can happen.

And if the Voice from the Bush is not here (and it may be, subject only to the discovery of Time) it is not the fault of these poets. Such clearness and passion as theirs has not been heard in a long time, in our land and in our language. If the Lost Son with the Angel's tongue does not dwell in these pages, let us regret it doubly, for some of these lines hint how he might speak. These young American poets are with and *in* human experience as poets have not been for a very long time.

DEDICATION

This anthology is dedicated to that young poet who happens to come upon it in some bookstore or in the apartment of a fellow poet and who may feel hurt or angry because he wasn't invited to submit work and be included among his contemporaries. The omission of invitation was not intentional. Requests for poems were sent to every young poet—some 300 in all—who was recommended either by an older poet or one of the young poets or by a poem I read in one of the quarterlies or little magazines. If in a few years from now it seems a service to the literary community to publish a second selection of *The Young American Poets* devoted to work by poets not represented in this collection, I hope to have the chance to read your poems and if I have sense enough I will include some of them among the poems of your contemporaries. In the meantime, may I wish you delight and truth and success in your writing.

NOTE ABOUT THE SELECTION

Almost every editor of an anthology must struggle with the tough question: Should the book be devoted to the maximum number of pages for work by a handful of the best poets? or should a broader selection of good poets be made with less space available for each writer? Happily, the poets themselves made the problem largely irrelevant for this anthology. The poetic generation to which they belong is still in the exciting phase of being defined. Although some of the poets in this collection will obviously become leaders of their generation I doubt if anyone knows which poet will develop in important and influential directions or which will fizzle out and end either in sterile silence or in boring imitations of his younger self or his more recognized contemporaries. Most of all, nobody knows which of these poets may expand into a major writer. Largely because this generation is still brand new, then, the problem of selection became in one sense simple: Include only those poets who seem genuine and exciting; and include only those poems or that one poem by each writer which you admire without reservation. After I had made the final choice to include the 54 young poets represented in this collection, the range of their achievement seemed so various, stimulating, technically interesting or at least competent, and so often more good-humored or witty than previous generations of American poets, that I found myself at odds with the wise and wry observation which the young William Butler Yeats offered one evening in The Cheshire Cheese to his fellow young poets in the Rhymers Club: "None of us can say who will succeed, or even who has or has not talent. The only thing certain about us is that we are too many." Clearly the first point applies to any generation of young poets; but the next two hardly apply, in my opinion, to the 54 young poets in this book.

Regarding the exclusion of several well-known younger poets: Since the purpose of this anthology is to introduce work by young poets largely unknown at this stage, I decided not to include such celebrated young poets as John Wieners or David Meltzer. To have included their poems would have given more comprehensive definition to the generation represented in this book but room could have been found only by excluding other poets whose works I admire. Such exclusion seemed unfair: to become known as a poet is hard enough as it is. Regarding the absence of two famous younger poets: Invitations to submit poems and be included among their contemporaries were sent to Bob Dylan and Ed Sanders. In fact, both were invited twice. Neither poet replied. The absence of Dylan seems particularly unfortunate: in the purity of his tenderness and anger and in the authority of his imagination he is one of the best poets of his generation. Regarding eligibility determined by age: Originally, the age limit was 30 years; as I came to know work by the twelve poets in their early 30s now included, however, I realized that it would be foolish to sacrifice such poems for the sake of an arbitrary nativity date; still, an age limitation had to be set if this anthology was to fulfil its purpose and since good but as yet unrecognized poets now in their late 30s or early 40s belong to an earlier generation I chose 35 as the maximum age for eligibility.

A final word: To that reader who may wish that there had been more poems by a writer whom he likes, may I say that I've often felt much the same when reading an anthology; and I can only hope that the work of the young poet you've read here will encourage you to buy all of his future books.

—*Paul Carroll*

TIC

Here, I stood by the pole, while, before, I had stood by the water and, also, by the law. There, you sat by the bird and by the judge, and, as well, by the person posing. In place, he lay by the valley; soon he will lie by the motives, but now, if anywhere else, he lay by the country. In position, she settled down by the cake by the gaze. In such and such surroundings, by the play, they folded their arms by the paper.

Suddenly, things are poles apart, as already something has made my mouth water and the law has been laid down hard. All at once, the bird is in your hand, while the judge in boarding a ship hears the case and the person poses a question. At the same instant, the valley dips and hollows, it becomes drained, before the motives are about to drive him, and even now the country has a side, it is wide, it dances. Promptly, the cake comes out of a mixture of flour, sugar, the eggs are beaten, the milk stirred, when the gaze grows intent upon her. Without warning, as soon as both ends are played against the middle and played into their hands, the arms are taken up and, open, receive them, the paper cut and hanging and at work.

By this time, I am running with the vine, the stocking, the faucet, the story, the eyes, the fence, the days, the family lines, having already run with the train and the breeze and the thoughts and the price. At this, you are walking with the hour and the baseball player, and, not stopping with that, with the basketball player, and walking on with the beam, and on with the papers, and walking on and on with the fern, too, the stick, too, the delegate, too. By now, he is flying with the colors and all the way with the buttress, the Dutchman, and once this motion is passed he will fly with the sheet, moreover, and with the trap, moreover,

though, when he flies at this time, he still is flying away
with the column, and, also, with the saucer, also, with the
start. In the same breath, she is sliding with the pond, then
with the scale, then with the trombone, then with the rule.
At the same time, with the kitchen, they are sinking with
the voice, and they keep on doing that with the lake and,
further, with the cost. In time, you are plural, you, too, are
walking with the hour again and with the hour you walk
away, you are shuffling with the deceiver, again, with the
board, again, with the cards . . . In all, we are leaping with
the frog that, in turn, is leaping with the year that, in turn,
is jumping off.

RE

(here)(   )(   )
(   )(there)(   )
(   )(   )(here and there—I say here)
(   )(I do not say now)(   )
(I do not say it now)(   )(   )
(   )(then and there—I say there)(   )
(   )(   )(say there)
(   )(I do not say then)(   )
(I do not say, then, this)(   )(   )
(   )(then I say)(   )
(   )(   )(here and there)
(   )(first here)(   )
(I said here second)(   )(   )
(   )(I do not talk first)(   )
(   )(   )(there then)
(   )(here goes)(   )
(I do not say what goes)(   )(   )
(   )(I do not go on saying)(   )
(   )(   )(   )(there is)

(   )(that is not to say)(   )
(I do not say that)(   )(   )
(   )(here below)(   )
(   )(   )(I do not talk down)
(   )(under my words)(   )
(under discussion)(   )(   )
(   )(all there)(   )
(   )(   )(I do not say all)
(   )(   )(all I say)(   )

KAY PRICE AND STELLA PAJUNAS

5

black gain a whit (e;)   (jetty):(a color again
            -st(op)(down)
un(done)to fasten(up)a skirt as quickly
what(*I don't like to talk*)about   (the paper bent
(into)a blond (de)rived)
                            of, in, around
(where)I talk down(while)upon it   (*two walks
a pout* her luck)   (SICK
LAWYER:thus the woman far out un(rolls)(really)a
tobacco wound . . . no doubt some(thing)(ells)
                                    (an arm's
length in the DAY   JURY . . .   "The least, one
can off"

58

With two sleeps dropped, one's
"able to put off the head" at one's
head 1 2 3 4 day's

times(over the color under what would
((be the ranged heat))under the collar
for a spy) — to take it tall — two have
(the law on)
one's frontal lobotomy, (one)back-

8

(wards) — (swivel-
eyed)(mope-eyed)   Correct: "I see
through a glass, barking: 'The bark
glazed through a sea' "("I was

86

caught in my favor till pneumonia")The
woman let he(jetted
what else he had down
a shirt):   present(ence?)(in hurt walks I
high I mean)(the pout her lands)(the can in
the bay I can't know at bay)"Not a white

680

rate"/not
"Knotting the sail-
or"/not even the ink, though

68

even, pronounced a lit something
behind   (the two-) back
"O" wound(-)up to "rose" around

her letters of surprise HERE:LETTERS OF SUNRISE
   (after the (*sic*)-best poet(h))("after
       the largest in
       the largest number((is
able))to sleep the can

    102

    off"(from the first-bet
    language)(the long furs beat((the tongue's be
       blond's))(b)
        bent((ELON-GATE!DOORS . . .))

2

LOCK:floccipaunihilipilification:head-
                         (/)
edmouthlivelongsuggestinglyslawtoucancannonslipping

      312

      (longe:to a railroad)(mouthful:in the head-
               man) A(t)   B(in)   C de-
leted he took the/burial service to Oulu and then
                  lighted the dirt-
     y la/dy to bed with a shovel/

   213

              caw, a mouth gesture
      sheet simplification
        fact, ahead slip)

(a flock specific
/to be(near)(about)
its entrance(it)and ex-its(that is,

12

"to argue on the print(er)left(in)by
the page be-

neath" or that henceforth the thing is
the other

strikes arrest")

(the look-out in)
hence, for the function of "tick"

204

here it changes to "glass"
("clangs")

205

here, a fish-
erman's battery"(I can bat in
another place where the far-
ina woman walks mean)
812look be-
hind, here, "toe rubber"

29   92

here-"tic"   here "unction"

974

"I am he(re)
that drops letters(he banks; he banked; he was
banked; he can, will, might,, may bank;((can
he be banked on?)); he has been
banked; he will be, have been, banked((it is not the on-

74

ly "he"))((as were his bin, his can for your
thing that was, she was more than he))
)*I look here*
across the line crossing the look-out and my eyes moo —"

67

(lied)Rather(it ran also),
looking out I cross the line(mine)
to cross my eyes(lies too)lying
(LAYING)as being so as that line before or as tearing(on behalf)up
the sentence(f)(law)/but not pro-

507

nounced, above(bounced), as

410

(has)to the LINE OF RAISINS YOU
     MIGHT EXPLAIN ON YOUR FOREHEAD/but
(as)here(you)hear 'Knot the pronouns,
be(they)four at best, as a best

71

lie'/but
as in/cross

18   81

purposes   the porpoise answersa at this end

812

(in)(inform)(informal)(infromality)
     (*fun*)(*fund*)(*fundament*)(*fundamental*)(*fundamentally*)

626

(the colors a gain
undue to be fast about a shirt "as
     what" I don't talk up wanting)(He moved
          him.)

296

(He, with two letters on the fact
of it, nobody in back, and his ground clear

　　　　　　　　　　　(He moved, taking, talking
on the print, moved him.)　　　up the face
of it, tall first in a sense and then short in
sense, him.)
　　　　(He moved him,
who had apart from it a fake of three
parts, without any mile in water,
　　　　　　　　　　　　without any
weight to lead over — without, in
fact, much of an idea at all.)

937

:empty

1,706
hands put his head in the loving: "I.C.
　　　threw a lass and I was
dry about the certain bark he timed down her thighs."

63

(in time　　　　(of)taking(up)space(out)
(of)it he cut her(down)(to)the size he banked
(on)being barked(for)(a derivative blond
up)(that I followed the coal or the cob or to cope
or to cool belongs)

34

　　A core — erect — (there):"With two
　　　　was slept the busy street
　　of the just supposed　　Two bed-
　　ded too　　to bead the shift

(not"slipt"into the passive of 2 3
4 lines above or the bed ends . . .)

47

or sides: a beady size

3,879

Some thing of the past(not 27 inches out to sea)for the right
                                                eye —
                                                creamed cold
                                                the maker's news
                                                an aye-aye upright
                                                outbrothership
                                                a beadsmanry
                                                a wool performance
(don't look where-   the well's fare
fore)   bare a skin to
        get a bead on the other(though booked too soon, through
    it though it is "easing the jar" now proceeded in
      the war that the other had a shadow with and is just
    returned to tour else with her arms receding with
    what's left —

692
lifting heirs
split(to spor-
        rans lit)

296

climbed as I'm(over
          town)

26

to two("2 to an
     apron maker)
   (I fell into the middle numb the same just

      7,465

         then)(just as now, then, while you are redder past
                 it and are passed before it as it I fell an ax
            with three strokes(out)(of the mine)*the right
         reason why(being meant because to be)* THE NEW MOAN

               485

               (BREATHING)could not be left
                                   (either)

                    580

                    any to more angles, reason-
               ably — in a report — of noose:
                    (*old change*)   Choose?

100

To have to be heard in half(
)with the correct "ear" nor
having the loss on her sighs?(!)

703

Again, par in this is
              (the former clam(A — T — on
thereupon,"TO GAINSAY:v.1.earn your(chance)to speak"
                        (our)   (pea)
as you dipped before or(change)"pneumonia"   (ear)(n.)
          (edit)   (an)

                        39

                        (to me(an))(the wrecked core:"lobotomy"
          3:you   the gain sags(over and under)

95

"The highest price ever paid on the open market for a single
letter is $51,000"
              in your language(H — I — G — H
    P — E — N — M — A — R — K)($5, 151,000)

715

The vegetable is his
(reason to speak;)(hearing it kept,)
(he earned)what you say to theirs "you
saw(vege/table; ear/ned)
LLLLLL

21

"Physically the	(over six-tenths	adding machine
longest letter	of a mile in	roll over a
ever written was	length. It was	period of a
one 3,200 feet	written on an	month in 1954,"
		etc.

128

(redivid(er)re:*chr-*
zaszcz(with a pole it may bug
you)   (thrzaszcz)

281

reentry:BACK AGAIN WITH A JET OFF-COLOR
(on, you color it back to you:a.full heart;
b.hot head; c.slow burn; d.deep sense; e.thin
time; f.finer feelings)

83

An edition of 150 copies of *The Rubaiyat of Omar Khayam* was published in 1956 in Massachussetts, and weighed (or that something else can be seen to it) a total of 0.34 of an ounce.

On Dec. 1, 1963, the intention to publish an 800 lb. plexiglass "art book" of 3 pages 7 ft. by 3 ft., and priced at $5,000, was announced in New York City (in front as what of behind you.) It was to contain the works of Karel Appel.

The largest encyclopedia ever compiled was one of 11,095 volumes, written by 2,000 Chinese scholars—(no longer but at length elsewhere) in 1403-08.

The world's fastest novelist is Earle Stanley Gardner, who dictates (above and both at double-time) 10,000 words a day and works with his staff on as many as 7 novels simultaneously.

The longest English poem is *PolyOlbion or A Chorographical Description of Tracts, Rivers, Mountains, Forests,* etc., written in Alexandrines (in the opposite direct to what goes away for it) in 30 books, comprising nearly 100,000 lines, by

Michael
Drayton
between
1613 and   346
1622.   . . . once
                 wrote 2
                 books(in
                 the com-
                 ing that
                 goes a-
                 cross)in
                 a week
                 with a
                 half-day
                 off . . .
                 (half once
                 and the
                 rest eith-
                 er) had
                 been pub-
                 lished in
                 7,893 ed-
                 itions . . .
                 lifetime
                 output
                 (likewise
                 or all day)
                 was at least
                 72,000 words
                 (to the way
                 as this
                 you can)

41

he is against, right, or another so
    sure you do(I mean, crossly, that
fast, he skirts up   (a.*tickled pink;* b.*cheesed off;* c.*like*
  tinder; d.*dead-pan)*
              to that he has really gained blackly
and mean: *the sub-jet avers* a.— b.— j.— e.— t.—

9,871

        and it is(there)that(then)after all you can see
      for yourself for your sides that do not do
             ever after all . . . *all off* —
    set at rest — played out — to the end of the chapter —
 clocked out — in fine — to the bitter end — once for all

Among the more adventurous of the young poets who experiment with fresh, contemporary techniques, VITO HANNIBAL
ACCONCI was born in 1940 in New York City and earned
degrees from Holy Cross College and The University of Iowa.
His poems have appeared in *Art and Literature, The Paris Review,*
and several small magazines; translations of his were published
in *Poems from XV Languages* (Stone Wall Press: 1964). Currently a teacher at Brooklyn College and the School of Visual
Arts, Mr. Acconci is married and lives in Manhattan, where he
edits the little magazine *0 To 9.* Of his poetics he says: "Hypoth-
eses about ways of writing, ways of reading—if a book is defined
as writing on paper, discuss a hand-writing lesson; if reading
takes place one word at a time, then discuss each word (defini-
tions, functions)—can be the form of a particular piece of
writing." His note about the title of the long poem "Kay Price
and Stella Pajunas" may offer a clue to one way of approaching
the poem: "Kay Price, of Adelaide, South Australia, typed, non-
stop, for 53 hours, ending on June 13, 1962. Stella Pajunas, in
1946, typed 216 words per minute on an IBM machine."

FLOWERS: *Calabria*

Brown fingers
the salt
sun peels
touch,
tend.

Butter
cool lips
wax
open.

Enter
air
of the mountains,

yellow wings.

PERIOD

Oak leaves holding on
scrape the vacant window glass.
The moon is bright & hard.
Her belly swells. There are tears.
Love, I'd like to say
that you . . . buried
in sleep in the next room
her breathing flares, falters.

Blood seeps into the cotton pad
darkens the silk briefs I bought
in Paris . . .

The thought of her body
fresh from a hot bath, sleek
with the sheen of oils immersed in water
set me hunting
through lingerie shops, watched
by Gendarmes, eyes that knew what they knew.

That was one version.
                              And I have seen
her blood closer to home. Rage
I'd turned my back on
exploded through glass—
the kitchen door. I stopped
the pulse at her elbow.
Layers of cut muscle
drew back from the line
of incision, baring
taut yellowish bands. *My teeth've ripped*
the same tendons from a turkey leg....

Something pulls together inside her sleep.
A slow, heavy sentence.

Darkness has cancelled the furniture.
The oak leaves are black against the window.
The moon is a bald girl who's never been laid.

THE SUN-SHOWER

for Robin Hoople

"... *Miracles occur*
If you care to call those spasmodic
Tricks of radiance miracles."
                    —Sylvia Plath

Down the street
a sunday of empty parks.
Clouds assemble
like the grey stones of a prison,
and the river's blown ripple-patterns
grow suddenly still
as restless men grow still
before the world's great battles
or a hanging.

All day
I have watched myself move
through dirty windows.
Whenever I thought to ask,
puddles would back me
with a sky whose light was thickening
toward rain.

When it does come,
cold, drowsy as hemlock,
the drizzle packs me
into a doorway's upright box.
To the right, to the left,
clocks display
their blank, numbered faces
cared for by spider limbs
behind my face
which hangs, a faint ghost
about to evaporate,
in the glass between this universe
of wheels, wheelings, whirrs, insect speech,
and a town wiped out by rain.

Strange thoughts
begin to breathe at the back of my mind
like the unshelled bodies of snails.
But the rain's effects change

from mouselight and hypnosis
to long spattering bursts
of relief. The overcast breaks up
like an ice field in april,
and wherever sunlight lights the bouncing rain
on the sleek tar, on the rinsed
roofs and hoods and bumpers of cars,
even on dead water,
it surprises thousands
of horned creatures the color of glass
whose looked-through lives become visible
only when they have something to dance about.

GEORGE AMABILE was born in 1936 in Jersey City, New Jersey. At present, he lectures at The University of Manitoba in Winnipeg, Canada, where he edits the poetry magazine *The Far Point*. After study at Amherst College he received the Master of Arts degree in 1961 from The University of Minnesota where he won the Anna von Helmholz Phelan Prize for Creative Writing. Work of his has appeared in *The New Yorker*, *Choice*, *Paris Review*, *Harper's* and *Minnesota Review*. When asked about his poetics, Mr. Amabile replied in a comment which echoes the response made by many of the other young poets: "I can't think of anything that wouldn't sound pompous or absurd."

from THE SUMMER DEATHS: III

Christ, I was twelve
when I gave up my love
to you & burned in your streaming
wounds. I was the skinniest
kid in camp; I dreamed;
I faithfully wet
my bed. Only your wilderness,
berries and nuts, red
bushes gone to flame,
kept me apart
from each ordered day.
For one whole month
(August) I imagined your delicate
hands, your red mouth
pushing at my flesh. But,
in truth, it was your marvelous,
intricate pain that was temptation.
My dear Christ,
how often you came at night
redeeming some of us
(who *knew*)
from the counselor's planned salvations.
How I loved you.
Out of the dark, your pale, intense
teenager's face
swayed behind our tent.
O, I'm here, come out, I'm here . . .
Whatever we learned
we learned through our disgrace
at being twelve, and not yet
willing to tear at
our loins, or to burn
in our private, downy hair
for love of you.

ENTRANCE TO A MIRROR

This is a still life,
shadow beneath which

configurations
come forward to you.

I am coming
toward you. The deep

chairs, the piano
and thin glass vases

darken behind me,
coming to the door.

Here is evening, here
are white roses, and

my hand. The windows
stand very straight, as

if amazed, but are
closing now against

us and the light. Here
is your glass hand. In

our faces, roses
like whitened wax, shine.

THE FRONTIER

for Jim Tate

When I ask for Lao Tzu
it's you.

The Masked Ball
to which everyone came dressed
as a telephone. No one

was left to answer.
That was the weekend of

The Continual Celebration of Retrospect.

Mother,
Homecoming, the best
of the Big Ten, the Illustrated
Index to Pound's Cantos.

But you were the loneliest poet alive.

That is: the old Chinese lawbreaker
facing the lavish weather
at Land's End.

THE HISTORY OF PSYCHOTHERAPY:

I find many dishes
lie on the dark lawn, waiting.

Now for the history of love:

A man found a locket
—or amulet—
anyway, a real disc, cold
silver in his bed.
He opened it.
Much of the rest

is an underground journey, soft noses
    of moles,
running water,
the occasional
distant emergencies: holding aliens
    or ships, in time of war.

In the end, he might arrive.
His childhoods
surprise him:
                    Thousands
of motionless, small toads.
But each sleeps, for love, in a dish.

The entire scene
is opening.
Clarity, I think I am
coming toward you, I bear
myself with such indifference.

LOOKING FOR JONATHAN

Before sunrise
the sky whitened. I said
to myself: "Whatever troubles you,
leave it."

            Then we're speeding
into the fields,
    corn, white houses,
buses at daybreak: the same eyes
we've brought along before.

    But the yellow light
looked
    in at us: "That discomfiture;
give it here."

O, I knew what
had been planned, but where?
    And in whose name?

Non-Fiction, happiest man, ran alongside,
    then right-angled "See you—"
into the white woods.
    We followed, of course, on foot.

There, various women (Some I knew,
    or had known) were dancing, filling
    a clearing.
                    The pond:
We swam in the old way, lit
    the green leaves to grow warm.
Our smoke rose into the sun.

When I saw America, she had danced all night,
she was chalk-white,
leaning on her husband's arm.

            I could see
the orange home town, coming.
I leaned honestly
    into my own reflection.
I had no more stories of God.

THE GIVING-IN

This afternoon
a nil wind
didn't blow *me*
home. For no
good reason, in
another town
stones overturn,
rabbits run
wacky on
the loud tin
roofs. I see
your point, I'm begin-
ning to agree: we
need a friend.

DEATH'S ONLY SON

I wanted to be
brilliant glass, worn
at my throat.

Whoever I faced
would become clear to me.
I wanted to be Death's

only son, the favorite,
constantly refused.
Ritual, our bond.

I stand among friends,
representing them;
their flesh, like

damp bread, softens.
Now I am lonely.
And when they turn,

their mouths small
and old, I think
it is to speak of me.

Memory, we grow
restless, you & I,
and accidental.

TOTEM

In a pitched bed. I
am pink, in love with
heat. Out in the afternoon
a red barn shifts, turns
down Beacon Street.

I am gliding amidst
foghorns and in a dream.
Oars lock in my high
secretive skull; I
drift between doors
into the flooded dark.
Here is the home
of nighthawks and owls.
A massive protection
opens in my head—

indoor afternoons:
the house smelled of
dampness, the shadow
of the piano reached
across the living
room. *Mom's
gone upstairs*. Now

the echo of water
knocks about, the odor
of pine-pitch and cedar
lolls all over. Stripped
to the waist, I touch
for the snouts of seals
in the dark. Somewhere
trees are bending in
an afternoon; also my
face, sticky as a leaf bud,
opens. I am truly tired.
My mother mentions me.
Two or three times, I
am arriving home.

AVIATORS

We learned, and slowly, only
that we fell in the blue spiral

of confusion. The millionth run—
and now our lives unwound.

Well, we had always had bright flak at heart.
And when we stalled our bomber under

the brown moon, and emerged—Who could have known?
In that musical dangle, jukebox angels

fed us their sweet compassionate bread.
Our bellies grew round as the red moon,

And we starved. Who could survive
desire? They have wired

our wild hearts for sound. We are falling down
forever toward your blue receding town.

THE MONUMENT TO RESIGNATION

Then I was crazy,
wearing my solitude lightly—
the colored duck

breeding war in a thatched hut—
but I couldn't have loved you less.

I washed my weapons in
the day's events; went out,
armed, at night.

My door
opened on the new unknown.
I threw stones

at the houses of starlets,
then ran off, colorless,
into the shadows.

But the danger wouldn't disappear.
No one would let me in.
My house
was a column of salt.

So I left, living
for years on water and grain.

And one spring morning
I passed by, and
laid this poem, like an ordinary head
on my old doorstep.

Although he admits that "I don't have any formidable objective
feelings about poetics," JON ANDERSON states that many of
his poems "seem to come out of a need for some kind of personal salvation. Although it's not much in evidence, I believe
most of them come from imperfect memories of childhood—or
maybe it's just an attempt to regain the thickly textured, personal images that a child does not have to put into (arbitrary)
contexts. There's a great deal of permissiveness, secretiveness,
fantasy allowed here—at the same time, the healthy ability to
grow by unconscious needs." A graduate of The Program in
Creative Writing at The University of Iowa, Mr. Anderson was
born in 1940 and raised in Lexington, Massachusetts. His first
volume *Looking for Jonathan* was published in 1968 by The
University of Pittsburgh Press.

AFTER A LOBSTER DINNER AND PLAYING LIKE KIDS ON A KING-SIZED BED

if I take my own excitement
and the willfulness of your mouth
doing all those crazy things it does
and your body jumping against mine
like it does. and the fine hair
that drifts over the small of your back
just above the swelling of your secret ass
I really dig going in and out of this delicate forest
and feeling your skin
bring some of itself even closer to me.

THREE

          For the first time
I draw your full and solid legs to my lips;
your hand; your mouth. I draw blood
to each nerve and gently
touch their tips:
you move and I am over you,
you stop and I lift you close,
you watch and I lick your eyes.

. . .

In this corner of my life can I build your house?
In the water of your past will you trace my name?

. . .

I will cling to your musk,
your music and your skin.
When you go
I will steal your dreams,
burn fires in the hills of your long memory.

THE NEW SOUND

Herds of carrots cross the river
tame gazelles are grazing
my eyes shiver in the shuffle

I bull my way in the wake of beavers
my mouth breathes
in the shadow of your breath
my fingers
flank your hands
I am sorting the colors of whales
I have you clowning and climbing the sky
we melt
floundering for a deserted glove
wishing for an immense hand to hold our sex

In the poplars crows are calling
in the rain an orange
in my mouth the new sound of your unfailing tongue.

"A poem is a diver that longs to levitate," ROGER APLON
writes. Born in 1937 in Chicago, Illinois, he studied at Roose-
velt University and The University of Chicago. He is the man-
aging editor of *Choice*, the important magazine of poetry and
photography. Currently he lives in Sausalito, California.

MY GRANDFATHER'S FUNERAL

I knew the dignity of the words:
"As for man, his days are as grass,
As a flower of the field so he flourisheth;
For the wind passeth, and he is gone"—
But I was not prepared for the beauty
Of the old people coming from the church,
Nor for the suddenness with which our slow
Procession came again in sight of the awakening
Land, as passing white houses, Negroes
In clothes the colors of the earth they plowed,
We turned to see bushes and rusting roofs
Flicker past one way, the stretch of fields
Plowed gray or green with rye flow constant
On the other, away to unchanging pines
Hovering over parallel boles like
Dreams of clouds.

                    At the cemetery the people
Surprised me again, walking across
The wave of winter-bleached grass and stones
Toward his grave; grotesques, yet perfect
In their pattern: Wainwright's round head,
His bad shoulder hunched and turning
That hand inward, Luby Paschal's scrubbed
Square face, lips ready to whistle to
A puppy, his wife's delicate ankles
Angling a foot out, Norwood Whitley
Unconsciously rubbing his blue jaw,
Locking his knees as if wearing boots—
The women's dark blue and brocaded black,
Brown stockings on decent legs supporting
Their infirm frames carefully over
The wintry grass that called them down,
Nell Overman moving against the horizon

With round hat and drawn-back shoulders—
Daring to come and show themselves
Above the land, to face the death
Of William Henry Applewhite,
Whose name was on the central store
He owned no more, who was venerated,
Generous, a tyrant to his family
With his ally, the God of Moses and lightning
(With threat of thunderclouds rising in summer
White and ominous over level fields);
Who kept bright jars of mineral water
On his screened, appled backporch, who prayed
With white hair wispy in the moving air,
Who kept the old way in changing times,
Who killed himself plowing in his garden.
I seemed to see him there, above
The bleached grass in the new spring light,
Bowed to his handplow, bent-kneed, impassive,
Toiling in the sacrament of seasons.

JANUARY

Snow on ground and
brown weeds above; reddish
light now panes one
washboard wall of a farmhouse.
The other, shadowed
wall holds skim-milk light
as a bedsheet hung out to dry
and catch cold's cleanliness
holds blue sheen from the thin sky.
Chinaplate fragments of snow
in hollows of the ribbed bank
are touched by sun with color in it
of clay waved over by broomstraw,

will be blue, steel
blue, toward night.
The white boards seem
translucent, like a mother's skin
when she is old enough
to be left at home by her sons
the January afternoon.
Seem translucent with enclosing
up there the sky's blue
air I see through an upstairs
window held in a dresser mirror;
or see from looking
through two windows
all the way through those rooms,
through the still air of
this afternoon in her life and back
into sky where sun slants
down invisibly without
clay, broomstraw, boards to flush, there
where wind's too thin to be seen.

BIRTHDAY, WITH LEAVES

Housefronts rough with brick proffer
Plants to my walking. Tendrils move
In the delicacy of the air, leaves gesture
Like clean fingers folding clothes.
Children watch me covertly.

Heat is a glaze in light, street-vistas
Are flat, like hazed forms in a mirror,
Far cloud hovers by the shagged pine.

As if I'd newly come
From my mother's house I see
Weed-slant shadowed on clay,
Willow leaves by a culvert;
Crossed sticks, stems, shine magical.
Beyond colonnades of a grove
A tombstone stands like a door in dreams
I dare not enter.
Summer brings my birthday.

Then the high field I hardly have courage
To climb, past cherokee rose
Under the indian eyes of a small boy alone
In a tree house, where bob white call
And two run before with high interrogative heads—
Where there is scent of the hot pine sap
Where there is moving shadow of clouds.

I have lost my name again
In the beginning of summer, the old initiation;
In wonder at knowing from so long before,
Knowing as if to know forever,
Hot pine sap and moving clouds;
Smell of leaves from a tangled branch,
Startling, new.

from STEPS FROM THE STREAM: IV,
LAWN AND LIGHT

His mower whirred cut grass like dust
Through daylight gray as if seen through windowscreen,
    spun
Raw cut scent of wiregrass into the warm and failing dusk:
His taut muscular figure was strained erect

And I was laid on the sideporch studio couch
Sick with fever, but I knew from intensely seeing
The gray raining light over his stiff effort
Bringing the night with lawnmower sleepier than crickets
That his image was becoming a part of me forever.

I knew even then the sadness of a memory
To be, even as the shape of his strength
And turn of his mower, sweet
Like the strained music of a summer fan,
Held me from dying.

from STEPS FROM THE STREAM: IX, CHURCH AND CLOUDS

Church out, I walked over town.
Dark based cloud measured calipers of light
Through mist, drawing up water as people would say.
My grandfather had stood in his pew and prayed for rain;
He spoke for farmers dressed by the weather.
I passed young corn in crumbled rows
Curled thirstily to tubes.
Please God bring rain.
I walked past hedges and ditches bordering fields,
Where far off in the water-shimmer rimmed by trees
A clapboard church gleamed
Its steeple white as salt in the sunlight.

Heat stifled. I thought of Saturday night
With Laurie, my cousin's friend, who seemed her sister.
Forgetful of who we were, what we must be
We had pulsed in the cocoon of night
In my father's car
On a dirt road that ran past trees.

My vision through the clear air distilled
Its water, I ached for drops
To thud like spent bullets into the earth.
I was not my father, not like him.
I knew an intenser prayer than his.

I felt the sky's blue curve alive like a skin,
Turned toward creek and the rich thrusts of trees;
My blood was a veil that throbbed in sight.

I stepped through vines careless of snakes,
Brushed past fretwork leaves. Gathered
Overcast had wet the sun in swirls,
A few drops spattered to circle
The wood-brown polish of the stream.

As if through answered prayer my eye
Grasped smooth fish under
Images of cloud upon water stable as stones.

LEAF MIRRORS

Along a dustless clay road in wet weather,
        from the wide leaves there radiates
a presence of coolness and green, like water.

And the field of white weeds, delicate
        flattened umbrellas or mushroom heads;
Queen Anne's lace, so nearly flowers,

white sprays of unkempt blossom
        cocked in numberless angles to one another,
strung as if by invisible attraction

to the scattered clouds; and those soft-brushed
    billows seem deeply filamented,
potential with rain.

Such leaf-mirrors of water ineffably unite
    with clouds in this light deepened by haze,
like leaves regarding their figures in a pond.

The cloud-caught weeds, leaved clouds, shimmering
    holding a water-depth, connection
like consciousness, diminish

me shaped into the mosaic foliage,
    summer that is summer by passing; but mirror
my shared life between them, beyond me; promise.

TREE IN THE RAIN

I came out into the wet night
Wondering if windows of my car were down.
Keen drops needled into the slick grass.
The town was deep in a rustle of rain
Fresh-smelling as flapping wash.
I settled into a chair, willing to wait,
Thought of the earthworms stirring—

Still, in spite of my drowse
The young tree shaped like a cloud
Across the street seemed poised, aware.
I sensed the inside of it rain-rubbery,
Clammy like a wet raincoat,
With scratching branches and with leaf-edges
That would tickle like bugs;
And yet it dreamed itself

Listening like the ears of earthworms
Under their lids of mud.
A sensation trickled into me of it
Risen like an earth-pulse into the showering
Sky, like a single cupped palm
Catching drink, or cupped, hearing.

I felt the cold sound naked on my skin.

"I once had a visual impression of a poem as a procession of
men and animals moving within the edge of a forest," JAMES
APPLEWHITE recalls. "Vines and crooks of branches against
folds of the animal bodies (they had come to be elephants, I
believe, as the idea began to please me) created a natural inscription upon the live and moving statuary. The animals represented the direction and unified shape which there must be in
the initial concretion of impulse into scene and action. The inscription represented the hints of significance which poets insin-
uate, but now I mistrust this inscription, for the combination
of interpretive words into shapes as natural as vines, branches
and folds of skin is rare. Now I seek to make the clear shapes,
and to trust the reader to guess or invent the words he will see
upon their moving sides . . . I want the words I use to be absolutely clear in specifying the sights and other sensory impres-
sions which will be part of the total design. If there is to be
obscurity, it will consist in doubt as to how this organism, by
which I mean the whole unified thing seen and felt by the
reader, should be interpreted; there should be no doubt at all
as to what is seen and felt." Mr. Applewhite was born in 1935
in eastern North Carolina. The farmhouse behind him in the
photograph is the birthplace of his grandfather; his father now
manages the farm. Currently he teaches the Romantic Poets at
The University of North Carolina at Greensboro.

that crouched
           in the green day waiting
for evening.
If I had told you would
you have known?

So I sat
           on a bench among flowers
and trees facing
the traffic   surveying all

I knew of impalas, cougars, falcons
      barracudas, mustangs, wild
                              cats,
marlins, watching cars
go by.   I named them
all.

YOUR EYES HAVE THEIR SILENCE

Your eyes have their silence in giving words
back more beautifully than trees can rain
and give back in swaying the rain
that makes silence mutable and startles nesting birds.

And so it rains. And so I speak or not
as your eyes go from silence suddenly
at love to wonder (as those quiet birds suddenly
at rain) letting, finally, myself be taught

silence before your eyes conceding everything
spoken as experience, as love, as reason
enough not to speak of them and my reason
crawls into the silence of your eyes. Spring

always promises something, sometimes only more
beauty: and so it rains. And so I take
whatever promise there is in silence as you take
words as rain and give them back in silence before

there are ways to say that more beauty is nothing
for you before my hands can memorize
the beauty of your slender movements and nothing
is beautiful as words nesting in your eyes.

SECOND DANCE POEM

This (vestige of woman's animalness is the open secret that
   riddles & ruins me &
     cheated of the evidence by
shaved limbs & armpits I bless the perversity of those
     whose arms & legs trap
   beads of light & break
them into component hairs. Ruined by riddles too I see
   the gesture of her walking
     & dancing & think of
the way her brush does invisible things to the air
     Draws . Paints . with the artistry
   of the part-woman civilized
by cosmetic sterility. A little madly because it ruins me
   I think away what she
     wears hoping to think that
her wiry   silky   tangled   feathery   or whatever she
     denies climbs
     her belly & spreads over
   her thighs like wheat fire
night or earth. & even hangs bearded from the triangle
   that begins & ends my

doom. Because I'm no good
at riddles.
            The gesture of her knees is another kind
        of dance   .   a   Sacrifice. I
    go because her glory doesn't
crown but conceals & she hides so beautifully I'm reluctant
    to find her. I think
        of being lost & having
to part through the cushion that breaks the fall &
        sudden stop of flesh, going
    into not what is hidden
but what hides. What she wears or denies is not
    enough.
            There is this fear
        each time: that the resident
beast of her jungle will not be the friendly mongoose
        I expect, but an avenging
    vicious half-lion & I will be skinned
& sacrificed because I'm a
    failure as a tempter & no good at riddles.
            Call it what you will
but it)
        ruins
me.

Born in 1933 in Attalla, Alabama, GERALD WILLIAM
BARRAX is at present in the Master of Arts program at The
University of Pittsburgh. From 1953-1957 he served in The United
States Air Force. "I can't make any profound statement on
poetics because I never know what a poem is going to be," he
explains. "The poem is me as I write it. Anything else I might
say about poetics would be a posture and a lie."

THE PERFECTION OF DENTISTRY

Guanajuato, Mexico

Here I am, an industry without chimneys,
looking for an alternative
to abandoning privilege,
looking out from my long floral porch
which is not a porch but an expatriate
way of life (he hates her, she hates
him, but they can't leave), leaning
over the intricate stone railing,
over the caretaker asleep on the ground,
toward the haciendas on the opposite hill
which seems so luxurious without cactus.

Surviving "turistas," the physics of the fiesta
and the intimacy of our schizophrenia,
we have arrived, not without mercy,
to render unto trees and flowers and hills
our unnatural, filling-laden homage.
Across the way, they may be watching,
mineral water in hand, the spectacle-clad vermin.
But we do not think ourselves unhealthy,
if afflicted. We do not think ourselves visited
but visitors, without undue recompense.
If the trees bow slightly, that is alright. And

if the flowers bloom indiscriminately,
we can accept such favors. We knew before coming
we must restore to its altar the spine of the tree,
and the ebullient blooming to its rightful position.
We knew before coming that notoriety was wrong
everywhere, though trusting the wealthy North American.
But the causes of suffering are like impure water,
which one must walk beside and ingest

until one is covered completely in the sweaty afternoon.
And the momentum of the rains is like the momentum
of the bells, penetrating and cleansing the lush cover.

Here, every workday is part of a pilgrimage
for which the church tolls the approximate hours.
It's true, we have paid too much attention to our mouths.
We have the expression, "like pulling teeth";
we have words for the cabinets of our emotions.
But the caretaker has pulled his bad tooth
without fuss, and now weathers his senses in sleep.
And we, compensating witnesses, lead his concurrent
lives, take place in the garden of his salvation,
in the hierarchy of anonymity, and in
the masterful units of his siesta, and always did.

THE ADDRESS TO THE PARENTS

The children are not visas, sure to enter,
anymore than your dry carnation
intimidating past the doorman.
But they are the solace of not living in objects,
the very mechanism for believing belief,
Oh I can't convince you the way they want to;
I can't complain to them about you!

The process of election is gentle,
though it causeth you to go unheeded.
They wanted you to become a Bible
so they could read you,
they wanted you to become a beacon
so they could follow you,
they wanted for your education; as you, theirs.

You had an old-fashioned notion, or
I had an old-fashioned notion, of labor.
Its division was not immodest
when you accomplished everything,
by which was revealed your benevolent
and restricting nature, though no country
you can imagine will be left just like you.

It is always another time, a new face,
though you were gregarious and did not want.
You will have the immigrant's
terrible conviction, not far-fetched and serious,
that the children are out to lose,
but they are not. You honor the Sabbath
and keep your mother and father,

to which they add a feeling for saints,
the restoration of animals,
and a final solution to the problem of Nazis.
They have passed beyond the lovelorn
and industrial revolutions, beyond syllogisms
and the buttons of determinism.
Now the fishermen bring their nets in full of gold.

But you are afraid to stop breathing
and run out of money, and you are afraid
to support your feeling for the facts.
What will you say when I tell you they have changed,
that the comedies were tragedies
and noon was night? The children, themselves,
are out flying their kites, long ago.

THE ISRAELI NAVY

The Israeli Navy,
sailing to the end of the world,
stocked with grain
and books black with God's verse,
turned back,
rather than sail on the Sabbath.
Six days, was the consensus,
was enough for anyone.

So the world, it was concluded,
was three days wide
in each direction,
allowing three days back.
And Saturdays were given over
to keeping close,
while Sundays the Navy,
all decked out in white
and many-colored skull caps,
would sail furiously,
trying to go off the deep end.

Yo-ho-ho, would say the sailors,
for six days.
While on the shore their women moaned.

For years, their boats were slow,
and all show.
And they turned into families
on the only land they knew.

ON RETURNING TO TEACH

At a distance, young voices are whooping,
to which my stately, fostering mother
pays no heed. But as the moon bears
with great heaviness waters to itself,
one tongue reissues for attention.
It is mine. I have come back to win
the National Book Award, but am locked in
the English Department, let me out!

My friends rally round. They were expected to
do this. With refrains. Tunes. Lips.
With brace and bit and biting epigram
they bore the walls, release and welcome me.
At once I wish to share in their spirits,
their fitting wits and sensual nostalgia.
The short lines in my palms seem to lengthen,
and the slapping of their thighs sounds tender.

I have been rescued before by black angels
and merely observed their disappearance, have walked
in the corridor when the one door opened—
and entered, and asked for the moon, and laughed;
have wanted for a hand, a back and a brain,
and have wanted my women to tell me again.
In the second childhood, there are not more children.
In the second semester, the teachers are older.

THE DANGER AT FUNNY JUNCTION

a going-away present

A gallon of gas at a gaudy igloo
and you. Where's to go? Where's Tokyo?
Did we agree not to say "Whoa" to?
Are you using my telephone, I'd like to.

Operator, get me someone who can help,
before Father, long distance, dies laughing,
before Mother Invention is fear and farewell,
and the silence is a journal for nothing.

Of course one lives in an envelope
to go to far places. And a friend says,
Good Luck, that's what a friend says.
The title of this poem is "Toys",

for James Tate.

THE GROWTH

It's the great leap forward,
starring Marvin the Merrier.
Love, you said, is a bag of junk.
Well, *I* could empty into that.

I was going to write to you
of my life as a rubber plant.
It began, "Forced to submit to
the flowering of indecency comma,"

or: the tests we face
are such overwhelming premises,
the beauty of the vegetable
and the best years of our lives.

AN AFTERWORD TO MY FATHER

Still the wood I knocked on
is the family tree. I'm not a god,
I haven't the face for it.

Devotion is my disease,
or a way out. That accounts
for sons, and for everything.

Not so much "enough,"
there is more to be done,
yes, and to be done with.

You were the sun and moon.
Now darkness loves me;
the lights come on.

VERSES *VERSUS* VERSES

First, there's the courtship
and that's seven poems,
and the marriage costs three,
and then comes the first birth
which costs more than just several,
although succeeding births

grow less expensive, but more
routine, but then there's the
children's schooling, which
costs two decades and three or four
hundred and thirty seven
poems, with some interest,
and you worry about borrowing, until,
one night at dinner, there's the
possibility of retirement,
and you have them disconnect
the utilities, and there
go four poems—gas, oil,
water and electricity—and
a good meal in a restaurant
by this time costs one hundred
lines with a sonnet for the tip,
but you wouldn't have it any
other way, and you *wouldn't* have it
any other way, so you're held up
and when you sell out, you throw in
six thieves and a title
for good measure.

THE DELICATE BIRD WHO IS FLYING UP OUR ASSES

The delicate bird who flies up your asses
is flying up mine
also, with no express invitation.
The bird who likes the lean and hungry
is making me sweat.
I have delusions that I need a job,
that I will waste away
unless I eat the bird,

and that my family will remember me
only as a poor provider.
That bird means to straighten me out.
The bird in favor of fathers and sons
is cropping up insidiously.
Once I could be lazy;
now he turns up everywhere I sit.
Each day I have a feeling of the bird
higher within me.
Once I declined burdens;
now I jump to be responsible
for ones I haven't yet.
I can tell that bird
means to stay with me forever.
Hire me. I have another mouth to feed.

HOW I CAME TO RULE THE WORLD

It was easy.
I was appointed, from the very first
my qualifications put me forth
to be easy
to get along with, and I
had pull. How better
might I have risen
than just so divinely,
like one who comes up floating, where
others had the fortune
only to disappear? I, alone,
aboard ship or continent,
have not watched my step overmuch,
nor thought to. I could,
if I had to. Also,
I might mention my looks, also

my disposition toward this sort of thing.
Now that I look down,
there are those who feel equal to me.
But they are young and foolish.
And they will love me when I ask them to.

THE GIVING IN

Once I could ignore
birds everywhere,
though they were everywhere
I had to go.
Now I go wherever
birds are everywhere;
now I go anywhere
birds go,
having gone nowhere
they could not go.
That is the half of it.

MY HATE

My hate is like ripe fruit
from an orchard, which is mine.

I sink my teeth into it.
I nurse on its odd shapes.

I have grafted every new variety,
walked in my bare feet,

rotting and detached,
on the fallen ones.

Vicious circle. Unfriendly act.
I am eating the whole world.

In the caves of my ill will
I must be stopped.

THE 3 CORNERS OF REALITY

One might speak to great length
of the three corners of reality—
what was seen, what was thought
to be seen, and what was thought
ought to be seen—and forget it.
Or one might argue the relative
merits of looking back, as opposed
to looking ahead or looking in on,
and in no time be willing to end it.
Who has that kind of time to spend?
—they asked when they had the time
to ask; and it seems there was a movie
which flickered successfully
in behalf of these very questions.
Ever, the very very are among us,
appearing to ask for our lives.
Well, I give them the right answers:

"How do you recognize poetry?"
—It looks like poetry.
"How is prose different from poetry?"
—Prose goes by another name.
"Why do you write poetry?"
—Because it feels so good.

And I freely give samples of my pleasing.

THINGS WE DREAMT WE DIED FOR

Flags of all sorts.
The literary life.
Each time we dreamt we'd done
the gentlemanly thing,
covering our causes
in closets full of bones
to remove ourselves forever
from dearest possibilities,
the old weapons re-injured us,
the old armies conscripted us,
and we gave in to getting even,
a little less like us
if a lot less like others.
Many, thus, gained fame
in the way of great plunderers,
retiring to the university
to cultivate grand plunder-gardens
in the service of literature,
the young and no more wars.
Their continuing tributes
make them our greatest saviours,
whose many fortunes are followed
by the many who have not one.

Both as a student and now as assistant professor of poetry,
MARVIN BELL has been one of the major figures who have
made The Program in Creative Writing at The University of
Iowa the most seminal and exciting workshop for young poets
in the world. "I'm not sure that I chose to write. I write to make
discoveries and inventions, as a necessary strategy to get certain things said, to confront the irrational, and because I must,"
he explains, in a statement which reflects both the integrity
and enthusiasm he brings to the job of writing and teaching
poetry. "My reasons, insofar as I realize them, are a little cranky
and peculiar, I suppose. They have nothing to do with standards

or necessary truths. I think one ought to write primarily to
affect what one thinks of oneself. Of course, that happens to
a certain extent in terms of what others think of you. Also, I
believe in writing as a way of understanding what would otherwise remain irrational. But a work of art doesn't need a purpose
to come into being. My most cranky answer to the question,
Why do you write? is, Because it feels so good. I write to change
my life." Mr. Bell was born in 1937 in New York City and
raised on Long Island. After study at Alfred University and
The University of Syracuse, he earned the Master of Arts
degree in 1961 from The University of Chicago and his Master
of Fine Arts from The University of Iowa in 1963. In addition,
he spent almost two years in The United States Army as a
Foreign Military Training Officer and was discharged with the
rank of 1st Lieutenant. "Twice married," he states, "I now have
a Polish wife named Murphy and two sons named Nathan and
Jason." Associated with several literary magazines as editor or
publisher, Mr. Bell is currently poetry editor of *The North
American Review*, and he selected the poetry in *Midland II*
(Dial: 1968)—the anthology of writing by alumni of The Program in Creative Writing at The University of Iowa. He has
published a first volume of poems *Things We Dreamt We Died
For* (Stone Wall Press, Iowa City: 1966) and a pamphlet *Poems
for Nathan and Saul* (The Hillside Press: 1966).

DIVINE LOVE

A lip which had once been stolid, now moving
Gradually around the side of the head
Eye-like
The eye twisted on the end of somebody's finger and
    spinning
Around the sun, its ear,
And the brain aloft over the lake of the face—
Near the cataract of the body—
Like a cumulus cloud enlarged before a rainstorm:

A sound
That grows gradually in the East
Driving everything before it: cattle and rainbows and
    lovers
Swept on
To the table of the body at which five men and two
    women are casually sitting down to eat

THE EUROPEAN SHOE

The European shoe is constructed of grass and reed,
bound up and wound around so that it may slip easily
over the wearer's head.

In case you are an aircraft pilot, you must take care that
the European shoe does not creep off your foot, and begin
to make its way carefully along the fuselage.

The European shoe pressed against the fugitive's nose,
preventing it from imminent departure.

The European shoe spends summers in delightful ways.
A lady feels its subtle and unexpected pleasure the length
of her decolletage. (It winters in pain.)

That time I lent you my European shoe you departed with
a look of grandeur, and in total disrepair.

The European shoe knocks on the door of the carefree
farmerette. "The harvest has been gathered in, ha, ha,"
it says, moving shyly forth along the edge of the couch.

I pointed to the European shoe. I ate the European shoe.
I married the European shoe.

Tears fall from the eye of the European shoe as it waves
goodbye to us from the back balcony of the speeding train.

It helps an old lady, extremely crippled and arthritic,
move an enormous cornerstone. It invents a watch which,
when wound up tightly, flies completely to pieces.

It was a simple and dignified ceremony, distinguished for
its gales of uncontrollable laughter, in which I married the
European shoe.

If it rains, the European shoe becomes very heavy. I failed
to cross the river, where thousands of European shoes
lay capsized.

And so we lived alone, we two, the envy of our
neighborhoods, the delight of our lively hordes of children.

I saw a flightful of graceful swallows heading to distant,
half-forgotten islands over the distant seas; and in the
midst of that annually questing company, I saw the
European shoe.

It never harmed anyone, and yet it never helped anyone.

Gaily it sets out into the depths of my profoundest closet,
to do battle with the dusts of summer.

JOY

How can I get through that innocence?
Jump through, and land in a damp swamp—?
No, I'd rather go bicycling

Around, and enjoy its transparent squalor
Starred with flowers so magnificent
Only the most rotted self-deception could impel them.

Another thing I like doing a lot
Is helping you across busy boulevards
With a specially enlargeable hand

Implying friendly aid at first,
Secondly, a growing degree of passion;
Then I inflate it and make it throb! I also enjoy

Watching you tremble in deserted underground tunnels
Your wonderful trembling, too, when we are side by side
        at midnight,
And kayaking in mid-Atlantic, alone.

THE EYE

The narcissist's eye is blue, fringed with white and covered
with tempting salad leaves.

The purse-stealer's eye is yellow.

The eye of the non-combatant is white. In the center is
a target rendered in green and black.

The voluptuary's eye comes to a point. It is like a silo,
the echo of a halo.

The gravedigger's eye is hollow. It is surrounded by a
thoroughly contemporary serenity.

The dynamite salesman's eye is like a pool, in which he who
leans to drink may be lost. Drifting forever, like a cloud.

The maiden's eye is tucked under.

The billiard-player's eye comes to a point. It is like a
mild wine. Each billiard-player suffers from imperfect
nostalgia.

The ghost's eye is green.

The poet's eye is like a candy.

The battleship captain's eye is like the light that falls
in a glen, when the doe has done with drinking.

The eye of the realist is inflatable.

SOME LITANIES

1.

Was the arrangement made between the two couples legal?

No.

Did they spread the word around?

No.

Have you visited the two couples lately? Did you have an interesting time? Was it illegal?

No.

What was the decoration like?

It was furnished in Swedish "modern." Strings were hanging down in the living room. A bird flew in the window and out again.

Will you ever marry?

No.

Have you ever been married?

I don't remember.

Do you love your husband?

Yes.

2.

May I please have this dance?

No.

May I please have that dance?

No.

Aren't you going to wear anything to the dance?

Yes.

Are you a good dancer?

Yes.

Do you know how to dance?

No.

May I in that case have your company during the dance
they decide to play exactly at midnight, whatever it is?
I have fallen in love with your eyes, lips, hands
and hair.

No.

3.

During the lapse of several years, during which I spent
most of my time in Barcelona, was the magazine published?

Yes.

During the lapse of several years, during which I spent
most of my time in Barcelona, was the magazine published?

No.

Aren't you absolutely sure?

No.

Aren't you absolutely sure?

Yes.

Will you ever come to Barcelona with me?

No. I am afraid to leave behind the business affairs
of the magazine, of which I am general manager.

Are you really that conscientious?

No.

4.

Would you care to deal him the death-dealing blow?

No.

Would you care to pay him a little visit?

No.

Would you care to improve his laundry service by
making persistent inquiries?

No.

Are you really his legal guardian?

No.

Would you care to hand him this large can of
fortified beeswax?

No.

Do you have a favorite hobby?

Yes. Devoting myself entirely to that boy.

A BELOVED HEAD

A beloved head, truly, but the mouth part was operated
By a small treadle
Located just outside near the corner of the lawn;
The ears by a lightswitch
And the eyes by two faucets mounted inside the
    writing-desk.
The hair was operated by a kind of abacus
Upon which one tried not to lose count of possible
    developments there;

When it hung down loose it could envelop the attention
    of the operator.

The body of the beloved was operated from an enormous
    panel
Covered with hundreds of dials
One had to climb up to it by means of a ladder,
Daring that only after a refresher course from the
        handbook which came either with the previous
        instrument, or the previous beloved, the operator
        can never remember which
How often that body would suddenly whirl around
With a gesture so gentle and rare
One could not seriously comprehend that one had created it

—Nor even the way it arched its back and stretched
        in the commonest of yawns; or adjusted jewelry
        come slightly awry (one had accidentally brushed
        against a small throttle located near the knee)—

And sometimes the controlling mind collapses.
Just look at the way the operator is slumped over now.
He is tired, his head hurts, his hand is exhausted,
        in fact he has fallen asleep there in his chair.
And the beloved, head and body, is passing the time until
        the next awakening

By sitting around and sewing, presently the sleeve
Of a doll's kimono which she is going to give to a Japanese
        friend of hers who collects such things

MICHAEL BENEDIKT'S first volume of poems is *The Body*
(Wesleyan University Press). In addition to his poetry, he is
known as a frequent contributor to *Art News* and *Art International* and as the editor of four anthologies of modern drama,
including *Theatre Experiment: An Anthology of American Plays*
(Doubleday: 1967), and three collections published by Dutton:
Modern French Theatre (1964), *Post-War German Theatre* (1967)

and *Modern Spanish Theatre* (1968). He is also the translator
of the XIV and XV Century verse published in *Medieval Age*
(Dell: 1963) and he edited and translated *Ring Around the
World: Selected Poems of Jean L'Anselme* (Rapp and Whiting:
1967). Mr. Benedikt describes his sense of the poem and the
direction his work is growing: "A condition in which all possibilities are open, offering the widest range of choice, including the choice of not choosing at all—not writing, I mean—
strikes me as a very spiritual condition. I want poetry to be a
way of both creating and experiencing. I want my own poetry,
increasingly, to contain a maximum of spiritual information." He
was born in 1937 in New York City where he now lives.

EAST END

Sometimes I think it's here too,
　　which is to say the joy your dress
　　　　　　　drags in with it.
　　　　　　To go from that to the nearest consolation
　　is enough to tear my soul apart.
　　　　　　　　　　So stay.
　　　　The mystery has been proven.

OUT THERE

　　　　　Rain and the thought of rain:

but reality won't make itself over for the fact that you
　　　　　　　sense something—won't in fact
　　　　　　　wax miraculous,
though it's right—that responsibility belongs to the outer
　　　　　　　ether whose fragments are
　　　　　　　gummed together
so as only to be analyzable *in toto*. So
the man who cries "Marvellous!" is only human, putting
　　　　　　　out his sign. But the ether
　　　　　　　doesn't need this sign.

cloudburst to terrace to drainpipe backalley sewage to river
　　to sea—

　　　　No need, my love, to complain.

　　　　　Quieting down.
　　　　　Going on inside.

SURABAYA

Are you coming or going? The opening
                    pages of a scream may thin your blood
but you are a champion of equidistant parts
                                    the spreading eagle of death
            would you like to die in my arms
            don't worry I will die too you
            will never be alone but then
                        and then I take off your hat
                        to look a glistening cobra in the eye
                    grand the destroyers
                            are shuddering in the Caribbean
                    you wouldn't vote a lover of yours
                        into Congress would you?
                        You would die first wouldn't you
                    Later history will praise you
                                    for being succinct

VARIATION

        Half-ended melodies are purer.
        To no longer perform in broad daylight,
        the apple's a radish for it,
        the winter chill a living thing.
        But take your brother into later learning:
        Let the girls who will smell the buried cloves
                there.

        So I am only beginning to learn what I from
                time to time forget.
        But throw away these childish things!

Barney's coffin disappeared,
and luckily you said the right thing
for the sky mentioned for the last time.
The little master of small talk
is really the seducer of your every move,
taking you into his confidence the way a cat
    his mouse.

And still young Lycidas cannot express himself
    fully.
(And) "Everyone is the same"

even down to his jockey shorts, *dolce far niente*, as they
    say.

When he was still in his teens, BILL BERKSON was the young-
est member of the exciting and influential circle of New York
City poets and painters that included the late Frank O'Hara,
Kenneth Koch and John Ashbery. Educated at Brown University
and Columbia University, he was born in 1939 in New York
City. In addition to his book of poems *Saturday Night* (Tibor
de Nagy Editions: 1961) and forthcoming books—*The New
Life*, a long poem, and a collection of shorter poems written
since 1961—Mr. Berkson has published art criticism in *Art
News*, *Arts* and *Art and Literature*. He teaches literature and
creative writing at The New School and was associate producer
of the series "Art New York" for WNDT-TV. Most recently, he
was the editor of the illustrated volume of poems by Frank
O'Hara: *In Memory of My Feelings* (Museum of Modern Art:
1967). He makes his home in Manhattan.

TAMBOURINE LIFE

for Anne Kepler

1.

FUCK COMMUNISM
                    it's red and white and blue
in the bathroom
                    Tuli's
            One dollar, you Mother!
            Make all your friends
                        STOP!
            (now there's an idea)
                        ARTFORUM
                        723½ North Cienega Blvd
                        Los Angeles, California
                    *
Back to the wall
                    (it's all in California)
                                Thanks to Jack
I mean it's all right here
        it's morning
        and I'm looking   over the wall
        at Mr. Pierre Loti   and his nameless dog
        they work well   together
        on paper
chasing a tiger across white expansiveness
                that is not lacking in significance
what is?
                        The Russian Revolution
                        CIRCA   1967

2.

The apples are red again in Chandler's valley
redder for what happened there
                                never did know what it was
never did care
                        The End
                        on a pillow
                                    naturally
    a doormat   lust   steam   a hiss   Guilty!
            I see the handwriting on the wall
                    of the bridge
                        intersection
            New York Post   ten cents
        tip the newsboy
                    over
                    a million
                        laughs
            that's the party line:
                                    yes
            he's working on the paper:
                    Mr. Horatio Alger
    (he has a lovely talent)
                        thank you
                    here's your change

3.

I'm touched
            here, take this penny
                            there is no need for the past
            the sun is out
            it's night
                    I mean
                        it is night
                    and I love you better
            since

this seizure / of my eyeballs
                    *
        Take off those Fug panties
    Go ahead
            it's a big world
                        The big guys do it
        TO ANNIE
                    (between Oologah & Pawnee)
    Guillaume Apollinaire

                    4.

    The bodies of my days
        open up
in the garden
            of
            my memory
            in America
                *
        I have had the courage to look backward
it was like polio
        I shot my mouth off
                *
        I NEED MONEY
        that money
        that at last
        means less
        than a band-aid
        or a toad-stool
                *
        OUCH !
        that band-aid had an OUCH ! in it
Who notices a toadstool in the street ?
                            Everyone
            who has on
            a band-aid
                    That toadstool had a

band-aid on it

5.

(to Brett deBarry)

"He doesn't know how to take a vacation"
Dick
doesn't know how to take a vacation
either
That is not to infer
that Dick is a toad
under a band-aid   far from it
a toad is a cold-blooded fellow
Dick is warm and full of blood
When you leave, Dick
turn the refrigerator
to vacation please

6.

Now I'm going to read 3 cereal poems:
CORN FLAKES
OATMEAL
RY-KRISP
they were composed
excuse me
I mean NOT composed
using the John-Cage-
Animal-Cracker
Method of Composition
(this seems to be mushrooming
into a
major work
of high
seriousness
*
I'd fight for that !

I didn't have to.

8.

True Love

           there is only one way
              to describe
                    "True Love"

   does anyone know
       that one way ?

           *

          Mr. Nelson Algren
          1958 West Evergreen
          Chicago Illinois
           *

In Chicago Illinois, you
   are really at home
      whether you like it or not, baby,
            and, whether you like it
               or not
         You Are My Friend
           so don't pees me off!

9.

     Come into my house
     tonight
     Dick
and I will show you
      this new work
         "Houses at Night"
   It & this page, there not here, are not the same
            except in a
              manner of
                speaking
      it is not
      "A Portrait of Jean-Marie"

tho it cd be, sir
it is also not
"A Portrait of Barbara Harris"
whom I don't know
though I like her plenty

she's a lot like me
(my own name is
"Mr. Brigadoon")

10.

I am constantly being caught up
in my own commotion
it is now a slow commotion
The radio turns me on

11.

Commotion over, clothes in hand I wait
in Mr. Ron Padgett's furlined
bridge-jacket
who shivers now
in Paris, Oklahoma
between Galveston &
Mobile a word
incidentally
invented
cross that out
coined
by Mr. Marcel Duchamp
to describe a
lady finger

12.

it's too cold in here but not for me
in my present balloon state to write this love song

"Cold rosy dawn in
New York city"
hovering over the radio

13.

I woke up this morning
it was night
you were on my mind   LADY BRETT
looking for a home
for the boll weevil

        nothing like that in New York city
        it's all in Oklahoma
        where you-all
        can learn to talk like me
        if "you-all" is
        Mr. Ron Padgett, "The
        American Express"

14.

He's a good friend of mine
although   he fears he is unable to love
        people
      who have no politesse
           whatever that may be
thanks anyway, Frank
you're not without *con brio*
n'es ca'fe?

                (thanks, Ed)

15.

    I quote
    from "The Code of the West"
    a work
    by Mr. Ed Sanders

whose "Poem From Jail"
I highly recommend
On second thought
I quote instead
this work
by Mr. Marcel Duchamp
which
oddly enough
I also give high
                recommendation

16.

THE CODE OF THE WEST

1. Sob when you read "Black Beauty."
2. The true test of a man is a bunt.
3. Dare to do your duty.
4. Press the tip of the tongue on the gums
   behind the upper teeth as for t, and expel
   the breath with vibrations of the vocal cords.
5. He went to the windows of those who slept
   and over each pain like a fairy wept.
6. Halt!
7. Loosen your snood.
8. Close your eyes and doze.
9. Jove! Jove! This shepherd's passion
   is much upon my fashion!
10. Drill.

17.

you know
        once people paid no attention to me
MAYAKOVSKY
                        in the garden of my memory
& now
    passion's flower

wilts
constantly
because
                    my lady love is a Holy Roller!
                    Her body is a sponge
                    it has no mud

Tonight's heat
will dry that mud
and it will fall into dust
                              I'm already in it
                              the body I mean
                              not the dust
                    however if you are in the dust
                              kindly hop into this tub of
                                        black water please
now hand me that quail
lean me against the belly of a woman
                                        (you are that woman)

                    18.

knock on the door of her house
                              knock-knock

the sun is out
river flowing in a window
a geranium trembling automobile
droning
across the screen
                    Turn back to look
            you dont see
            the door open
            you are   standing there
                                        I mean
                                        I am sitting here
                              between the door
                              to a world full of others
                    like yourselves

and the droning solitude of this here Los Angeles
        Freeway
            How to get off?

                    19.

                Hi, Bears!
do you believe in magic?
                    good!
                    because I am here
                    to make a monkey out of you
The best way
to make yrself a monkey
is to jump down
(spin around)
pick a bale of cotton

                        if you don't understand
                        that
                        you will never understand
                        your country's history
            1000 volumes a year
            ooze from the minds
                            of dead monkeys
                    and yet
                we are still too dull
                    to understand
                        them
                            or that
                        *
Kiss me!   it is not at all unpleasant
                to be kissed by a monkey
            if you are a monkey
                            I am not a monkey
                    I do not have a monkey on my back
            I am not a monkey's uncle
                    turn page

20.

Only a monkey would read this
                    THE ENCYCLOPEDIA OF FLIES
                                over 250 flies
                        photographed
                    in living color
These 250 flies were tied "up"
        executed
by hand
                    Not my hand
                                The Little Sisters

21.

            There are no flies on me, New York City
                        oh

22.

There are, however,
            two sorts of landscapes
                the interior
                and
                    the exterior
        as well as the other
                which we will not go into here

23.

One song I have always liked
                    is
                        "Hope you Happy Monkey"
            that's the truth
            it's by Ruth Krauss

24.

There you are
There I go
                    past The Majestic Men's Clothes
                        slightly dissheveled
            is a nice phrase
                    it has impact
                    like the three pricks
                        Alice gave
                    to Joe Gould
                    in 1933
                            MOTHER
                        that's Alice's idea of Wonderland

25.

She happens to be a sex expert, among other things
if you are squeamish I'd better not tell you
WHAT other things . . .
                    "How did Red China get the "O" bomb?"
                            no one knows
                            No one will ever know
because no one
        is a tautology
                        let's have no truck
                            with tautologies

26.

                    This poem
                        has no truck
although it does provide
a sort of Reader's Digest
of Oriental sex practices
                            under the sheets
                            Who threw the panties into

Mother's Tea

is a good example of one
of the many unanswered questions
life provides

Where did the beautiful
British secret agent
lose his nightie
is another
it was not a Majestic nightie
nor was it a man's nightie
unless of course
the Beautiful British
secret agent
was a female impersonator

Perhaps that was his secret
There has always been a
quick turnover
among British secret agents
Look! there goes one now

27.

I am here today   a gentleman
with time on my hands
you are in my heart
during
The Four Seasons
which are
1. springtime
2. bedtime
and so on

28.

There is a revolution going on in my skin
I have the gift of young skin
no pimples

which is why I am here today
I would like to introduce myself
However
it will be better
between us
if I don't   cheat
The victory is always to the sweet
so keep on the ball, buddy
I mean "the button

29.

COME ALIVE
Meet Me At The Smoke Ring
(Get Your Piles Out of Vietnam)
Let's Love One Another
(Equality for Homosexuals)
YES

SUCK
Stand Up For Dikes
Commemorating The Visit
Of Pope Paul X   We Won't Go
to NYC
1965   I'm for Legalized
Abortion
NO MAN IS GOOD THREE TIMES

30.

Life certainly is marvelous
when you're in love
isn't it?
Consequently, it is important
to be in love
most all the time
but not all of the time
When you are in love

all the time
        you get bored
            because life is boring
          when it's always the same
    that's a strange theory

31.

    It's a theory of strange
  I am in love
    right now. I am in love with
    <u>(fill in name of person in room)</u>
see me about this later, (ditto) .
I am not in love with Mr. Walter Steck
        He was or
        was not
           recently elected
      to the assembly
Just for the record   I found Mr. Walter Steck
          recently
           at five o'clock in the afternoon
           on Garcia Lorca's birthday
     lying in the gutter
           on his button

33.

   O ship of states!
 Sail on allegorical poem
       about wispy affairs

34.

Branching out
shooting all night
he grounded
himself
on a button

35.

you stand
hitting upon things
you hadn't thought upon
when you get into the pictures
you wake up
inside an oval
portrait
I mean a woman
A beautiful reminder sitting on a line
it could be a steamship line—   or even a ferry
line
you take it right
down the line

36.

Life is boring when you are Tarzan of the Apes
e.g.   You step out from behind a bush
and say
Yes, I am M'sieur Tarzan

37.

Dick Gallup arrives at this point
and says
"Life is too boring"

38.

Jacques Louis David is crying in his crib
he is not bored
Jane has given him a banana

39.

Dick reads those lines
they bore him   but I laugh plenty

40.

David is sobbing bitterly
in the jungle

"Shut up
or I'll kill you"

He doesn't want to

41.

He wants the white
tempera
paint
with which I am painting out the words
in this here comic book
"Tarzan of the Apes"
so that I can fill in the words

42.

"The Words" is a good book
it is the autobiography of Mr. Jean-Paul Sartre
from age zero to ten
In it
he tells what a little shit he was.
"I'm going doo-doo" says Jacques-Louis David
we have words
and he falls asleep
unexpurgated

44.

Life is long

its sure been a long times
crossword puzzle
since I last
was here

That Spring of '65
that was

my best year
that was also a good year for
Dancers
Buildings and
People in the Street

*

in the cell block
a boy
invented
the mahogany cage
before he rested
The climate was a song
Crowds disperse my
purpose
my great calm

Dim lights
turn me off
the radio parts
the curly hair
me on the floor
saying

45.

"Go now
and get me a vast band-aid

46.

I'm sitting here thinking that these words that I have been
borrowing from Mr. James "The Rock" Proust and son
should stretch to the end of at least one
period in my life.
They did.

48.

"What I really like is new girls to fuck"
            that's a good line
                        it was said by Dick Gallup
                  who let it drop there
                        that to be explained later
      in the backroom
            of The Peace Eye
                        that's all I know

49.

Cow a is not cow b
      Dick
                        Count Korzybski said that
            that Polish cocksucker
            is what a drunk called HIM
                        He didn't mean Korzybski
                              though
                        He'd never heard of Him
                  I don't know what he meant
                        I was drunk
                  He was speaking Polish
                        He didn't like Counts
That's a fact

50.

According to FACT
                  William Burroughs
                        studied under
                        that Polish cocksucker
                              in Chicago
I've always admired Count Korzybski
and, in fact, I've always admired William Burroughs
                        Hi Bill!

I do not, however, admire FACT Magazine
because it costs too much money
and probably for other reasons
too vague to be present

51.

After all, this is art, not life
or, on the other hand, after all,
this is life, not art. Please
check one of the two. In any case,
it's six of one and half a dozen of
"the other"

52.

Listen

Is there a Pseudotsuga Menziesii
in your house ?
if so, there is
nothing to worry about
it would be hard to find
a house
in America
where Pseudotsuga Menziesii isn't
all over the goddam place
it has a lovely talent

53.

cross something out here

54.

Imagine yourself
driving on a super highway
with your friend

Mr. Bob Harris

besides being a genius
he is also a perrennial
problem child
            who mooches off his friends
            sleeps with any available women
            ignores his children
            and drinks ceaselessly
                        like yourself
    you may have to stop often
    to relieve yourself
    because your friend
    suffers
    from a terrible disease previously
            unmentioned
    but not in this poem
                    nor by anyone you
                        have ever known
            in this vale of tears

55.

back on the freeway   the cars pass
    over your eyes ears nose and throat   and hairs
        no interviews   no photographs
            no autographs
                    in this dream
which is so realistic
    you can almost hear my voice
                in your ear
                    which is on the level of your back,
                                    dear

56.

Fish and Cheep Pet Shoppe
The Pioneer

Block Drug   Manhattan
Fox's Corner
Martha's
              are all places I have never visited
                                though I keep meaning to

                              *

the mist of may
              is on the gloaming
        and all the clouds
                          are halted still
                  fleecey
            and filled with holes
                  They are alight with borrowed
              warmth
                          just like me

                        57.

            Italy is a boot in the atlas
                          The snowball centuries rolling
                          collect only the tiny footprints of
                          hens
        the burning bush attracts
            the hen

                            One comes to take one's
                            place in the sun, only
                            to smother inside the
                            hide of a hen
                  These passages were taken
                    from the works of a man
                        who was once attacked by a butterfly
                            in broad daylight

58.

Come in !

Hello Lee   Mr. Lee Crabtree
                                    of The Fugs
                            just came in

59.

Rhetoric
is what we make
out of our quarrels
with others

                        out of
                        our quarrels with ourselves
                        we make poetry
            Yes, that is true,

60.

                        In my house, every cloud
                        has a silver lining
            there is only one cloud in my house
Inside that cloud is a joke
                        it is an inside joke

61.

on every mirror
in my house
            is a big kiss
                        placed there by Mr. Joe Brainard
                    *
            it's very exciting
                not to be asleep

62.

If Joe Brainard were here now
he'd be excited
             about giving me those kisses
that's a lie
                  clickety-clack   William Saroyan

63.

What we do in life
in New York City
                    in 1965
        we "get the money"

64.

                    GET THE MONEY !
        that was Damon Runyon's favorite expression
the heat is coming on
like gangbusters
                  (Eric Partridge
                        History of American Climate)
                  I guess that means
                  it's time to burst,
                  eh,
                        M'sieur Cloud ?

65.

Speaking of Picasso, he once said
        that for him
                    true friendship cannot exist
                  without the possibility of
                  sex
                        That is true
        I have many men friends

I would like to fuck
               However, I am unable to do so
               because I am not a homosexual
fortunately
this makes my life complex
rather than simple
          and vice versa

66.

Dream on O impudent virgin
               Guillaume Apollinaire
     you too are aware of the duality of nature and of
the spirit
       and you too prefer the visible
              to the invisible
      I salute You !
          (Salutes)

67.

the true Guillaume
is a great deal more interesting
than many of those people
whose misfortune it is
not to be so true

68.

           the logic of that is
       lost
          but may be recovered
   in the theory of Mr. A.N. Whitehead to the effect
that a human being
        may possess two kinds of perception / that
    as it were
      work from opposite ends.

69.

So, in conclusion, may I say
that this is what life is like here
                    you drink some coffee, you get some sleep
                    everything is up in the air
            especially us
                    who are me

70.

Now
in the middle of this
someone I love is dead
                            and I don't even know
                                            "how"
                    I thought she belonged to me
How she filled my life when I felt empty.
How she fills me now.

71.

games of cribbage   do you understand
            with Dick   that?
        filled this afternoon

72.

What excitement !
                    crossing Saint Mark's Place
            face cold in air
                    tonight
                        when
                                that vague someone waving
                                on a bicycle turned me
                                            back on

73.

What moves me most, I guess

/   of a sunlit morning

is being alone

with everyone I love

crossing 6th and 1st
at ice-cold 6 a.m.

from whence I come home
with two french donuts, pepsi
and the New York Times

74.

Joy is what I like
That, and love.

January 1966

Due to poems like "Tambourine Life"—which may turn out to
be one of the milestones of the generation—TED BERRIGAN
is considered a leader of the young American poets. He says
about his work: "I like Frank O'Hara's *Personism: A Manifesto*
and his statement on poetics in Don Allen's *The New American
Poetry* [Grove]. I tend to exhaust my poetics in a given series
of poems, such as *The Sonnets*. Then I wait. In the meantime,
I simply assume everything & go on my nerve." Books of his
poems include: *The Sonnets* (Grove: 1967) and *Bean Spasms*
(Kulchur Press: 1967) in collaboration with Ron Padgett and
Joe Brainard. He was the editor of the important "C" magazine
(which also published pamphlets by some of the young New
York poets). Mr. Berrigan was born in 1934 in Providence, Rhode
Island. "I went to lots of Catholic schools," he writes. "Then
in 1954 I quit college and joined the Army and was sent to
Korea. In 1957 I began attending the University of Tulsa. College was easier to take as a 'Korean Veteran.' I felt most of the
time as if I were 'On the Road.' In Tulsa I met Ron Padgett,
Dick Gallup, David Bearden and Joe Brainard. In 1960 I came
to New York and lived in a store front with Joe. In 1962 I took
a trip to New Orleans, met my wife, got married, and came
back to New York," where he now lives on the Lower East Side
with his wife and son David and daughter Kate.

OKLAHOMA PLATES

The ground lives out its days as a landscape of refusal,
     begging its purpose from the feet of slaves
Dawn levels its forehead, its eyes
My heart takes aim
The light outdistances me
Leaves wake to tear themselves free from the horizon
     at uncalculated velocities,
velocities of grief . . .

Your youth goes up in smoke in front of the rising sun
My hands grow old

I am ready to pass out of my body
I surpass myself
I am leaving you behind
with your entourages of sadness
(this poem is really
in French)
Today I feel French
Tomorrow I'll feel Danish
Next month I won't feel
The world is passing out of itself
     into history
A wind hurtles   lame dial

This country is guarded by the logic of pain

DREAMS OF THE ACCUSER

All day the rain on this long voyage into wreckage plunges
inside the distance of my sleep, these lands that have cast

themselves down from a high place. Chickens riot on the roads and abdicate the provinces of grief. The hog dreams of absence. Great Americans rebuild their vistas of unpopulated landscapes intersected by telegraphy and ESP. Coinage flocks inside the heads of the farmer's daughters. Savings dry up slowly in the angry light that is breaking the farmer's wrist. Someone is battening down my hatches by happenstance. I allude to "you." Outrageous green, you have not strewn my path with flowers, nor thrown yourself for silver at my feet.

THE DYNASTIES, THE SKY OVERHEAD

Principles of aerodynamics converging in the light,
As if the blueness of the day existed
Only to prevent it, the way you follow in the snow,
The berries of the future in your grown-up hands.
You look in on
The spectacle, a frail glare of loaded . . .
Others had gone ahead
For plunder. A jazz musician is dead
In your sleep, the dreams worsen.
Some new weather breaks on the horizon,
You lean against me near a yellow tree.
I go on studying a manifesto
For the identification of obsolete
War planes. In it a Chinese-built fighter is cruising
Over the mainland. Below, on the mountainous terrain,
The test pilot's countrymen fought to repulse
The invaders. Now a light rain is coming down in the street
Of the festival. We enter the zone of the unbearable
Secrets, fear of sudden reparations.
"I love you" was a promise in the slowly falling sun,
And the world the world belongs to no one. The flowers
    are for you.

A BOOK OF SHELLS

Mornings you trudge these beaches with misgivings,
as great colonies of giants
unfold alliances nearby.
Defiant, you spurn their treaties,
and the world goes on like this.

You search through all the grains of sand
for the mystery of stone.
You might try
Oriental magic,
to help you experiment with your true intentions.
Someday soon the sea will reveal itself
in its own tongue.
The sky leaves you empty-handed,
like a feeling of joblessness you find
you're unable to accommodate.

Otherwise you require
that days take on the appearances
of commemorations.
The smudges of evening will swarm up
against you and all
you stand for: propensities, favorites,
and, as a rejoinder,
smallness even—those ways you have
of alerting yourself to ceaseless developments,
such as vast crews of workmen putting up
apartment buildings down the coast.
You are disadvantaged
by foreclosures, the newer tactics
of rescue-artists.

The year closes its grip on the defunct
subscription, waves behave along the lines
of the title, that dour secret you withheld
as a key to its logic:

now you have everything you want, but mostly
you act as though your life were really a movie,
with huge outdoor crowds looking on in the night.

RANDY BLASING writes: "The poem defines its own reality,
its logic or continuity being fixed by the shape of the poet's
imagination at a given time. There is nothing to be decoded or
translated: the poet does not communicate in terms of symbols
but attempts to create other worlds of experience which are self-
contained and which are accessible only through the use of
language. The reader enters at his own risk." Born in 1943 in
Minneapolis, Minnesota, Mr. Blasing attended Carleton College
and The University of Chicago. He is married and teaches at the
College of William and Mary.

HIM: THE ROACH

I know now. It has been him
after all, the same one I
have burned, flushed down my toilet,
crucified beneath my thumb

with equal redundancy.
I have never seen more than
one of him at one time. I
know now. I have watched him eye-

ball to eyeball. It has been
him: the roach. I have found him
in my pants, my hair, my soup.
I have lain in bed and seen

him tottering over me up-
side down on the ceiling. I
have tattooed him with pins and
buried him across town deep

under. And he has returned,
knock-kneed in an overplus
of paranoia. At night
I have risen from behind

locked doors only to know his
fullness. I have gone by touch
across this room, myopic,
and I have crushed out the face

of that one inkspot mismatch
on the floor, imagining
the horror of his silence,
his holiness, him: the roach.

THE GLOVE

In its absence it has become beautiful,
    my black-leather, my rabbit-fur-lined glove,
given over to the foreignness of strangers,

    of mad dogs thieving away to the deep woods
       with my lost glove. I imagine even
the hunger of hobos and the coveted taste

    of leather in their infamous mulligan stews.
       I consider my lost glove. I consider
the copulation of rabbits, the precise instant

    of conception of that hapless mother's son
       who would inhabit my lost glove. I think
of the busy, unknowable chain of commerce,

    the wholesale and the retail of my lost glove.
       And today I leave my home uncertain
which will effect attention to itself—the one

    gloved hand or the one gloveless. I revisit
       my itinerary of the night before:
Huffy's Sinclair, the Eagle Mart, and Tic-Toc Lounge;

    no one has seen my lost glove. Later, I find it
       grease-stained behind the cash register of
the Campus Grill. I pull it on, my slipped skin,

    and it fits like a good metaphor in that
       fortuitous gathering of elements:
cowhide, rabbit fur, the five fingers of my hand.

THE MENAGERIE

You say you know me. I am the one
who appears suddenly at parties.
When I am late, which I am always,

you cry *procrastinator*, and flap
your ears like any old basset hound.
Your jellyfish women take my hand,

feeling the hoofed fingers stuck with glue.
In our various wars of attrition,
you come paddling up your Rubicon

with nothing but a jackass' jaw
to lay me under. You cry *stopgap*
over the potatoes I have dropped,

the fumbled passes, the killed smalltalk.
And when I huddle in some corner
and hunch my shoulders against your clear

plastic tombstones for warmth, sir, you cry
schizophrenic. I am your burlap bag
of glue, your palomino frothing

at the mouth. You carry me around
with you always. Do you understand me?
Say it. You understand perfectly.

FOIBLES

I: *HP*

You were always a one to
call a spade a petunia.
Your forbidding tongue lashed at
our vernacular, that the
iron lungs we tenanted

were not sardine cans: they were
"respirators." You saddled
the wrack of our bodies with
exercises, heat treatments.
Behind your back we called you

amazon. You envied us.
You told us the afflicted
are assured a place in the
hereafter. It was vaguely
Biblical, like clear water

over stone. Would you have thought
my laundryman years later
would label my shirts with an
"HP"? Or that the state of
Massachusetts, year after

year, would issue my license
plates with an HP also?
It was right somehow, neither
a euphemism nor a
fish can: handicapped person.

You would envy me my glib
identification, my
clear waters flowing to the

hereafter. For you I would
sell my car and go shirtless.

II: *Acquaintances*

Grocer, tailor, all my stock
acquaintances, behind your
elastic smiles there is the
assumption I am less than
intelligent. You watch me.

You equate my clumsy walk,
my paralytic hands with
my intelligence. And I
disappoint you. Always there
is the expectation I

will drool or make guttural
sounds or have convulsions. I
can do all three but I will
not let you see me with my
hair down in public. I will

remain articulate and
deep-throated and immensely
ethereal. Yet I am
grateful for your improbable
amenities. I am "sir"

to you despite your knowledge
of my madness. You ask me
for the weather. You smile when
I tell you it is snowing
in July. I will sustain

your fable. I will have you
all in my home. I will squat

for you. I will scratch my arm
pits and grunt like an ape. And
you will say, Thank you. Thank you.

III: *The Game*

You are my friends. You do things
for me. My affliction is
your hangup. It is yours more
than it ever could could be mine.
You spread my affliction thin

enough to go around once
for all of us. You put my
coat on for me when I ask
you. You put my coat on for
me when I do not ask you.

You embrace my shoes with your
compassion. You tell me I
would be less apt to fall with
rubber soles. You carry things
for me. You tell me they are

heavy things. How it would be
difficult for anyone
to carry them. You open
mustard bottles for me. You
tell me how hard it is to

open mustard bottles. I
agree with you. I will not
destroy our game. At night I
dream I am Sampson. I will
topple coliseums. I

will overwhelm you with my
brute power. I will knock you
dead. I will open mustard
bottles for you. I will show
you how easy it really is.

DREAMSIDE BESTIARY

Home has been a tree-house all
      along, I find, somewhere
off in the woods. Going there, I say
      to myself, why have I not
         before thought of it
in that perspective. At the dream's edge,

      later, I turn. I hear them,
         first, the raccoon, his
paws frisking the room like shovels, then
      the girl, the tall, beautiful
         albino girl who
follows the raccoon, her milk-white skin

      and silver, shoulder-length hair
         dazzling the room.
Her intention becomes apparent:
      to order the animal's
         rummaging, the stove,
breadbox, bureau drawers spilled open,

      knowing, in fact, the precise
         position of each
rummaged item. When the animal stops,

he sees me in her light, and
   as I see him, a fox
now, he turns from the girl, sidling

  back to the furthest corner
    of the room. The girl
nods yes and yes, her pink eyes like suns.
   And the raccoon, later a fox,
    breathes deep in his heat,
witnessing the silences between them.

Now working as an editor for a book publisher in his native
Boston, HAROLD BOND was born in 1939 and earned a Master
of Fine Arts from The Program in Creative Writing at The University of Iowa and an AB in English-Journalism from Northeastern University. Work of his has appeared in *The New
Yorker*, *Saturday Review* and *Harper's*; and he won a first prize
in the 1967 *Kansas City Star* Awards for poetry. His first book
called *Dancing on Water* is scheduled for publication in the early
future. "I've never really given much thought to why I am a poet
or what my poetics are, and I do not think I would want to,
either. The poets I read and the poems I write reveal my tastes
in poetry, but I have no aesthetic bag to expound," the poet
states. "My obsession the ten years I've been writing poetry has
been how and when I am going to write the next poem."

THE PLAINS OF ABRAHAM

A man puts your hand on the small
of her back. Just where the shirt rises
back begins to play. The mind
can't stand the pressure for long, however.
It boils down, and waits to be poured
over the faces of the very plain, the homely
no one thinks "I'll possess."

                Thought! it turns
its back on the very skin that gave its birth
and even toes become exceedingly strange
like a man exiled for his resonant face
to the smallest of the Carolines, the edge
where a leg takes on the shape
perception forgets to track down, and adds
to a file the ocean holds up.

The ocean, fertile bed with sheets of real foam.

Legs bare in the photograph
a place we've never seen by itself
and would like to visit, maybe even stay:
there are the senior visitors.
One separates himself from the rest
he ambles over and takes your hand
and the hand of your girlfriend, golden in the sun.

"Ambiguity is pleasure," he says.
"Anything we are sure we can never enjoy.
The mind does its best with the passing days,
adding up to something at best. The faculty for heat
survives on the lawns of the coldest academies
burning our fingers as on a stove
children are transfigured through pain
to a surer grasp stiff with pleasure."

The girl grows into a young girl.

You ride past her in a train of thought.

He helps himself to your food
and under the stars will lead you back to her
lovely and tanned but somehow inconspicuous.

DIAMOND

A heart speaks and you are spooked
Coming to rest above Mt. Olympia
Instead of thirteen miles across noisy brown glare
                              to Bridgeport (in eastern U.S.)

And you rest your arms, a lemonade in blue glass
Soothes as if I soothe you
Like a factory in the night

Large factory: Lhasa toils gigantic
inside a cup you are drinking mountains
. . . a pork barrel hidden from
quiet vegetarians digesting the sun . . .
flutes called up through gauze
of the Pink Brick Motel . . . freedman
caravans focus slowly over your clover bed . . .
clearing your throat you disturb another virgin lake

Small factory: rancid yak butter
cause you to laugh unawares as a testy goon
smites you in the rolling dawn of a particle . . .
gun slides on a far wall . . .
piles of bored newsmen in the corner
serve irritations begun as a closet

by taking up space ... Pica
lettering the cat obscures
if you have a cat ... I have a cat ...
I have a small ink eraser without my hand ...
I have, here on the table as I write,
several new books and the death of Stephen Crane

You shoot out of the lamination of a chair
To verify, not lists, but the sake of a list
In white porcelain cup, leaves

Of never having to carry your heart
Toward a storeroom that forces it to speak
Because actually you and I are always speaking

AGAINST THE GRAIN

... either, over the shoulder enjoy leaning. Don't
Touch it. Skyway pumpkins lounge
Rocking beside me but I thrive straight
Away. Large early centers blur off (Look, Johnny
See the Indians at home on their Maine blankets
Lobster smoke disappearing between the
Tree. Don't knock it over.) looking over.

Would you turn it down a quarter inch?
Now I rest between the teeth of
Courage, silence, gold. I pass the lines
Painted below the pilot's "Otto" window
Like a lake going up from gasoline
To drowning above the clouds (of starch beauty).
Probing a border the police sighs
The trestle agh agh agh over the train late
Mathematics pass hot trees. Dutch door. Don't move.

I wander the banks and Wanda was.

Sounds not so much mingle curtains
Yellow against green and then of course
The perfect right green has against yellow
In the dusty white pod against here
Beside your wife who is too sinuous and tall
To be a real Dutch . . . little men in pocket charms
Made her. She travels . . . an easy window
Sunlight on Bavarian cottage window
In natural southern Bavaria. Large blue
Against the Pittsburgh sky. Sky.
Summer in the pedigree under Moscow's dome.

Take the summer.

She delivers a folded postcard to the hill.
Mingling feeds rain and forest an afterthought
As I am planning to feed astronomy
To the turkeys here for a year
(Light snows over the eighty mile ear)
Pure ground plum stew chugging up.

Early in the morning it quieted down somewhere
Among the flamingoes. Suddenly I realized this was
    because
They had no place to sit. I shaved for a while in the mirror
And crawling out of the tent (take the summer) I crawled
Out of the tent and talked over to the shore
Most of the people were eating already.

Born in 1943 in Philadelphia, Pennsylvania, MICHAEL
BROWNSTEIN was raised in New Jersey, Tennessee and Ohio.
Study followed at Antioch College and The New School for
Social Research in New York City. In 1966 he received a Poet's
Foundation Award and currently he is a Fulbright Fellow liv-
ing in Paris. A selection of his poems was published in 1967
by C Press.

THE LAKE: CODA

Last night I dreamt I saw
Your face in the lake   I hid till
With the sun the small
People in the lake awoke   And shook

The dew from their silk jackets
Aloft to flowers and grasses
Like a morning lamp, and swept
Sleep from the woods with wings

Like tiny brooms   Until the ways
Of the minor world glowed
With traffic in each inch, and day
Rung from pool to hilltop like a bell

You live with the pale and weak
And meek ones in the mud
To whom the keys of the air are given
And lights rising throne on throne

YOU (I)

The door behind me was you
and the radiance, there like
an electric train wreck in your eye
after a horrible evening of waiting outside places in the
      rain for you to come
only to
find all of them, two I know, the rest scullions, swimming
      around you
in that smoky crowded room like a fishbowl

I escaped from, running away from you and my André
      Breton
dream of cutting your breasts off with a trowel
and what does that matter to them or to you now, but just
      wait it's still early
to the children embroidered in the rug, who seem to be
      setting up siege
engines under a tree house full of midgets who look like
      you.
Where are you in this sky of new blue
deltas I see in the drapery, and your new friends wearing
      bamboo singlets
what are they doing down there in the moat waving
      tridents like stalks of corn?
Me, I'll be happy to see their blood spilled all over the
      bedspread
pavilions of your hands as an example. If you come home
      right now I'll scrunch your hat
between my thighs like a valentine before you have time
      to wipe them.

SONNET

The orgasm completely
Takes the woman out of her
Self in a wave of ecstasy
That spreads through all of her body.
Her nervous, vascular and muscular
Systems participate in the act.
The muscles of the pelvis contract
And discharge a plug of mucus from the cervix
While the muscular sucking motions of the cervix
Facilitate the incoming of the semen.

At the same time the constriction of the pelvic
Muscles prevents the loss of the semen. The discharge
Makes the acid vaginal lubricant
Alkaline, so as not to destroy the spermatozoa.

STATIONERY MOTION

Sleep is great. To be
valuable in a tundra, tundra lightning, etc.
The malevolent legacy of dreams . . .
All the time we are discussing this
they are lighting fires under us
with our hands—but pressing close
to the gate of trees we approach the mansion
and cannot be shelled by the light . . . The shade
offered by a sleigh is artificial but the young Russian
men have been falling down the steppes one century,
    a topic
for disagreement among the historians and women. But
    we tire
of the linen animals of reading, and lie
a little on green paper to liven things up,
followed by a stork and a girl in gracious
greens, tall and stately, looking to be fucked
by an Ambassador. We cannot do that, I'm afraid.
But we do the next best thing, shave and
go for a ride in ourselves through the goldenrod
ooh-ing and ah-ing at the deer that came down to drink
at the imagination. They came to load the gazebos with
    tubes of cream
and we were awake all the time, but didn't notice we were
    falling asleep.

Now the landscape has been dialled, but its sentence

fell apart like a baseball hit by a sultan, the poor
cover changed to rags and ending up in the lap. For
    female boys
there are swords, but for men there are only butts.
So I go on smoking, and tears fall out of my
the face, which makes the same impression as my bulbs,
or their babies. As in a parade, the ribbons, pigs, and
    fiddles
increase as they come nearer, and then growing more
    distant from us recede, as in a
program. But don't cling to my every word as if you were
thinking it might become an aspirin. Luncheon before the
    business of the game
of moonlight, a statuary of day, girls stretching first
thing in the day, the dormitory crowded with the smell
    of their
darkness—under a full moon, tea, or moon.
That's a catalogue, not a display. The bear inside
the lion inside the man sows violence but falls asleep,
or sows dragon's teeth but forgets to brush its teeth, and
already shadows creep towards the rented rooms from the
    sheep from
which the ideas have gone, so all there is is breakfast
    and deafness,
wind, truculent azalea, and forms. The whole trouble with
    this academy
of dreams is its possession of a fire exit into reality, whose
flames are really as cool as a bath in dreams. Great
consciousness of truth, a blaze of white, and dreams—
    everlastingly
faint lakeside in salad—no solution, nor hope of a boot
    to clean dreams.

"Poetry goes on all the time, in talk, sleep and thought," TOM
CLARK says. "The other, 'real' poetry goes on pieces of paper.
I could live without it, I guess. But its unnecessariness sometimes

makes it delightful." Currently Poetry Editor of *The Paris Review*, Mr. Clark was born in 1941 in Chicago, Illinois and attended The University of Michigan and Cambridge University. For four years he lived and travelled in Europe and lectured on American poetry at The University of Essex. He is now active among the poets and painters who work on the Lower East Side in Manhattan. Among his books of poems are: *Airplanes* (A Once Book: 1966) and *The Sand Burg* (Ferry Press, London: 1966); he has also published a play *The Emperor of the Animals* (Goliard Press, London: 1967). Harper & Row will bring out a collection of his poems, called *Stones,* in the fall of 1968.

STYRO

quite is high
quatic

deliverance rates   dial   3

in ex

trees palling steins ing

snail of it, acrid, the dumps

the "sill row"

to knees smoke

sir fins

drub in minnow the illicit of haunt (bite)

crust, stub, crayon, chives

Galatea dumbing hard

cawl o'wrist it?

nubs

(Nile)

an green   and ever attack

styrene mistachio dubloon

rack sun correct ratchet

Dumbo in   size

sign or hone win

gold when aft

whom   whine

it, state

BLUE KINDS

soda block flange flume slim
donut at all
sorghum dew pat ermine leaps
doctor row

farm & blunt
tap locks & bloom fins cabal
panned heat in float of rest
nuages

time lap tarn   gone pens
crate add a rest mountain
Galapagos firm in treatment
which all ace low

fur notcher pant blur seeds
coin lean blue
mist oat a match
cape & nine

scab granite cab bow pole
elm tent paste rift
crane packs
summit

crotalus
dew hone dome load
palm trunk fringe
garb
pins mass lucky
                    lock

just road choice fifty ditch   away above pipe peers noon
        chance not hysterical laugh   it lap just car been
slowly & factory wearily   petrified call room   state him tion
        walks stops aura dow   banks room arms   and not and face
sits up kiss moves   white water waves white   looks strikes
        under away apart closes   away remain   out shouts out
cushion style same blonde cushion style   road pats late
        kiss while comes slowly puts still   upstairs is comes
    too   him that stairs mad   heart roof better bends
        that that tell that at it's   very there by starts sound
goes   squeezes   less looks flawless leafs   pulls two too
        lakes   distilled didn't concert gives go   takes shaken
    bottom when light   thing   left looks   loft   pelts sof
        things soled fringes   morphine morphine   must differenc
under arm package   flowers   towards jokes   wig house
        don't fifty print house   please please & steps   a   can
    seat   wind upon besides   climbs   is closed cold
        goodby final nearby shack   keep keep to quieted large
        a fin   pit caps copter quieted come down   soons
    or runs   clapboard door   of liked   face clam drag st
    brokes of and sacks   back sorry box goes   aren't?
        sound mud storm dress   thick is short a haze   haze
    under until depths oar   already breasts   usual rubberized
        lust shark   sailor fit   away a few sand and then
        bulk room   sea boat   gifts guitar   moves slight aw
        pitch after   landscape   were all throws piqued
        encircle   by number abashed   number sleep to last
        cod pounce   shot saccharine   yacht   not the at bo
        grabbed   swim   lanks sleep at looks   isles a tred
        pump part enter kiss   backwards the a nude turns third
        pocket ing down   same aroundthird   slanted nude
        tight sand blonde   fifty held   masses   slant
        bite glass   lame very time lawn   elderly by wings
        walks she she   is angry form   at the I say
            lump number   carry cold only   red glasses
            cent day!   coes   ent there   cap thing
            fleeting spare   eads   and sion pulls
                erable   ment   onds   knees
                    po   sent   tion   aged
                    him is thing had a him is had a him

Now living in San Francisco, CLARK COOLIDGE was born
in 1939 in Providence, Rhode Island. He has published *Flag
Flutter & U.S. Electric* (Lines Books: 1966) and *Clark Coolidge:
Twenty Poems* (Lines Books: 1967). He offers these comments
about some of the exciting dimensions in his work: "As Stein has
most clearly & accurately indicated, Words have a universe of
qualities other than those of descriptive relation: Hardness,
Density, Sound-Shape, Vector-Force, & Degrees of Transpar-
ency/Opacity. I am attempting to peer through the lines into this
possible WordArt Landscape, work within it & return with
Wordscapes, WordObjects to light & refresh the mind so currently overloaded with centuries of medial Language-Tape."
He is currently working with word-structures for electronic
performance.

WHAT IS GOING ON INSIDE HIS HEAD

Angel Hair sleeps with a boy in my head.
She says: School is a drawing of your body,
and she paints lectures on paradox when she screws.
The boy has blue eyes but looks like me.
He says my beauty comes from lectures—
especially when they are boring.
In fact, this love of theirs is boring
and sometimes I cover them with mist to feel
"this true fair world of things, a sea reflecting love."
Below, there is an island where thousands of white balloons
float above a class of high school girls learning grammar.
Earl-Jean sings after supper to the envying nightingales.
And when Angel Hair wakes up, even she looks lovely,
and she spends time with me.
The boy is nice, too, and I like him to adore me.
Sometimes I let him in to walk with me by the fountains
and skyscrapers and listen to "Sexy Ways."
He pays court to me, but I am distant every time.
Then when I tell him about our Lord Tennyson,
wrapped round with a cloak while dying in the moonlight,
he has Angel Hair to turn to for his mad yearnings.
But I am jealous when they kiss and I hear their
        breathings.
They surround me in their sad bliss,
and I watch how the ideas of my legs make them move.
My arms are homework and my blood runs for thoughts.
Still, when I sleep, they watch me, and once
they slept next to me.
They even got used to the smoke in my lungs,
and my heart does not wear them out.
When I read books, they take part in all of it,
and when I want to be alone, they go out for a walk.
They can never leave me, and I hope I will never go away.

HE SPENDS TIME IN SOUTHERN CALIFORNIA

I could ride the Disneyland sky ride forever.
It is always tea time or perpetual autumn,
my Duino, fireworks above my head.
The poets' girl friends ride the bobsled—Maud, Milena . . .
Fenimore sits alone.
I see them all blondes, flighty pink ribbons,
threes in their convertibles zooming home.

Down south, a love note on my door:
"Your intellectuality is so strong it destroys my
    womanhood"
or "Your mouth renders me mad."
Instead, they open up the surf with their dizzy teeth,
thousands of sprinklers light rainbows on the lawn,
even poison pink oleander trees make me cling.

They come again and stay.
In twenty years they look up, mild with pleasure,
and in fifty, too, back like the sea,
back with their careless limbs.
They are always coming to me like Friedrich's
great beautiful lonely cats of prey.
How they leave me with their wrists,
yet I fly above it.

In my heart of daughters they look lovelier than
                                        wild peacock feathers,
shoots under moss, arms, stems. . . .
They come to the breathing names, watering the brush:
Borrego Springs, Mesa Grande, Escondido, Solana Beach,
and there is always a happy day,
and now you abandon me.

[UNTITLED POEM]

You are lighting yourself
The steps in the papers
take "blench" into the tapestry,
watching the place
as happily as you can

The opening of the sleepers are skin boats
A shower is colors held inside,
dark cares behind the shell
The hoops of dressers,
vaseline sticking under your nails,
clear dreams lighten autarchic scratches

You write
        grazing buttons
        spinal cubes in the frost
You are high as lances saying
        Butterflies change deaths
        they are becoming cool
        As the sun passes behind the clouds
        I have made the world dark
        I walk upon half the sky

FORSAKING THE COURSE

> *To forsake the course is to die.*
> —Hobbes

I will be nice to you.
Glaciers move the sea carefully.

But here is a bouquet of angles:
full-bearded faces,
snow lines turning to black acres,
holding fast by another.
If you wish to light the course,
you can only see the dryness far away.
There, weights are placed on the field.
Rings hardly turn against the sky.
Like a bracelet, charcoal fillets
coat the melting glasses.
Someone says: I can't even disintegrate.
Perspicuity, like letters, moves like a crystal
to give you just an hour more.
Fathers are drawing circles on the ground.
This forms our gentleness,
mutual law just above the lines,
a cheek under my skin.
But there are two of you inside, even there.
They have made shirts to stop this,
they have covered sticks with fur
And the warmth belongs only to one form.
Icicles point down to the tracks.
My brothers will cut him up and leave.
You say: you only feel like that at times,
when her legs are lovely—
they melt into the snow—
just wait and you will join them.

[UNTITLED POEM]

There are words that slip out of you
                              (thinking:
        the action of a "leaf falling"

      helps you lie with her
      in slower fucking)
like "erect" (hearing "direct")
or "green eyes" which is my own rising.

"Earth" . . . your blue veins flow to the side.
Your hips are too small.
"I guess they'll have to cut me open."

Jacob fought "his" angel.
"Today I feel nothing
but am afraid of losing you."
Other times, when you light the oven,
bending down,
I have you close the curtains in a night shift,
as I stand outside and ask you to come in.

The Big Bopper told me:
"Girls are mirages."
"Trips cross country are mirages."
"Eyes through the head are mirages."
Still, I want to walk through West Berlin with you,
near the opera house, listening to *Moses und Aaron*—
losing our words.

ANGELS ADORING

1. Praxis

It's a likelier requisition
to see you here.
Draughts entered the walls

when R said
Hell's Angels reach esthetic dehumanization
like poets and saints.
Syrup of Tolu calms you down.
It is not adaptive,
this commutation,
balsam odors, curls slighter than rosettes—
the entities are emblems of exacting symptoms.

Everybody is one
so I do not take you, or even selections.
It is more like imperceptivity,
injuries which preclude the aura on your hand,
playing dead, instead.
Nothing enters into this way,
no balking, no partners   or else hundreds
under a grate.

On a paten he brought a word
"information".
It faced the air between transepts,
ignored its units
as it refracted the spaces' lights.
The hoe's spikes rested it
and the word became a jagged stone.

Your name is leaning behind me.
carol   linda   pythogenic lines,
cilia on embers
shield your songs:
heart feels sad   love gone bad
if you can't find a partner use a wooden chair.

2. Walking Away

From the hills the smog,

measured with petunias,
coats gray and white air
gunmetal blue.
At sunset the water is orange
down the coast.
About midnight trains cross
Sacramento Avenue:
Frisco   Sante Fe   Wabash
an old NY Central.
At the airport the clocks say
Lake Regina 4
Rhinebeck 2
Sydney 11.
The imputation lies with you.
The lake is the vagina,
the hill, mons veneris.
Your name forms your skin
and a homophone thinks your arms
as others.
Only lust specifies this.
As changes appear
they occur first in viewing
before spillways turn them down.
Then like the fire
that leaves no ashes,
love holds itself steady under car lights
and moves west.

3. The Bearer

The strangest part—
everything seems simpler.
Your slippers change,
the bedspread's just like mine,
your hair's longer.
It gets easier to come over.

When the night ends
I get over you
just saying *ragazzo* to myself.
As if tubes are in me
water smells get deeper.
It is what J calls "light
weight", simpler than arms
where the walls are inside   inseparable.
You are sleeping   painted
from your mouth.
The surface melts away.
You are left of me, exactly   repeating,
just saying it again:
I shall never exist.

4. *Quasi-feu le romantisme*

In the roots of the landing
the caiques through the nets were bound
like you   in shades.
They turned you clearer, haughtier
round an isinglass sky.

The last dinner of our stay
someone said, he's a little bit like that.
All he did,
when we had nothing to talk about,
was glance at the cracked lobster shells,
empty green bottles.

The dinner table,
supposititious, dreamier for a final moment,
cleared out the molding
where bars caught our ankles
on the steps.

Near the section of a thousand jails,
the beds displayed switches
for your short Swedish hair.
Where we lay
you imagined the children
turned into three white dogs.
The smallest, most deformed
moved into the tombs.
The shrubbery moved for him,
the pines nestled him closer down.

JONATHAN COTT is a leading member of the stimulating
group of Lower East Side poets who publish in *Angel Hair, The
Paris Review* and *The World* and read at the Poetry Project
at St. Mark's Church In-the-Bowery. Born in 1942 in New York
City, he was graduated from Columbia College and The University of California at Berkeley, and currently lives in London
as a Fulbright Scholar. He has produced programs of contemporary music for WNYC (New York) and KPFA (Berkeley),
written film reviews for *Sunday Ramparts* and articles for
Ramparts; he wrote the essay "New American Poetry" in the
book *New American Arts* (Horizon Press: 1965) and his essays
on Theodore Roethke, John Berryman and James Purdy appear
in *On Contemporary Literature* (Avon Books: 1966). This past
year he has been European correspondent for *Rolling Stone*
magazine.

FEATHERED DANCERS

Inside the lunchroom the travelling nuns wove
sleeping babies on doilies of lace.
A lovely recluse jabbered of bird lore and love:
        "Sunlight tints my face

        and warms the eggs outside
        perched on filthy columns of guilt.
        In the matted shadows where I hide,
        buzzards moult and weeds wilt."

Which reminds me of Mozambique
in that movie where blacks massacre Arabs.
The airport runway (the plane never lands, skims off)
        is bleak—
scarred syphillitic landscape—crater-sized scabs—

painted over with Pepsi ads—
as in my lunar Sahara dream—giant net comes out of sky,
encloses my open touring car. Joe slumps against Dad's
emergency wheel turner. Everyone's mouth-roof dry.

One interpretation. Mother hated blood!
When the duck Dad shot dripped on her leatherette
        lap-robe,
dark spots not unlike Georgia up-country mud,
her thumb and forefinger tightened (karma?) on my
        ear-lobe.

Another interpretation. Motor of my heart stalled!
I've heard truckers stick ping-pong balls up their butt
and jounce along having coast-to-coast orgasms, so-called.
Fermés, tous les jardins du Far West, I was taught—tight
        shut.

So you can't blame them. Take heed, turnpikes.
Wedgies float back from reefs made of jeeps: more offshore
    debris.
Wadded chewy depressants and elatants gum up footpaths.
    Remember Ike's
"Doctor-the-pump-and-away-we-jump" Aloha Speech to
    the Teamsters? "The —"

he began and the platform collapsed, tipping him onto a
    traffic island.
An aroused citizenry fanned out through the factories that
    day
to expose the Big Cheese behind the sortie. Tanned,
I set sail for the coast, down the Erie and away,

and ate a big cheese in a café by the docks,
and pictured every room I'd ever slept in:
toilets and phone-calls and oceans. Big rocks
were being loaded, just the color of my skin,

and I've been travelling ever since,
so let's go find an open glade
like the ones in sporting prints
(betrayed, delayed, afraid)

where we'll lie among the air-plants
in a perfect amphitheatre in a soft pink afterglow.
How those handsome birds can prance,
ah . . . unattainable tableau.

Let's scratch the ground clean,
remove all stones and trash,
I mean open dance-halls in the forest, I mean
where the earth's packed smooth and hard. Crash!

It's the Tale of the Creation. The whip cracks.
Albatrosses settle on swaying weeds.
Outside the lunchroom, tufts and air-sacs
swell to the size of fruits bursting with seeds.

JAPANESE CITY

Centennial of Melville's birth this morning.
Whale balloons drift up released by priests. Whale floats
        parade
followed by boats of boys in sou'westers jiggled by runners
followed by aldermen in a ritual skiff propelled by "surf"—
        girls.
In my hotel room with its cellophane partitions (under-
        watery)
I phone down for ice-water, glass, tumbler, and the cubes.

Cattle for the X-mas Market fill the streets.
Black snouts—a rubby day indeed. Bump the buildings,
        herds.
A Mexican seamstress brings back my underthings shyly
six, seven times a day. One sweats so, lying about.
She mentions marvelous pistachio green caverns
where one canoes through cool midgy Buddha beards

where drafts of polar air sound like cicadas, where—
About the partitions. The other travelers seem—
there were beautiful hairs in the wash-basin this AM—
thick, and they smelled of limes
(good, that jibes with mine—ugh!—)
but mine, how perverse! Form a hoop, you there. Mine,

mine smell like old apples in a drawer. Jim the Salesman
and his cohorts are massaging my feet—a real treadmill

example.
They're in lawn decor, ether machines, and nocturnal
    learning clasps.
And Jim? Plays cards in his shorts, moves black fish
    around.
Black houses, the capitol. Hotel chunks. Sky chunks. The
    squeeze:
green odd numbers—white air, amputations and eagles,
    respite.
Red even numbers—body sections, the ocean sac, the great
    beach.
Green even numbers—oval jewels, quicksand, the haven
    behind the falls.
Jim's stammer is contagious, zen smut about hatcheries in
    the suburbs,
how the women in the canneries came down with the
    "gills",
hence bathtub love-makings, couplings in the sewers.
    The ice-water comes.

The room-clerk's pate shines up through the transparent
    floor.
Soon the sin couples will start arriving, and the one-way
    mirror teams
and the government professionals with their portable
    amulets—
shiny vinyl instruments that probe and stretch.
Much visiting back and forth. Pink blobs. Revels and
    surveys.
Many olive eyes'll close in a sleep of exhaustion. More
    ice-water!

The celebrants in metal regalia jangle and tinkle
moving past the red-roofed villas of the Generals,
past the cubicles of the nakeds and into the harbor,

past glum stone busts of the Generals, sitting in the water.
Out they go, (Jim etc.) into the sweet emptied city,
    leaving behind
the red odd numbers, untouched: pleasure beaches,
    monsoons and sun.

For some years KENWARD ELMSLIE has been an energetic
figure in the New York City literary and art scene. In addition
to two volumes of poetry—*Pavilions* (Tibor de Nagy Editions:
1961) and *Power Plant Poems* (C Press: 1967)—he has collab-
orated with the artist Joe Brainard in two volumes published
by Boke Press: *The Babybook* (1965) and *The 1967 Game Cal-
endar* (1967). Boosey and Hawkes published his three opera
librettos: *The Sweet Bye and Bye, Miss Julie* and *Lizzie Borden*.
In 1967 The New York City Opera Company performed *Lizzie
Borden* which also has been shown over National Educational
Television. Mr. Elmslie has received an award for his creative
work from The National Foundation of the Arts. Born in 1933
in Colorado Springs, Colorado, he now lives in Greenwich
Village.

POEM IN WHICH MY LEGS ARE ACCEPTED

Legs!
How we have suffered each other,
never meeting the standards of magazines
                              or official measurements.

I have hung you from trapezes,
        sat you on wooden rollers,
        pulled and pushed you
                              with the anxiety of taffy,
and still, you are yourselves!

Most obvious imperfection, blight on my fantasy life,
strong,
plump,
never to be skinny
or even hinting of the svelte beauties in history books
                              or Sears catalogues.
Here you are—solid, fleshy and
white as when I first noticed you, sitting on the toilet,
                              spread softly over the
                                      wooden seat,
having been with me only twelve years,
                              yet
as obvious as the legs of my thirty-year-old gym teacher.

Legs!
O that was the year we did acrobatics in the annual gym
        show.
How you split for me!
                One-handed cartwheels
                from this end of the gymnasium to
                        the other,
                ending in double splits,
legs you flashed in blue rayon slacks my mother bought

for the occasion
and tho you were confidently swinging along,
the rest of me blushed at the sound of clapping.

Legs!
How I have worried about you, not able to hide you,
embarrassed at beaches, in highschool
                    when the cheerleaders' slim brown legs
                            spread all over
                            the sand
                            with the perfection
                            of bamboo.
I hated you, and still you have never given out on me.

With you
I have risen to the top of blue waves,
with you
I have carried food home as a loving gift
                            when my arms began un-
                            jelling like madrilenne.

Legs, you are a pillow,
white and plentiful with feathers for his wild head.
You are the endless scenery
behind the tense sinewy elegance of his two dark legs.
You welcome him joyfully
and dance.
And you will be the locks in a new canal between
        continents.
                    The ship of life will push out of you
                    and rejoice
                        in the whiteness,
                            in the first floating and rising of water.

SONG FOR A MAN IN DOUBT

for Jack

The sweet cake tongue
oh women are grounded in the stuff of

without apologies
I offer myself, a thing to hang onto

a place to detour the eye that turns
in on itself

all that space a man makes
impassable with pulleys

Look
you touch my arm and you've touched

all of me, waves inside my skin
The talk of dark places

becomes a conjecture
except as it is the shadow of

or the hollow in
(it has ends it has beginnings)

I am here to fill and be filled
My feet grab the soil like radishes

GRASS

Grass! That's my grass
green poking
cool in hot summer and
yellow under the washtub.
From there I've seen
stars falling. The grass is
my second skin. Drawers opening,
spilling with green.
Or doors. Each blade
the entrance to the grass city.
Lie in it. Open slowly to it.
The creatures moving there
are among endless waving forests
of green. Their tasks, cool
as through tinted glass.
Moving along the natural order.
The names of grasses
have their own smell:
beach grass
beard grass
Bengal grass
bent, bent grass
running barefoot grass
Eric Satie grass
Bermuda, back bent, bluegrass
bluejoint and bog grass
bristly foxtail
bunch grass in bunches
canary grass singing
China grass, ping!
and tiny figures floating in it
cocksfoot grass with splayed talons
cotton grass, cotton grass
crab grass, claws and colors

eel grass, green grass
English rye and feather grass
finger grass for slipping hands on
fly-away grass, with-me grass
four leaved grass with leaf plans
gama, sesame
grama grass

guinea grass for shilling
shalling
hairgrass washed by the rain
hassock grass, the resting place
Japanese lawn grass
sprouting calligraphy
Kentucky bluegrass with
horses and riders
little quaking grass
(what does the green fear?)
love grass I love you
meadow grass will bury me
myrtle grass, orchard grass
pampas grass/oh who shall ride there?
pepper grass and pepper-grinding

pony grass where colts are born
ribbon grass by yards and inches
for necklaces and the ankles of girls
squirrel-tail grass with
small eyes blinking in it
grass called star
grass with stripes
sword grass, inflictor of pain
and Tears for Timothy
the boy who said Yes
tufted hair grass
from hiding in fields and
wooly beard grass
on the chin of the hill.

Oh yellow-eyed grass has known
laughing and whirling
and the stalk of the zebra,
the stalk of the zebra.

CHANGE OF ADDRESS

When the ring gleamed white and your chair hugged the
        edge of it
and I led an elephant into the tent
with my skin like gold lame and black mesh snaking
the length of my legs and hair of pomaded waves curling
        red
to the waist; when I leaped to the back of the elephant,
scaling his five-thousand wrinkles,
yes, feeling his huge bones lurch
and the canvas ripping up
night near my neck (and all the lights blazing);
when I slid down his hairy trunk
to lie flat in the sawdust under the five-cloved foot,
waiting, with the old silk handkerchief over my face,
did you think you were at a circus?

Or the year I wore purple velvet and a torn wedding veil
with a little blue fan spread over my pale thighs
and hovered near the ceiling pouring tea (and good omens
were predicted when the oatmeal cookies were passed)
and you cried out: the recipe, the recipe!
And then when I hitched a ride on that Spanish rooster,
        waving
goodbye with one hand, the other holding tight to his
        blazing
comb, and seven candles burned on the wedding canopy—
did you think it was a painting you were looking at?

You can tear up your lecture notes now, erase every phone
    number
under my name and go shopping in someone else's
    suitcase.
I've changed my address again. And don't waste your
    money
on bi-lingual road maps. After a six-day ocean voyage,
a train ride and three Metro transfers you'd only find
    nights
where the breath churns to snow after dark
and a bench with a man making blankets of his arms, his
    wife
in her black wool nightgown and a three-legged cat
in her lap. And then would you know me?

A CHILD DROWNS IN THE SEA OF ITS OWN IMAGINING

No taller than the grass
she swims in a sea
that is wet and green behind the house
where nothing moves
but the wash. It is Monday.
The only noise is of bees
spinning webs in the sky,
and she's sitting bare
with her skin pressed green
to the ground, faint shapes
of pigeons flying through her eyes
and a dream of fine ladies
bathing.
The idea in her head is to swim,
an impulse of pulling clothes down,
of skirts spread over the sea.

Oh coolness of legs Oh
lettuce and clover morning.
There are waves of dew on the lawn
and my mother is coming.
My mother is coming to chase the sea
with a towel. She shakes
questions all over the grass.

REACHING-OUT POEM

You cut your hair and it made me very shy.
I wondered if you were rich that year you pretended
to be poor. I wanted to please you.
Do you know how many days I thought of it?
Your hair as a roof
might have been a comfortable relationship
but now that you've grown it we don't speak
the same language. I don't care about the alphabet,
only accents. If a person's from Oklahoma,
I assume we understand each other. If I said to you
"Hey you'n down yonder in that sharp outfit"
you might smile if you had been a child there.
But I keep forgetting history. My Colorado friends
climbed mountains together. The hunt.
All that meat cut and wrapped in butcher paper
and stored for winter in the town freezer.
Elk steak. Venison roast.
If I sang "Live Wires for Jesus", a whole line of
pictures would start moving through their heads,
drawn in crayon, at tables in the church back room
where it was cold.
I am talking about understanding. And I think
my life has gone wrong. I mean wanting the wrong
things, but not even admitting it.

LETTERS: *To Barbara*

Why must my life be as obvious as an elbow?
Feelings stick to me like expensive glue—
adhesive, persistently
not pulling away for years.
Little words and big words are flying,
are flying. Red exotic birds
in a history I ooh over, myself above the page,
a wishful face with tear ducts under the bones.
Good bones
I've been told. High. And skull
following the fitter dictates of survival.
Will my child inherit this measurement
and myself the pain?
Do you know what I mean? This plenitude
of silence. This fullness and emptiness.
This stranger who moves wherever I move.

SOUNDINGS

Honey! My mouth is full of it.
Honeysuckle white and yellow
trumpeting from my mouth.
Sweet blossoms, honey blossoms.

And the sea too, at my feet,
at my ears. It comes and goes
with its power.
How can I comment?

It moves in spite of me,
as my life does,

and I am thankful
for the clear details

that ride on its surface—
the sailboat, small and white
and pure of shape,
the honeysuckle in my mouth.

Now I have delivered of myself
a child called David.
Six months of breath
and already he is himself,

afoot, arms stretched to the water.
His energy doesn't require me
or care that I care.
He is all of him urge.

Fearless before the sea's
sucking and unbalancing beauty,
he makes his sounds,
his respondings.

I can only guess that
there is joy in the gutteral cry.
I give him honeysuckle
and he admires the whole flower,

his mouth desires it.
Neither goodness nor evil
enters into it.
The eye beholds a rushing of blue,

breaking on rocks.
The skin feels a cool wetness,
a small wind.
It wants. It wants.

KATHLEEN FRASER'S first book *Change of Address* (Kayak Press: 1967) was distinguished for celebration of everyday realities, joys and heartbreaks. "I write poetry when and because I have to," she explains. "The need simmers and grows to a boil and the inner struggle must be put to paper. Sometimes it is specific things that need out, need expression. Other times it is simply a pure joy sensation that wants celebration. And sometimes it is simply the need to write, not knowing what. This particular urge finds pleasure in play, many times. Play with words and syntax and arbitrary categories of edible luscious verbiage . . . this quite apart from the other thing of trying to get at that puzzle you so need to explore and discover in yourself." Born in 1937 and graduated from Occidental College, Miss Fraser is a redhead married to the poet Jack Marshall and since 1967 the mother of a "polymorphous perverse boy named David Ian who makes my life a joy." In the spring of 1968 her book of children's poems and game chants *Stilts, Somersaults and Headstands* was published by Atheneum. After having lived among Lower East Side poets, the Marshalls now reside in San Francisco.

EARLY DECEMBER IN CROTON-ON-HUDSON

Spiked sun. The Hudson's
Whittled down by ice.
I hear the bone dice
Of blown gravel clicking. Bone-
pale, the recent snow
Fastens like fur to the river.
Standstill. We were leaving to deliver
Christmas presents when the tire blew
Last year. Above the dead valves pines pared
Down by a storm stood, limbs bared . . .
I want you.

COTTONMOUTH COUNTRY

Fish bones walked the waves off Hatteras.
And there were other signs
That Death wooed us, by water, wooed us
By land: among the pines
An uncurled cottonmouth that rolled on moss
Reared in the polluted air.
Birth, not death, is the hard loss.
I know. I also left a skin there.

THE EDGE

Time and again, time and again I tie
My heart to that headboard
While my quilted cries

Harden against his hand. He's bored—
I see it. Don't I lick his bribes, set his bouquets
In water? Over Mother's lace I watch him drive into the
        gored
Roasts, deal slivers in his mercy . . . I can feel his thighs
Against me for the children's sakes. Reward?
Mornings, crippled with this house,
I see him toast his toast and test
His coffee, hedgingly. The waste's my breakfast.

THE INLET

Words fail me. The ocean travelling stone
Returns turquoise; small animals twinkle in a haze of weed
As this or that sequence of pod
Rattles with complete delicacy on the rotten vine.
I know what's slipping through my fingers.
In Hatteras the stones were oiled with mud.
The sunset leaked like steak blood,
Sank, and my companion weaved his fingers
Through my fingers. Wood's Hole,
Edgartown, the Vineyard in the rain,
The Vineyard not in the rain, the rain
Fuming like snow in Worcester, like gas in the coal
Country. Grass and goldenrod
Come to me, milkweed covers me over, and reed.
But this riddle has no name: I saw a blind baby try
To fix its fists in tendrils of its mother's hair
And get air. The air burns;
The seaweed hisses in its cistern. . . .

        Waveside, beside earth's edge,
        Before the toward-death cartwheel of the sun,
        I dreamed I was afraid, and through the din

Of birds, the din, the hurricane of parting sedge
Came to the danger lull.
The white weeds, white waves' white
Scalps dissolve in the obliterating light.
And only I, Shadrach, come back alive and well.

Although still in her early 20s, LOUISE GLÜCK has published
a collection of poems *Firstborn* (New American Library: 1968),
won The Academy of American Poets Prize at Columbia and
read at The Guggenheim Museum, and appeared in *The New
Yorker*, *The Nation*, *Tri Quarterly*, and *The Atlantic Monthly*.
She was born in 1943 in New York City and raised on Long
Island. After two months at Sarah Lawrence College, Miss Glück
studied with Stanley Kunitz at Columbia University. At present,
she lives in New York City. She is a 1967-68 Fellow of the
Rockefeller Foundation.

ON THE COAST NEAR SAUSALITO

1.

I won't say much for the sea
except that it was, almost,
the color of sour milk.
The sun in that clear
unmenacing sky was low,
angled off the grey fissure of the cliffs,
hills dark green with manzanita.

Low tide: slimed rocks
mottled brown and thick with kelp
like the huge backs of ancient tortoises
seemed to merge with the grey stone
of the breakwater, sliding off
to antediluvian depths.
The old story: here filthy life begins.

2.

Fish-
ing, as Melville said,
"to purge the spleen,"
to put to task my clumsy hands
my hands that bruise by
not touching
pluck the legs from a prawn,
peel the shell off,
and curl the body twice about a hook.

3.

The cabezone is not highly regarded
by fishermen, except Italians

who have the simplicity
to fry the pale, almost bluish flesh
in olive oil with a sprig
of fresh rosemary.

The cabezone, an ugly, atavistic fish,
as old as the coastal shelf
it feeds upon
has fins of duck's-web thickness;
resembles a prehistoric toad,
and is delicately sweet.

Catching one, the fierce quiver of surprise
and the line's tension are
a recognition.

4.

A strange thing: to kill
for the sudden feel of life.
The danger is
to moralise
that strangeness.
Holding the spiny monster in my hands
his bulging purple eyes
were eyes and the sun was
almost tangent to the planet
on our uneasy coast.

Creature and creature,
we stared down centuries.

ADHESIVE: FOR EARLENE

How often we overslept
those grey, enormous mornings

in the first year of marriage
and found that rain and wind
had scattered palm nuts,
palm leaves, and sweet, rotting crabapples
across our wildered lawn.

By spring your belly was immense
and your coloring a high, rosy almond.

We were so broke
we debated buying thumbtacks
at the Elmwood Dime Store
knowing cellophane tape would do.
Berkeley seemed more innocent
in those flush days
when we skipped lunch
to have the price of *Les Enfants du Paradis.*

BLACK MOUNTAIN, LOS ALTOS

Clumps of ghostly buckeye
      bleached bones
weirdly gray in the run-off
between ridges, the flats
in fog. Five deer grazing
on a far hill. The soft
cluck of mourning doves,
creeks running. I feel
furry as sage here
after an hour's walk
in the clear midmorning air.
                        Only
three species of tree in
all these hills: blue oak,

the buckeyes, and patches
of leafy, fragrant laurel.
In the old quiet the Indians
could have heard bells
at Mission Santa Clara . . .
They manufacture napalm
in the fog where Redwood
City sprawls into the bay.
I think of the village
of Ben Hoa, the early spring
death in the buckeyes
and up the long valley
my eyes flash like another
knife, clean as malice.

BOOK BUYING IN THE TENDERLOIN

A statuary Christ bleeds sweating grief
In the Gethsemane garden of St. Boniface Church
Where empurpled Irish winos lurch
To their salvation. When incense and belief
Will not suffice: ruby port in the storm
Of muscatel-made images of hell
The city spews at their shuffling feet.
In the Longshoremen's Hall across the street,
Three decades have unloaded since the fight
To oust the manic Trotskyite
Screwballs from the brotherhood. All goes well
Since the unions closed their ranks,
Boosted their pensions, and hired the banks
To manage funds for the workingman's cartel.
Christ in plaster, the unions minting coin,
Old hopes converge upon the Tenderloin
Where Comte, Considerant, Fourier

Are thick with dust in the two-bit tray
Of cavernous second-hand book stores
And the streets suffuse the ten-cent howl
Of jukebox violence, just this side of blues.
Negro boy-whores in black tennis shoes
Prowl in front of noisy, faggot bars.
Like Samuel Gompers, they want more
On this street where every other whore
Is painfully skinny, wears a bouffant,
And looks like a brown, slow-blooming annual flower.
In the places that I haunt, no power
To transform the universal squalor
Nor wisdom to withstand the thin wrists
Of the girls who sell their bodies for a dollar
Or two, the price of a Collected Maeterlinck.
The sky glowers. My God, it is a test,
This riding out the dying of the West.

LETTER TO A POET

A mockingbird leans
from the walnut, bellies,
riffling white, accomplishes

his perch upon the eaves.
I witnessed this act of grace
in blind California

in the January sun
where families bicycle on Saturday
and the mother with high cheekbones

and coffeecolored iridescent
hair curses her child
in the language of Pushkin—

John, I am dull from
thinking of your pain,
this mimic world

which binds us in
the analogues of grief our
spirits, made uneasy,

have elected in passion,
one brute to another,
like poems on a page.

What can I say, my
friend, thinking of you
I found old pain to live

I thought to hold in sufferance.
There are tricks of animal grace,
poems in the mind

we survive on. It isn't much.
You are 4000 miles away &
this world did not invite us.

A healthy aspect of the personal and direct approach favored
by many of the young poets seems to be captured in this statement made by ROBERT HASS: "I like poems for the peace
involved in reading and writing them. I began writing seriously
when I found that I could write about myself and the world I
knew, San Francisco and the country around it, in a fairly
direct and simple way. For a long time I felt a compulsion to
direct myself to large issues; this was mainly due to the cant I
acquired around universities about alienation. About the time

that the Vietnam war broke out, it became clear to me that alienation was a state approaching to sanity, a way of being human in a monstrously inhuman world, and that feeling human was a useful form of political subversion. So the exploration of where I am, in this place, in relation to that person—place and person both caught somewhere between the old movements of the unconscious and the brutal, accidental collage of one's historical and geographical presence in the world—and the writing about it, as carefully as possible, are a way of being for a while one thing: no personae, no middleman or structured ambiguities, no talk about the Artist." Born in 1941 in San Francisco, Mr. Hass studied at St. Mary's College in Oakland and at Stanford University. Married and a father, he currently teaches in the influential Department of English at The State University of New York at Buffalo.

LINES WRITTEN IN OBJECTION,
OR
THE LIMPOPO EXPRESS

I am dreaming about trains, perhaps
just watching a movie about trains
as they appear in dreams. A friend
suggests that we catch one

or the other, so we construct
a huge snare, largely invisible;
but they are wary, these trains.
A few run backwards, or maddeningly

fast. Finally everything comes true:
they could all be the same train,
endless variants on the Twentieth Century
Limited. By neither dreams nor snares,

commuters appear. As in a stopped movie
all their watches read 8:02,
but suddenly, either an elephant
chugs by, or I wake up.

MÖBIUS

It is unreasoning. Flat
in theory, yet circular
by inspection, it becomes
universal when considered.
I have traveled for days.

You were here yesterday,
or there, looking across
at me. Inverted as we were
to each other, it made

no difference. All traffic met
as I met you: head-on,
expectedly. This was no country
for Euclid, or love; there was
no direction but in.

POPCORN

for Frank O'Hara

it is very late.
my wife and i are sitting around
with nothing to do but watch
the old dead television set
and all the late movies
that were going to be over
are over
and so she says
I have a piece of popcorn
thats as big as a house
in my head, but I want
it to get bigger

and i say because
shes trying so hard,
Can you get it as big as
an old red warehouse
with peeling paint
and dirty trucks inside?

and she says Oh Yeah!

and i say Can you get it
as big as PS 93 on a friday
when all the kids are just
coming out for the weekend?

and she says Oh Yeah, Yeah!

and i give her the final
idea and say Now can you get it
as big as Yankee Stadium
with a capacity crowd,
last of the ninth, two
out, Yanks behind, and Maris
telling everyone hes going
to belt it out of the park?

and she says Oh Yeah,Yeah,Yeah!

But wait, she says.
something's beginning to happen
it's burning

SUBJECT, WITH APOLOGIES

> . . . *the singular potency which the subject*
> *has from the first possessed to excite*
> *controversy and breed divisions has in no*
> *degree diminished with the lapse of years.*
> —M.L. Lovejoy

This is a poem about Iowa.
It is also about pigs.

But the breeding comes first.

Pigs, you see, is just not pigs.
Nor are people, who also breed
Iowans: can there be any

controversy about the mud
on the sheets or the leftover
sliced ham? I think no more

potent beasts, men or pigs,
excite the corncrib for years
in breeding (Iowans, either kind,

or unkind); also lapse into degrees
of sleep; are undiminished
in the morning; also eat.

WINDOW, PAINTED SHUT

It was our room, that cold day,
somehow warmed as I watched
the sun, until the frost
grew dog-eared on the glass.

Snow in your absence figured
against the window as I slept.
Surely you had sent a clearing wind,
fresh with word of you.

A new wind blows clean, you said.
I have opened my window; the snow
lies on my bed like a torn letter.

SUPPOSITION AT 2 A.M.

> *"Real things, it is plain, have a fixed and real*
> *nature, which remains the same notwithstand-*
> *ing any change in our senses . . ."*
>
> —Berkeley

The cat, if cat there be, merely harmonizes
with the milk-run locomotive; the cars, just

because they are, acquiesce by perspective
to the clouds. Understandably, any cat

so hypothesized and unafraid might sing
itself at the moon; but the vision that is,

is Socratic, pure in the nominal extreme:
the long possible of the whistle

and the arched back of its conjecture
in diesel smoke, whose rationale is "sky."

THE POEM THAT TRIES TO BE A TREE

assumes it is true to put down roots,
invading land as it does the air.
Travelers for miles around
marvel at the open horizon, vapid
as all that is, and pass by.

If only for fantasy, there would be
birds if they saw it. Alone,
it is a fantasy of the pure earth,

belief in itself crass against the sky,
with twigs bent in their doing.

Resisting any roots, the land allows
it, ungrowable as old newspaper
in this latitude. Pushing past,
strangers to the climate see things
it is not, itself: a giant bower,

a study in ingrown longevity
resistant, as it is, to all disregard.
The circus, shrine, or promised land
still waits ahead, and what once
became a tree by its own definition
shows an edge of green, and is permanent.

One of the most cerebral and witty of the young poets, PHILLIP
HEY is another of the large number of good writers trained in
The Program in Creative Writing at The University of Iowa,
from which he earned the Master of Fine Arts degree in 1966.
He was born in 1942 in Dixon, Illinois. Mr. Hey is married and
father of a daughter Sabrina and currently teaches at The State
University of Wisconsin at Oshkosh. "I am a poet because
poetry carries the perpetual surprise of reality; I want to build
the Wonderland in which a reader—in everyday life—can
become Alice," he explains. "If I ever perfect a 'style', it will
be one with a simple surface under which odd perceptual shifts
are always occurring."

MY WORK WITH SNOW

My work with snow is crucial,
while yours, beautiful woman, is with water.
The part of me that is the wind
scatters the snow over the moon-deepened pond,
where I attempt to clarify these snow prints
of your lips and of your breasts.
You are evasive as roads that constantly fork.
Your virtue is of gently rising hills,
and your name, which I know by heart,
I call out as easily as the wind speaks at night.

SONG FROM THE END OF THE EARTH

Deny and what will be given you?
Sunlight on the rose bush, a breeze
on the green bronze gong of the pond,
a breeze sifting the thorns,
with invisible birds on white wings.
Deny the sun and you are fed to dreams,
a procession of beasts:
the blood-filled eye.
Deny the moon and you are given cathedrals,
spires, skeletons, death on wings;
the amputated arms of Hermes,
his marble stare, green tundra.
Deny the wind and you become deaf;
the wings twist within cloud;
the door is shut, the clock is stopped:
these windows give out onto death.
Deny water and sun sets.
Deny fire and the breath becomes landscape,

hollyhocks tacked on the closed door:
the lion shall be small on this design.
Deny and you will be given children, a son.
Deny and you will grow large in more than shadow.
Deny and the wings will not be consumed in fire.

AUTUMN IN THE PLAINS

Lying on your back in the chill of November
the map of the sky seems incomplete.
Through the trees there are only the stars.
In the well you would see them again.
In the blue house, that the moon surrounds,
the porchlight is like a bending head.
My wife is indoors singing to the cats.
Above the house the stars throb
as if I only partially watched them.
The cold ground makes me forget my bones.
On the trees what leaves are left
threaten to tear away suddenly.

WINTERING IN THE HEARTLANDS

The heart longs for a pickax.

At once off the ice, as if crippled,
each skater walks with his own style.
The lake horizon slit distinctly—
the long line between bodies pressed together.

Inside my shoes
a man curls up to sleep.
Again and then again curling around the sun.
His eyelids dark as green beetles
and maternal oceans.
Their delicate folds burnt shut.

This is a sketch from a child's primer,
where a hint of wind is made by three lines.
A row boat beached far back on the sand
its hull the breast bones of a crow.
We're near the edge where the fire beckons.

The ice goes on into a distance that is blue
with the weight of the snow.
There the thin sail of an ice boat thumps the air
and tilts like a knife in slow motion.

MOVING ALONG

From a train window hypnotized,
we observe files of wheat fields,
that telegraph poles halt.

The sparrow looks up and moves off.
The sparrow flies on an old bedsheet.
This is the story of the sparrow
and of the path that is narrow.
What Hart Crane saw passing by
passes by. This is silence.

The solitary bird
pauses in our reflections.
I am talking of how to hold you
and not suffer defeat.

The image is of the newly dead.
Their arms circle our necks
and our heads. We wanted to sing
(we hurry through the turnstiles singing).

I know the voice I wanted to use
with you, it said, "Tear
up this, its use was momentary"
(though the voice softens and states
we should reform the poem
in the folds of a bird).

THE DEAD KNOCK ABOUT

The dead knock about
not only in graveyards and in beds,
shopwindows, streetlamps, photographs
serve them almost as homes.
You'll want to be their friend.

In the dark
they've gotten clumsy;
they grope and don't understand.

They've no more substance
than all the breath
your life has left.

They empty the room.
The door they open
is your own.
Without your surprise
they won't come.

SO THAT WOMEN WILL TALK TO TREES

So that women will talk to trees often at midnight,
the cat rubbing their white-gowned and chilled legs,
so that this will occur when I am dead,
I talk to trees now. They say,

> *Our roots are not arms,*
> *our limbs are fastened on,*
> *but caught up in*
> *violence with the wind.*

There is no discussion when air fills with seeds:

> *It is our bridal day and wedding night*
> *shared throughout the world. Wind and rain*
> *are an aid.* I asked of the insects.

The trees in that autumn would only recall birds
and compared their grace to their own wind-blown seed.
Like a lonely wife its dream returned to its yearly youth,
the messages of wildly driven sex,
reminiscent also of the tidal motionings of the sun.
The door opens. The cat precedes the woman
to the tree. Where am I ?
The door into the tree opened long ago,
all that has been said by the tree I said and say again
to the woman who sits in the white gown of the moonlight.

WHAT YOU CAN GET FROM THE BODY

You can get all of the soul out of the body.
It rises like a corpse would from a lake's bottom,
slowly but obedient to natural law.
It is in a purple or possibly a blue
elevator shaft. Through the dense roar
of the water it calls your floor.

Except for the feet which will rest
in the eye sockets, as in stirrups,
while you want the soul to escape entirely,
it will only bend over forward,
precariously perched under your eyelids
facing a torrential rain. The soul wears a hat
and guards its face from the wet.
When you are blind it is free to remove its shoes
and run away over and over again.

The former poetry editor of *Chicago Review*, WILLIAM HUNT
was born in 1934 in Chicago where he still makes his home
with his wife and child. A graduate of The University of Chicago, he has worked as a labor union organizer and as a community organizer. "Experience is a wall; finally it excuses our
presence," he states. "I suspect that life should be a daydream
without dreams." In 1967 Mr. Hunt was the recipient of a
National Endowment of the Arts Grant.

LETTERS TO WALT WHITMAN

I

I hear you whispering there O stars of heaven,
O suns—O grass of graves . . .
If you do not say anything how can I say anything?

Let us tunnel

the air
(as a mole's green galleries)
toward the ultimate

cornfield
—the square of gold, & green, & of tassle

that rustles back at us—

let us burrow in
to a susurration, the dense starlings,

of the real—
the huge
sunflowers waving back at us,

as we move

—the great grassy world

that surrounds us,
singing.

II

Unseen buds, infinite, hidden well,
Under the snow and ice, under the darkness,
in every square or cubic inch,
Germinal, exquisite, in delicate lace, microscopic . . .

Slant sheen/wrinkled silver.

Foxtail & lace-fly out of the vast organic slough
of the earth,
& the exquisite eye
—as myriad upon myriad of dandelions—

seeding itself on the air.

MIRRORS OF THE DARK WATER.

Poems beginning germinal in the instant
—reeling out, unravelling, tendril & silken, into the air—
ethereal growths,

sudden, & peculiar as mushrooms?
Uncrumpling
as moths from cocoons—

under the darkness,
pale wings,
slight densities out of the breadth of summer nights?

A largesse!

Argus-eyed & insistent.

III

These I compass'd around by a thick cloud of spirits . . .

Solitary, smelling the earthy smell
. . . a handful of sage.

Here, out of my pocket—
twigs of maple & currant-stems,
copious bunches of wild orange, chestnut, lilac!

. . .

But I have come O Walt
for the interchange, promised, of calamus,
masculine, sweet-smelling root,
between us:

you, who lie in Camden, still waiting for death,
         still exuding an earthy smell
        —your pockets redolent with sage—

the pond-soil still clinging to your fingers,
         aromatic with plucking
              calamus.

         Calamus, 'sweet flag',
         that still thrusts itself up,

that seasonally thrusts itself up for lovers.

IV

*The press of my foot to the earth
      springs a hundred affections,
They scorn the best I can do to relate them . . .*

*(The moth and the fish-eggs are in their place, The bright
      suns I see and the dark suns I cannot see
            are in their place . . .)*

         I see a galaxy of gnats,
      close-knit, & whirling through the air,
apparently for the pure joy of the circle, the jocund
            inter-twinement.

         And through this seethe,
            I see the trees,
      the blue accumulations of the air
               beyond,
               perceived
         as through a sieve—

& all, through other, & invisible, convolutions:
         those galaxies in a head

      close-packed & wheeling.

      I am involved with the palpable
               as well

as the impalpable,

where I walk, mysteries catch at my heels
& cling
like cockle-burrs.
My affinities are infinite, & from moment to moment
I propagate new symmetries, new

hinges, new edges.

V

Earth, my likeness
. . .
I, too, have plucked a stalk of grass

from your ample prairie, Walt,
& have savored whole fields of a summer's hay in it—

I have known your Appalachian length, the heights
of your Sierra
—I have unearthed the roots of calamus
you left at the margin

of many, hidden ponds,
& have exchanged it with the few, select,
lovers.

I have lain in the open night,

till my shoulders felt twin roots, & the tree of my sight
swayed,
among the stars.

I, too, have plucked a stalk of grass

from your ample prairie, Walt.

VI

Hefts of the moving world

at innocent gambols silently rising, freshly exuding,
Scooting obliquely high and low.
Dappled concave pulsing to the cricket's scrape:

the scud & mottle of sudden
dilations, divigations & night-jars.
CHURR, CHURR.

Mackerel & Fleecy,

in alternate dusks &
brightnesses,
a restlessness tumbling its

meadows, yeasty,
churning,
its black & white heifers working the cosmic cud

—a moon-humped bulge, as of the sea,
swelling irresistibly—

CHURR, CHURR,
I, too, caught in its strange tussle
its tough, prosy commas

punctuating the surge of me, out, & out,

lifting & proliferating: drifts
elastic, supple,

effuse.

VII

A transparent base

shuddering . . .
under and through the universe

rides the brows of the sounding whales
& swells in the thousand
cow-bells.

It undulates under each meadow
to thunder in the hills, the crow's call,

& the apple-falls.

I hear it always, in a huge & earthy fugue,
from inner ear, to farthest owls:

the circulatory musics of all things, omnipresent & in flux.

VIII

This grass is dark
. . . to come from under the faint red roofs of mouths.
Dark as heat-lightning—

mirage of flesh!
—purifying the air electric.

The intimate kernel putting forth final leaf

from The Valley Of The Many-Colored Grasses.
An *Aurora Borealis*

'dawning'
incorporeal.

All day the figures continued to move
about
& to bend over the green mounds

in the warm air.

Shades limned exact in the prismatic spheres
of death.

O SPEARS! TRANSPARENCIES!

IX

Landscapes projected masculine,
full-sized and golden . . .

With floods of the yellow gold of the gorgeous, indolent,

    sinking sun, burning, expanding the air.

But are these landscapes to be imagined,
    or an actual
Kansas—the central, earthy, prosaic core of us?

Or is the seen always winged, an *eidolon* only to us—
    & never
    the certain capture
of great, golden, unembroidered

    slabs?

    All is Oz.
The dusty cottonwoods, by the creek,
    rustle an Emerald City.

And the mystic, immemorial city

    is rooted in earth.

All is Oz & inextricable,

bound up in the unquenchable flames of double suns.

    X

    The smoke of my own breath,
    Echoes, ripples,
buzz'd whispers, love-root, silk-thread,
    crotch and vine.

I have put my ear close & close to these lips, heard them
    to the last syllable
    spun out—
respirations of an encircling night
    —a cat-bird's ventriloquil
    'whisper-song'

interspersing melodics with soft mews, brushing &

teasing my ears with its intimacies
as if surrounded

by many muted birds in the dark.

And ever these nights of 'love-root', sweet
calamus, embrace me, elusive, illusive, their buzz'd whisper
ever
at my ear.

Echoes, ripples.
There are Camerados, Walt—still they come.
And nights yet to come

to whisper you
to the ears of others.

EMANATIONS

'I am a walking fire, I am all leaves'.

'I find I incorporate gneiss, coal, long-threaded moss,
fruits, grains, esculent roots,
And am stucco'd with quadrupeds & birds all over.'

I find I advance with
sidereal motions
—my eyes containing substance

of the sun,
my ears built of beaks & feathers—

I ascend with saps

& flower in season

& eddy with tides.

With every moon,
I come from the darkness into incandescence.

My tongue assumes the apple's flesh
& my skin, the infinite spheres of the thistle's prickle. And
    as I
breathe

the wind has its billows—& all the grasses—

in a combing, mazy movement.

THREE PAINTINGS BY ARTHUR DOVE

I: PLANT FORMS

Dove once pulled up a cyclamen
& tore it up
to show how the color went
down in the stem

& on into the root.

Color is a *condition* of the plant—
color of the flower,
& pod,

embedded in the bud.

At the perimeters of growth
the plant
has lines of force—

as the 'wind
has weight'.

If we could look at an orange flower long enough

it would become blue:

spathe, sheath,
petiole, blade,
stalk, & root—

'these moving circles, in which we walk'.

II: COWS IN PASTURE

What is wanted
is someone who can open the chestnut-burr
with his bare heel,

& bark, hide, the bull-calf's eye,
as forms.

Once open, form is wind, 'water in an old hoof-print',

but must branch an eye,
the bull's or buck-eye,
as if—

it grew bark. Give it hair, turf,
willow.

'Raw sienna, black & green'.

Form has no
size.
The burnt-out log
is not a whale.

Nor is it

'silver burnt brown
wood
color dark'.

And there are no cows.

We walk,
careful not to step on snails.
The grass is very
green.

'That the mountainside
looks like a face

is accidental'.

III: MOON

It is, of course, as great as any
Ryder.

The sensation of sound
as if someone
had hit a tree with a club,

fog horns, the *Ferry Boat Wreck—Oyster Bay*,
& all his

Dawns, Moons, Suns,

are a new form, 'boundaries of other
events'

such as cross-section
of sequoia,

scales of haddock, agate,
are.
'On the levels of the very large, the very small, the very
    slow,
the eye sees as constant, & at rest,

what our memory assures us to be fluid & moving'.

The moon is on a tree-trunk
& there are rings of growth & brightness.

At the heart of this
light
it is dark.

This is a man who has looked at a moon in the face, night
& day

dove, dove.

"The Ancients believed plants sprang, not from seeds, but out
of the lust of the earth," RONALD JOHNSON writes in a
lucid statement describing his poetics: "There were no weeds
then, nor at Walden, for the definition of a weed is a plant
growing where it is not wanted, and the lowest plantain is
succulent and has its virtues, meadows make the best gardens.
Poetry is the imaginary furrow where the words grow, out of
lust. We come on each one anew, and name it, but savor the
dandelions in our grasses." Mr. Johnson was born in 1935 in
Ashland, Kansas. Among his books are: *A Line of Poetry, A
Row of Trees* (Jargon Press: 1964), *Sports & Divertissments:
Translations from Erik Satie* (Wild Hawthorn Press: 1965),
Assorted Jungles: Rousseau (Auerhahn Press: 1966), *Gorse/
Goose/Rose* (Indiana University, Fine Arts Department: 1966),
and *The Book of the Green Man* (Norton: 1967). Forthcoming
volumes will be *New Hinges, New Edges*, part of a longer book
The Different Musics; a book of concrete poems; and a book
of verse about Thoreau and Walden Pond animals.

FACE IN THE ROCK WALL

                                        sun about to set
                                        be kind to
                                        all those who cannot

face in the rock wall
face in the rock all
rock has faces

                it is heavier
                to refuse
                to see them

than not to hear
music,

        as from a preliminary age undocumented by direct
            data
        the troop of Atlantean musicians comes
        brass kettledrums copper lyres well-tuned flutes

        or are they musical liars out of Steiner's brain
        Blavatsky put there, a realization, but tawdry,
        of the meaning of that splendid dark hidden im-
        ponderable Plato
                        we see in the Dialogues like a rough
        but recognizable face in a rock wall,
                                all rocks in their
        weatherings take on faces
                        that change as the sun moves
        or we walk past
                to be no face at all)
                                the weight
        of their music
                on us

                (my dream
                 under the ground
                 the City right on
                 top of me

                                 southward, the lake,
      in whose only waters I could breathe.

"THE MOON CLOSES"

The moon closes
                down on us . she rises
she enters her mansions & undoes our clothes

(Ishtar at the gates
                relinquishing form).
The only need
            is ritual   (men
had no original need of food : Adam
sinned not by apple but by eating
                                anything but light)

the only need
            is ritual . discover the metabolism of light .
Air He gave to us   & Fire   .   Water
                bore us down   .   Earth
                                hid us / hides us
in itself,
        our meat is fury & we stay.
                                What was in us was a
                                    mask
grew teeth inside it
                to grab & to die in pain,
                                    teeth to say
our names with,

           our names with,

                    our names the seedbed

                       whence this

                           other flower

But I know a hill where a tower stands

                     green over a whole

                      city

a woman lives there . takes

                what she needs . takes

the whole sun in her mouth each night

                    & dawn

          spreads from her thighs

FOUR SPELS *from* THOR'S THRUSH

SPEL IV

& all these years I have hidden it
lest they take my eyes away

ai, ai, what good were it
the crow could get there faster

away, away, watchers, I list
the things I see, animal pig, bird cock

fish salmon, worm blind as I, I
hear them crow, spill, root with tooth

white bodies I have hidden in the hall

SPEL V

now the meadow drinks
now drink I

cup, good cup be full

SPEL VI

mood passes
spring comes
an arm a leg
a cloud from
southward, making
rain
      hold to what
you know exactly,
make use

SPEL VII

sun spell
rooves spread

a house does not wait

the blue lake

what little we know

THREE ORGAN RITUALS FOR ERIK SATIE

Knowing too little
& feeling too much
with a new beard
throttling him
                    wrote
in the morning of what
turned out to be
a quiet day
                    three fanfares of the Rosy Cross

Like him
I am an inventor
of ceaseless alphabets
each more complex
than the next,
                    Shekinah
                    bent over Rouen
                    against an enormous sky
my Holy Guardian Angel machine-gunned against a wall
    in the rue Dante,
                                        my nauseating

black self on the other side of the Seine handling silk
    gloves.
This is the first fanfare of the Rosy Cross.

                    .
                .   .
                    .

Be hold.
What am I running for in the dark of your mind.
This is for the dullest & most precious work of Erik Satie.
Be hold.

I am handling France:
Your father outlined against the wroughtiron grille of the
      big Paris window
his features cancelled by the brightness behind him of the
      big Paris sky
is the first of two charred corpses I saw in London against
      the light
but the light came into the room to show
how each of them was very much meat & very much meat
      too long in the oven
& stood there finished by the blitz, unrecognizably
      anybody,
waiting for their child to come home & slowly surmise their
      hideous identity.
I have been things much worse than any I have seen:
this is the second fanfare of the Rosy Cross

.

. .

.

The beard my catches
purple Assurian light,
bowed down before the Lord unknowable in the best of
      his works
dimly perceptible in the worst, great horned Bull of Bethel,
you whose works banish the thought of You from my
      heart,
this heart made for subways, for the first light of day
      polished on windows,
for thighs immigrant hours, the armpits of the eternal
      poor,
the man I loved stretched out over seven states,
wet Kyrie of the single organ, Lord, as I have mercy on you,
at climax, stillness of noonday, everything stopped,
      everything gone
out from me into the other, I let you slip into my mind.
This is the third fanfare of the Rosy Cross.

SONG XXVI

Circle & wheel of   .   who cares what I'll
have to say of Time?
                              unless the fire
of   .   inform the heart
                                        (leave
spaces where we are not sure   .   pure
enough to use the words
                              without rime or system-
atic folly we contrive to
                              tell & not-tell)
                                             unless
fire know the heart
                        & Lot stands in his doorway again
What ill they speak of time, the angel said,
for Christ's sake open up & let us in—
(Lot's daughter shivered in the draught of the opening
      door)
Lords, there are no windows in this town
we stand up on the roofs & watch our time go down.
False rime. Only when the consonance of sound
discerns a doorway you had not seen before
can you go through . is it true.
Town does not rime with down. Purple
shadows beneath his daughter's breasts.
                                        Come up
& watch the systematic savages of the public street
taking their time. Downtown. They strut by the door,
jangle shekels in their jeans, reform, turn on,
shake their shoulders when they cry, cry in their friends'
      rooms.
Downtown, devils talk in their heads.
                                        Lords,
here I sit resisting their rich meat.

(The story of Lot is obscure; no one knows the sin of Sodom. It is a city & it was destroyed, destruction comes from sin, death has no birth but birth. Sinful city. What rimes with Sodom's sin? Was it prosperity?)

The angel said to Lot
My only gift is destitution   .   Give up your house.
The vine is a measure   .   Begin nowhere.

(Saint Poverty   .   with uneasy lute
tells rimes on her fingers one by one.)

ROBERT KELLY is a man of letters in the old tradition: he is active and influential as poet, editor, anthologist, novelist, translator, and teacher. His published books of poetry include: *Armed Descent* (Hawk's Well Press: 1961), *Her Body Against Time* (Ediciones El Corno Emplumado. 1963), *Round Dance* (Trobar Books: 1964), *Lunes* (Hawk's Well Press: 1965), *Devotions* (Salitter Books: 1967), *Twenty Poems* (Matter Books: 1967), *Axon Dendron Tree* (Salitter Books: 1967), and *Finding the Measure* (Black Sparrow Press: 1968). Doubleday published his novel *The Scorpions* in 1967. A founder and editor of *Chelsea Review*, *Trobar* and *Matter* magazines, Mr. Kelly was co-editor of *A Controversy of Poets* (Doubleday: 1965). He was born in 1935 in Brooklyn, New York. "Poetry begins with the KADOSH KADOSH KADOSH of the angels. It begins with the thighs & hips of random women (wch also are achoraim, the backparts of God wch only we can see & live). It begins with the movement of a small stream over its rocky bed," Kelly writes. "It begins with Sherlock Holmes and Bashô, with every being or impulse of being to notice, to be aware, to connect each thing with each other thing. It happens in the ear . . . No system. 'Accepting the universe as his bride, let a man attend to each thing as it arises, & speak to it what rises in him to be said. Scorn nothing.' Write everything."

TRIBUTE TO HENRY FORD—1

TRIBUTE TO HENRY FORD—2

TRIBUTE TO HENRY FORD—3

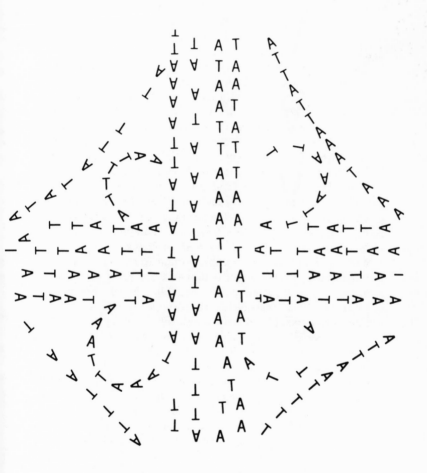

In addition to being one of the least conventional of the poets
who work with the graphic poem, RICHARD KOSTELANETZ
has distinguished himself for his prolific and varied work as
editor, essayist, historian, TV-Radio producer, and critic of
contemporary American art and thought. He was born in 1940
in New York City, where he now works and lives; he was
graduated with honors in American Civilization from Brown
University and earned the Master of Arts degree from Columbia
University, followed by additional study at King's College,
University of London, as a Fulbright Scholar. His ability in
pursuing the wide range of interests has been rewarded by a
Pulitzer Fellowship in Critical Writing and a Guggenheim Fellowship for history of recent American thought. He has published *The Theatre of Mixed Means* (Dial: 1968) and compiled
the following anthologies: *On Contemporary Literature* (Avon:
1964), *Twelve From the Sixties* (Dell: 1967), *The Young American Writers* (Funk & Wagnalls: 1967). Essays and reviews of
his have appeared widely in *New York Times Magazine, Village
Voice, Esquire, Ramparts,* and in *Hudson, Sewanee, Minnesota,
Chicago,* and *Tri-Quarterly* reviews. He was the producer-inter-
viewer of "New Release," film portraits of American intellec-
tualism, for the British Broadcasting Corporation. At present,
he is working on a history of American Thought: 1945-1965;
a series of profiles of the most important American artists and
intellectuals; a collection of critical essays; a prose narrative;
and a volume of pattern poems. Regarding his diversified activity, Mr. Kostelanetz feels that: "A writer should be little
interested in what he already knows and not at all interested
in what everybody knows. Knowing, or doing, the same thing
over and over again must be a terrible bore." Regarding his own
poetics and the term concrete poetry, he says: "I prefer 'pattern
poem' or 'design poem' rather than 'concrete.' I would identify my
major intentions in this medium as the discovery, or the devising,
of expressive shapes for individual words or groups of related
words that particularly haunt me; or the infusion of words and
letters into resonant and/or familiar shapes. In both these re-
spects, the ideal result of my ingenuity would be a word-picture
whose letters and shape were so effectively complimentary that
the entire image would have a unified integrity and an indelible
impact." He has also edited *The New American Arts* (Horizon:
1965; Collier: 1967).

THE CONCERT:
Oratorio for a Season of Wrath

1

She gave him milk and incidental comfort,
a mat for his wintered bones, a cloak
to hide him from the night. He slept.
She came to him across the tawny carpet
and drove a tent stake through his brow,
straight through until it rooted in the ground.
So perished Sisera at a woman's hand.

Nothing much has changed; the reedy fiber
of survival springs armed warriors out of stones.

I read the other day about a woman clothed
in virtue and a football helmet—
naked as truth, in a football helmet—
alone, she thought, in splendor at her laundry.
A muffled cough: alas, the gas man cometh,
(elders concealed to read Susannah's meter?)
he shuffled, blushed, summoned the word of prayer:
'Geez, lady, I sure hope your team wins.'
Violence is everywhere, survival knows its code.

In South Hadley there are never suicides
and only rarely murders. Small New England towns
preserve identity, define the subtle landscape
of the mind, discard irrelevance of blood.
Weather is expected to be poor where love
dies from unconcern. Yet anger pulses in the trees
like music, houses and the tired clutter
of the long stone walls conceal their violence,
their overcivilized facades. No suicides
and only rarely murders; death is by innocence.

The civil heart rejoices in its sinew, anger.
Without this sustenance, no longing and no subtle
aphrodisiac of scorn. A woman clothed in wonder
at her laundry wields an eye of weapon terrible
as swords. Survival by counterpoise: armed
warriors and the broken flowers of her hand.

2

Galaxies are big. Ours for instance,
one hundred thousand years for light
to pass across, ten thousand to pass through.
That big. They now and then explode.

Paradigm for lesser worlds (South Hadley,
any small New England town, a single mind);
whole galaxies have disappeared forever.

Lesson: the local curvature of space,
dependent on the mass of matter skulking
in the area, can ultimately close around itself—
isolate as any nervous breakdown—
provided that its density is high enough.
It sometimes is, and then
$2GM/c^2$ = matter disappeared from view.
With a bang. Energy enclosed portends
spectacular explosions. Class dismissed.

There is a law perhaps that helps explain
why dissolution keeps the chamber of the heart,
why persons most themselves set sparks
to a tinder world and constellations disappear.
One hundred thousand years have kept their silence.

3

We met a little beagle
and we beat his insides out
with one great clout
on his beagle skull.

4

In our cellar where my father paints
his witness to an ordered world—

my mother paints her private revelations
where trees shed night with a long sigh
and roosters summon dawn unseasonably white—

there is a respite from the law of things.
No television and no tent stake through the brow.
Only bicycles and hunting clothes and books.

(Recall though how Aunt Anne survived
the pressure cooker by a narrow margin;
how then escape the cellar boiler?)

5

But I, alas, whom love forgets
have sat beneath this willow tree
where in my heart sad time begets
maggots.

She sobbed a little and smoothed her hair;
examining her crimson nails, she sighed
and crushed an orchid on the morning air
as her dream died. Thus more maggots.

Cursed from its cradle, earth
has always tended to December:
antinomy and paradox and maggots
breeding in the ripened flesh.
Breughel knew. His cosmos playing
hopscotch in a village square,
hoops rolled against a wand of madness,
peasants dancing to unjointed music
of the spheres. Rejoicing follows
knowledge and forgetting.

I remember being human once.
It was, yes, April and the window
seemed to promise only Easters,
only resurrections from a painless
death. That was before I made
the offer. I remember it. A moment
caught between two silences.

Another start, another formulation
of survival. Even flowers violate
the rock and how shall I, tasking
of your nine month patience, not lance
the inner womb and force my birth?

Well enough to sing at summer matins
'I don't care if it rains or freezes
Long as I got my plastic Jesus
Sittin' on the ol' dash board';
there strikes an hour when innocence
reels drunken with the serpent's milk
and then the tongue will out and speak
the unforgivable. Love and destruction.

Everyone hates me, he complained,
my parents, the Ford Foundation, the dog
around the corner. Everyone. And I

loved him, black and beautiful
and full of pity for himself that he was
black and beautiful. He hated me
for loving what he could not love.

Survival is a death. Ask Lazarus.
Each casual day a tent stake
through the temple roots us firmer
to the earth, the windowfly becomes
our selves, its green head ground
to metaphoric dust. We tend
as always to become what we attack.

6

Forget. Forget. Put out your Pentecostal
fires and welcome back the long night
of our race. Milk and comfort are a way
to grasp survival. Racked on the dry wheel
of your affections, every pleasure tasted,
thirst alone will slake your thickened soul;
that cancer at your heart will finally win.

May all your enemies perish thus, O Lord.
Take them by the heels and dash their brains
against the wall. We are composed for prayer.

A BAT IN THE MONASTERY

We killed a bat last night
in our recreation room. Five priests
dropped their masks and newspapers, grasped
each a weapon—broom barrel magazine whatever—

and lunged and flailed the black intruder.
(Poor Luther, I thought) He soared, swooped,
swept the room with vine wings, fluttering
a hum of terror while priests laughed and ducked
and tried to capture him. He settled
finally from exhaustion and despair,
waited on the wall behind the heavy drape.

Big Ned killed him.
With a broom he whaled the hell out of that bat
that never hurt a soul. Cheers like canticles.
A tiny thing, a dirty mouse with wings
crumpled now and scudded to the gutter
like an autumn leaf. Farewell, bat.

The party ended. We picked our way
back to our cells, isolate again, estranged.

Well, anyhow, we got that intruder.

LANDSCAPE

When the hills collapsed, we went inside
the house and hated one another.
We listened while the frenzied wings
battered at the wind; waited, knees
against our chests.

And then the house collapsed. We lived
somehow. Summer that year was heavy with
bees. They melted golden on the humming
branch; molten, orchid, sound of bronze.
Bees were the beginning.

They gave us honey and the law, taught us
how to hear the light wingbeat of love
behind the storm. We learned to bear with
one another, found new earth, wandered
in the garden of our flesh.

Hungry, I grow rich with loving, give
my love, am given more until the weighted
vines go down upon their knees and we see
evening sunlight on the hills. There is no
hunger like the taste of you.

CELEBRATION

Voices of the vengeful dead curse
in the leaves sometimes. In autumn they do.
The smiling corpse reflects upon old hate.

I never left the rains of my deluge—
forty days of drowning. After that
blight clung to my clothes like burrs.

Courage and the creeping damp ached
in the branches and the roots; uncertainty
caught at my hands as I passed by.

Suicide solved nothing. I knew
it wouldn't and so I didn't fight
recovery. And then my faith returned.

Everything will wither in the end.
But have you ever died before, they said.
Only on the greater feasts, I said.

ENCOUNTER

The butterfly and wasp,
To both of whom
I bear a marked resemblance being
Both elusive and inclined to sting,
Accord convention small regard.
And rightly so.
Flower after all
Is fulfillment only in a sense,
Embracing as it does death's kiss
And falling petals.
Love should be quick
With a mortal life, involving
The dread risk and the social error.

The butterfly and wasp
Care little for
The patient spring that bore them
Since no nascent spring will bear
Again their birthings or their
Brief desires.
Never that raw
Terror which invades the bones
Invades their senses. Surely
This white moon
Mist soft as kisses
Will conceal our glances, quick
And suspect. The hour is cold, and I.

THREE AWFUL PICNICS

(as told by his widow
to *Time* magazine)

1

When his head split open like a rotten
cantaloupe and seven birds flew out,
we were surprised. We fell silent.
You don't expect a thing like that—
not even on a weekend in the country.

He muttered, bubbling from his split
left mouth: "Christ, I'm schizo now
for real." His sense of humor was appalling.
I recall we raised our eyes deliberately
and watched the seven birds describe
the circle of descending day, fly back
to consciousness again, again. We
memorized their flaming throats, their cries.
How long until we can forget this place?

His suit was ruined. So was our cookout.
We gathered up the picnic things
and left at once. Walking to the cars,
his friend remarked to me concerned:
"Well, he's never done *that* before."

2

He had been trying to imagine God. Still,
when his head split open like a cantaloupe
and three brown birds flew out, we were
surprised. One   two   three. Sure enough.
There they were: like a judgment.

"Only who are loved are capable of loving,"
he used to say, though he himself
never seemed the kind to die for love
let alone to split in two for it. We knew

about his thing with God only when he told us.
Counted   measured   prayed   watched: he had
done it all, scrubbed his patience to a gloss,
finally lost interest in God. Resented him.
Resented God's impervious omnipotence, love
computerized and lavished on the hateful,
impossible demands of law. He lived his death.

So when his head split open and birds spilled
to the sky, he would have thought it judgement.
Perhaps it was. Certainly there *were*
three birds. But he was not the kind for that;
never the religious type, really.

3

Nature ceased to war with grace in him.
Sometimes when that melon has released
its sparrow, appearances will shift and what is
will be revealed; decision will evoke response.
So when, after we had passed the wine, his head
split open and five green birds flew out,
we were less surprised. We half expected it.
He always seemed the kind to die in public.

He had spoken often of his name. "No one
knew it," he said, "no one ever would."
No hands tender on his secret body,
exploring hidden reaches of knowledge and desire.
No lips upon his eyelids blind from the light.
No total knowledge ever; his name unknown.
He talked like that, a little overwrought.

Still he made a good death. Undertakers
fixed his head so—except up close—you'd never
guess what happened. The birds return

sometimes in spring. Then we think of him
and his odd ways. He was wrong, however.
We all remember his name.

Ordained a priest in the Society of Jesus in 1966, JOHN
L'HEUREUX is currently in the doctoral program in English
at Harvard University. He has published three volumes of
poems and a journal: *Quick as Dandelions* (Doubleday: 1964),
Rubrics for a Revolution (Macmillan: 1967), *One Eye and a
Measuring Rod* (Macmillan: 1968), and *Picnic in Babylon: A
Priest's Journal* (Macmillan: 1967). Father L'Heureux was born
in 1934 in South Hadley, Massachusetts. "Poetry attempts to
bring order out of the chaos of our lives," he feels. "Its distinc-
tive language is symbolic; its form organic; its density mythic."

THE PIPES

You will not be like those who turn their faces away
when death moves toward them like an ocean.

You will know him. You will look at him,
slowly, opening your mind little by little,
just as you sat, as a child, with the water rolling
around your legs; staring until the ocean became known
    to you.
And you will go back often, carrying away with you
the strange moisture of that sea
and a desire to be luminous and unarmed.

I think of the Indians of the Colombian jungle,
and their pipes of gay colors.
They will dig clay for the pipes
in one spot only,
on the territory of their enemies—
a valley guarded by traps and poisoned arrows.
They say only those pipes are real.

FOR WGF WHO WAS TOLD HE DIDN'T PUBLISH ENOUGH TO BE PROMOTED TO ASSOCIATE PROFESSOR

The hell with universities!
For us, long ago
you were an associate professor of gentleness
who could play for us
the music we didn't
know how much we wanted to hear.

In the journal of gaiety
you published for us

                  entire nights!

that we will always
acknowledge in the obscure articles
our hearts may write.

Do you remember telling us
about the Highland Scots of 1746
—strange men with old loyalties—
blowing their bagpipes, marching
from the hills
to be slaughtered on an open field
by the modern world's artillery?

                They live in all of us. We
don't want the new king. But
this time—let the British
keep the lowlands. We'll stay
in the mountains, preaching,
singing, weaving and propagating
our own kind.

DRUNK, TWO AFTERNOONS

Drunk, two afternoons.
I am a tree gone mad because my tangled roots
have finally touched sweet water.

In the evening along the path from her house
I am blind with joy.
Her eyes sail in my veins like small, black fish
in a narrow stream.

O I will stay here forever
Growing higher
with snow in my hair.

SKINNY POEM

Skinny
poem,
all
your
ribs
showing
even
without
a
deep
breath

thin
legs
rotted
with
disease.

Live
here!
on
this
page,
barely
making
it,
like

the
mass
of
mankind.

I AM THINKING OF CHICAGO AND OF WHAT SURVIVES

In the shadows of old buildings, human bodies are opened
and fingered perfunctorily, like prayer books.

Near the mills, there are cash registers shining in the
    dimness
of bars, stolid as the helmets of soldiers at a crucifixion.

Along the railroad tracks I see poor men's windows
opening into a vacant eternity like the dusty mouths of the
    dead.

Yet, hidden in alleys the children practice their strange
    devotions
before the small churches of garbage and snow.

ALREADY LATE

Already late, we pull up to the house.
Shadows of the night stand in the doorway,
like Indians guarding the ritual place
of the spirits.
I pick up the child.

She is sleeping
and her body is like water.
She breathes very quietly.
She is like a brook that no one
has ever seen.

As I walk
the spirits come near,
stroking her hair and singing.
They plant four young trees
beside her shore, and in the air
they place two dragonflies
with scarlet wings
to be her companions.

An hour later when the TV goes on,
I begin to weep.

A WAY OF JUDGING POLITICS

*The relation of man to woman is the most natural relation of
human being to human being.*—KARL MARX

I

As usual, Election Day
                    approaches us

like a guerilla
war

We are all soldiers:

                         the unnatural candidates
                                    (hidden)

by the

perfect camouflage
of their
voices;

wildered

izens disarmed   in the
heavy
jung-   le   o
f   techniqu

e

s.

usual

W-E-L-L-D-I-S-C-I-P-L-I-N-E-D-T-R-O-O-P-S
BLOCKOFF
t   s
t
h   r
e
e
e   t
s

State trembles like a

oned child

iting black histories

the tanks
roll
toward
the rebels
who   shield
themselves

behind
an
over-

turned
bus.

II

Yet I have known the small, bright wars of love
fought by gentle soldiers
who lay naked in each other's sight despite all the risks.

Within me all the forces move toward you;
the cities of rubble forgotten,
the skin washed clear of the ferment and dust of barricades,
holding in their hands that solemn declaration the joyous body m

FOR kayak MAGAZINE

Our words are no steadier than our journeys
than the marriage collapsing
like a drunk over the wheel at 90 mph.

Our poems, full of halts, emergencies, far-off lights,
indecipherable smells, blind alleys,
I cannot apologize for them.
They are no worse than the thick traffic jam of losses
we are stuck in.

Our poems, shining and deadly, dense with emptiness
represent the dark interior
—the hearts of multitudes like factories at night
full of silent, black machinery and the smell of oil.

But our poems also rave at dusk, burn secretly in fields,
mad, nativistic, like hope's Ku Klux Klan
obsessed with reconstruction.

CITY SUMMER

Things come out.

After lunch, a young guy
in an undershirt
pisses into a pile of worn tires,
whistling.

Above the clinging adolescents
in the dark street,
an old lady watches from her window,
like a deposed princess
despising the revolution.

Under the trees
I fall on Joan by surprise,
like a caterpillar.

FANTASY FOR THOSE WHO HATE THEIR WORK

In the beginning will be the hand
of the tailor—
                gently,

very gently,

embracing the calf of a young lady.

Then shoe salesmen
will refuse to kneel.

Clerks will
vomit tables
of multiplication
ruining their
shines.

In the middle of America
assembly lines will be covered
by the Atlantic Ocean
of laughter.

The sealed gates of the mind
WILL BE SMASHED
by waiters with serving trays.
The old banner:
                    "I work therefore I'm weary"
will be minced. . . .

Then we will speak.
Then we will raise new flags.
Then we will learn.
And I will direct revolutionary
education,
teaching the politics of limbs,
the economics of valleys,
the psychology of the sea—
and the great disciplines of friendship and drunkenness.

THAW IN THE CITY

Now my legs begin to walk.
The filthy piles of snow are melting.
Pavements are wet.

What clear, tiny streams!
Suddenly I feel the blood flowing in the veins
in the backs of my hands.

And I hear a voice—a wonderful voice—
as if someone I loved had lifted a window
and called my name.

The streets wash over me like waves.
I sail in the boat of factories and sparrows
out of sight.

"I am interested in a poetry of directness, simplicity and passionate emotion," LOU LIPSITZ states. "Many of my poems
try to speak to the political and social problems of our time—
undogmatically but with grim and intense concern. And, not
separate, but directly connected with these, there are poems of
personal despair and gaiety. There is a poem of Mayakovsky in
which he says 'crossroads crucify policemen'—that is also why
I am writing." Now a teacher of political science at The University of North Carolina at Chapel Hill, Mr. Lipsitz was born
in 1938 in Brooklyn, New York, and studied at The University
of Chicago and Yale University, from which he earned a PhD
in political science. His first volume COLD WATER (Wesleyan
University Press: 1967) was one of the best collections of poetry
of that year.

RED RIVER

in memory of Frank O'Hara

Peter and Linda in my car gone to Easthampton.
In a bar on Third Avenue, The Rail.   Enough money
from this job for beer. Swampy, unpleasant day
Phoebe coming in mad, and rightly so. False claim of facts.
No one home on the lower east side, streets are filled
with me too, uptown to dinner. Peter talks poetry,
explains circumstances, the food is rotten.
Linda says at the funeral friends stood in clumps,
like people in galleries who know each other.
Fire engines go back down Broadway.
Peter downtown writing all the details.
Phoebe and I go home too tired to straighten out.
The girl is sleeping, I'm smoking, inelegant
as was never allowed in his poems
which spoke of the small graces we must master
to live in ecstasy in New York City.

SONNET

Phoebe runs in from the warm rain
wet, no umbrella of course (bumbershoot,
Peter would put it, in his charming brogue)
She borrows a blue sweater, dries off
her face with my white towel, and sets,
looking fuzzy to me, describing the casualties
of her closed-in day. My bed, a vision
of our own time marching. Everything
smacks of Hibernian magic, we practice
for special offerings, flowers to the

gods on the window-seat, all that, taking
the shape of the weather seriously.
we plan our own myths, where we will drift
under trees after the rain in dry clothes, and our eyes.

THE CLAES OLDENBURG STORY

Soft calls
Hello, yes it is
a droopy message

> au secours, you toad
> my road,
> my green and yellow road
> is folded
> > and tumbling straight back
> > at me.

POEM

There is lightning on the edge of the water
They are filling the cans tonight.
I'm not writing because I flopped
    so I'm driving.
In our relationship
    we multiply, like steel

> > (It's now hard
> > to get turned on
> > in Dallas, Chris says
> > But I laugh
> > kicking him in the night)

Conversations go like
>   send me the fabric
>   tell me how it feels
>   forget tape
>   and forget breakage

I don't care where *you* are
I ripped my jeans
but I got here, first, I think
>   Though I killed myself cutting corners

"Dope," you mumbled, "Dope"
I'm afraid I'll always move
  by revolving at night
and flatter myself
by saying: this is all significant.
>   my measuring rod
>   is in an empty milk bottle
>   filled with the warped version
>   of your sonnet texts. Hello.

A MEDITATION: WHAT IS A STOCKING IN ETERNITY?

What color is the hole in your socks? A kind of water mark brown. For September it is already cold and the task is already Herculean, being divided among masters whose brilliance fills me with longing for the peace of the sky. One tells me the proper road, another is selling coupons and the bridge, and a third is staggering down the highway, absorbing the hits and staying whole. As I am about to leave bed, my wife warns me never to mistake simplicity for ease, and rolls over asleep. I do not mean to be anecdotal, but the giant-man approach is wearing me down. Like, it is no longer a question simply of "big." That implies limits, as in "circumference of the known world." In a minute I will put

on my socks and fix coffee. At the kitchen table steam rises
from my special cup. Sounds and colors bend through the
wind screens. Something jostling the medallions has begun
to rumble in the brain. I take down a mountain of cereal,
send all hopes out to the corral, and pick up a huge spoon.
The day most clearly begins.

THE CLOCK WORKS

I

    Paint triggers the serene
a brush stroking the wall the wind through shreds of news
then the window
                & the folks outside flicker
That's why you make a home,
people the wind, hurt no living thing—
because you want it all,
                all life with that She
           in your hands. your life
              is covered
          with liquid sunshine paint.

Three of the thumb tacks are stuck in the thumb
a guitar plunges away into the soft hair.
Everyone has got a pale eye. In their blood
the landlords see winter coming on.
Behind the front, so many Indians
rows of pale scars on their bodies, wait.
A new swatch of paint on the ceiling. Will they
"get it done?" The hardest thing to learn is
It's real. I see your body

under two thick quilts in January
a book propped against the frosty window
and the forlorn birds in the snow.

The roof is empty, and a body lies at the foot
of the ladder.
Does the poet go to the rescue? Not
while there's work to be done.
    Dreams that do me best
            tend to surface in the daytime
These memories,
          they let you sleep,
a benevolent crowd of holiday shoppers after the gay fishe.
They leave your packages undisturbed
Why EVER leave the world?
                Sweet play of the earth
as you snooze on the convention floor.

II

Here is a list of rooms
completed so far—a bedroom,
    at dusk, thick with souvenirs,
    the cabinet slipping open
    the birds waiting on the shelf
as your skirt slips down
the walls are blue, painted a southerly blue
There's a slow flash
          and your body falls.

But look at the unfinished house, at the wife
with yellow paint on her tight red jeans.
Just five more seconds. She reaches up
and pulls him down. Fresh vegetables
in the double-broiler, the odor of the
bathroom as the shower blasts. We,
the paint brushes slapping against the corner, we

III

Your fingers like what they touch
the back of your hand against the wall
"You could hang anything here,
the antimacassar, the goose,
your Vassar posture foto,
or the zodiac for Harmonica Ed.
And the chimney there—
a hide-away.
                    they never betrayed
and they lived on so humble, & with some mercy
that now in Spring their face,
a reflection in the water vines,
& will not be bothered away."

Blue walls, a white frock apron, a violent set-to
in your life. Viciousness
is only a gap
in your perfect memory
of a home filled with peace
                    the kitchen lighted,
                    the stove,
                    when it gets dark early
                image of the rooms of the home

IV

Peace, morning, the sky is clean, has showered,
and my wife will sleep in the flow.
The dahlias
        are beginning to wilt
clean sheets
through the crashing and traffic of the night.

V

Where you been ? Your damn hat
got painted orange in your absence.
          MOVE it !
                    Your eye here, for instance
          it don't need *you*
          to tie it down
                         Like what if your eyes were *free?*
          with nothing to hunger for
          in the motionless light.

VI

People are looking to flee their homes. Who are
these people ? What have they born ? The fire,
where they live. A car quivers and pulls over.
It's a momma with the smoke of her child.
I want to take care of you,
to see you through
               the door to the bedroom.
Everything in sight is covered with white dust
from the spoon. There must be a big man.
He is older than me, a thunder,
like the heat of the mountain.
He painted a sequence. He called it
"First Dream" A fly buzzes into the paint.
You wander through the field to the pillar
to the kitchen You are filling up the air.
                              There is window
in everything. A relief for your eyes
               to be exact in ecstasy
then get out
               as the roof caves in.
to celebrate the lightning in the scattered buckets
and the neighborly racket of love
and the gleaming suitcases that are filling up this room.

THE ANIMALS

There is a green light which pets feel
that makes them vicious.
They leer from their haven *en carafe*
and detest your smell.
Right now, near the sofa,
animals breathe and glow.
The flowers are stiff
in the amber light.
We all miss you, tongue, in this room.

THE ACHE

A horse leans on a wooden fence.
Supper. The sky drains off somewhere.
A stetson rocks in the wind
"almost intact" I'll be twenty-three
in the moon. Mob-rule, the cities
where stoolies gape, is closing in. There are
documents. This evening is pearl gray.
Shall we dance ? Dear Reader, what's left to read ?

Dust-devils polish off the wind.
Ambition is wrecked, like that tract
of cabins behind the dusty pane.
You must not be surprised,
or surly, at the calm
which lives on near the war.
The wheels spin slowly on the plain.
I know you. I know who you are.
This is a conclusive time.

AFTER G. DE NERVAL

House of Cards, House of Dreams.
Oboes, bassoons, sisters, brothers,
I think my head is falling off now.   off

"I have no big statement on verse," LEWIS MAC ADAMS writes
in a note which echoes the attitude of many of his contemporaries. "I started writing because in high school I didn't know
what else to do with the feelings I was too embarrassed to reveal
to football coach-head cheerleader-trigonometry teacher. Now-
adays everything is so open there is no point in (poetic) manifesto." The editor of the influential magazine *Mother*, he was
born in 1944 in West Texas and raised in Dallas and was graduated from Princeton University, and has been teaching and
studying at The State University of New York at Buffalo. "*On
the Road* and *Howl* freaked me very clean in the eleventh grade.
I found out that what I was hearing was 'real': Buddy Holly
and The Crickets, Mr. B. B. King, truck-stop talk, everything
I was taught to exclude as un-literature," he states. "I like
sports in the Texas night. I like to hear everybody talk." His
first volume *City Money* appeared in 1966 under the imprint
of Burning Water Books published at Magdalen College, Ox-
ford. Two forthcoming books include *U.S. 40 West* (poems)
and *Get the Money* (novel). He is married.

"My contempt for you
You named ignorance and my admiration for you
Servility
When they were among the few things we had in
      common
Your trash and your poses were what I most
      appreciated
Just as you did

And the way you were free
Of me"
          from "Peasant"
          (A Prayer to the Powers of This World)
          —W. S. Merwin

:NEDETTA BARZINI

hen it is not yet twilight
          though the Italian girl
t of another life reminds me
          that I am not dead
the blue room the candle
ht pushed through our dream coming to life
that night
      disappeared into morning
kness she appears with
at she did not need
asons finding herself
      I have been before
th her

ut of another life
      her grandfather with Borghese
ming in the 40hp *Itala*
      through the rain and mud

in that transcontinental summer.
                                  Unable to find
the place she is hiding
                        out of contempt
for the young man who loves her.
She will wake up soon
                        not realizing all that
has happened. The truth that tells
all only once in a life
                        time the way she brings
nothing but her own radiant innocence
to the wide open field
                        clouds make shadows where she stands.
She comes back to me
                        in another life and I am not here
in the collapse of how many
                                  years from her death she will live
forever without turning to someone in bed,
turning the truth into a myth not to see
                                  two faces in love
in the black and white photo
machine.

She begins to live and die more when she could not
                                  explain how not to lie.
The dream taking place
                        of the small, private wedding,
the going away
                and coming back
changed into the features of her school days
                        the sounds of her class
mates dancing in gym class
                                  with and without her.

Benedetta Barzini. Benedetta Barzini. Benedetta Barzini

how strangely you lean on one leg in the full-color high-fashion sp
still living on nightmares of power and light

leaks. I try to remember your faults,

>> but know the top spinning

secret of looking at you.

>> It is all in

>> how you are living

the universe to which Dante

>> attributed your many sins

walking forward and back

>> through the sunlight rising to Paradise

the last faces

>> before going under the ice

>> return to enter my life.

—This poem is dedicated to Albert René Ricard

Poet and celebrity in the international Pop art-high fashion-hip taste world, GERARD MALANGA was born of Neapolitan heritage in 1943 in New York City. Three of his books appeared in 1967: *3 Poems for Benedetta Barzini* (Angel Hair), *Screen Tests: A Diary*, in collaboration with Andy Warhol (Kulchur Press), and *Prelude to International Velvet Debutante* (Great Lakes Books). His poetry has earned two prizes: The Gotham Book Mart Avant-Garde Poetry Prize (1961) and The Dylan Thomas Memorial Poetry Prize (1962). In addition to making five underground films and appearing in many others, Mr. Malanga was a distinguished member of Andy Warhol's "The Exploding Plastic Inevitable" when the troupe performed in New York and on the road during 1965-1967. Since the summer of 1967 he has been living and working in Italy where he is photographing and directing *The Recording Zone Operator*—the first American underground film shot in Technicolor-Techniscope. Miss Benedetta Barzini is the lady in the photograph with Mr. Malanga.

LOOK CLOSELY

I hold in my hands
one invaluable, unusually large, circular,
hydrated, cellular, fish-spined, shell-pasted,
molecular, wood-fitted, lilac scented, pollenated,
earth-colored, Katanga-mined, Bantu-smelted,
cleaned, polished, rough-edged, curved,
granite, gold-encrusted, filigreed, stamped,
platinum inlaid, green embossed, diamond-tipped,
rectangular, sculpted, Polynesian carved,
interconnecting, figure-locking,
beaten, Persian hammered, sheeted,
fur covered, feathered,
braided, Inca woven, lace trimmed,
stitched, beaded, Navajo embroidered,
Chinese inspired, Japanese designed, Brahmanic,
blue lacquered, hand painted, red enamelled,
impenetrable, soaring, mythic, hermaphroditic,
Hebraic, gothic,
mobile, eurythmic, mechanical,
non-plastic, free-spinning,
winged, elevated,
piece of myself.

If you look closely
you can see it.

WHAT I KNOW

What I know outlasts a tooth,
is larger than a year
or a wife pregnant with rain.

I know what words cannot spell,
intricate engines of light
alive in the middle of seeds.

I say, believe in common things:
the leer of a spoon, the knife
that gets straight to the point.

Have faith in weather, rocks,
the damaged screens of lust.
Become what your dreams create.

Platinum waters creep up the shore,
seasons are folded in a fan. Hands
and whispering heads are here, now.

I have come to this knowledge
with every tooth and grain of light.
Knife, spoon, even the rocks, breathe.

LETTER FROM THE GREAT SOCIETY

I cannot sleep in the weight of the year,
        nor in the gold weather
    flashing from a dissolved wrist.
            Red bombs in the blood
            allow me no peace,
            nor the arguments
            resolved inside a leaf.
That is what thirty years have taught me,
        and the months, the weeks,
            when Monday lowers its drawbridge.

But the nine shouts buttoned inside tuxedos;
the man coming toward me whose mind is a loose fit;
the woman of five arcs and the slack jaws of her womb;—
    these are something else.

    There are some, the old mostly,
who wear their loneliness like emperors' hats,
and others the land has done away with,
shoving them aside with the back of its hand.
    I speak not only of them
      but of the negroes
        who set their teeth
      on the steel of November
        and bite,
and the chickens of the Puerto Ricans' speech
    which scramble up the tenements
      and roost upon the roofs
    waiting for the heroin's empty eggs.

    On another street
the man whose mind is a loose fit
      walks on,
    and the woman of five arcs,
and the shouts buttoned inside tuxedos:
        here
        the Indians
    prowl the white rocks of my brain,
    the only land permanently theirs.

Oh, I cannot sleep in the weight of the year,
    each year a greater burden than the last:
      I cannot breathe—
  I want to open the mouth of numbers
      till they sing
        backward
    to the zero's impenetrable egg.

But I cannot subtract while the earth multiplies,
nor will the twelve expressions on the face of time
                    give me pause.
                Today
            bombs my taxes bought
        have taxed the breath of Asia.
            They detonate the dust,
                the yellow dust,
            which rises over Asia,
        an imperishable smoke
    that will sweep across the nights
    to hang like a smog above our cities.

No, I cannot sleep in the weight of the year,
                nor do I want to,
not when the commuter leans against the night,
watching the moon lay gentle horns upon the river,
        and hopes spilt moons of bourbon
        will lure a light behind his eyes;
    not when the merchant ship grinds in
                loaded to the gunnels
            with a cargo of eyebrows.
                Here
                the flat men
                folded in briefcases
            continue to hold their breath,
        and the voices trapped in clocks
                cannot get out,
                not even now
                at 8 p.m.

        Negroes hunting their names
            among grapefruits and shadows
                wait in the alleys
            flashing their switchblade teeth.
        The Puerto Rican dines with a vein and a spoon
            and watches the midnight fall

between the steep sides
of his hands.
And the faces wiped from grapefruits
leave anonymous heads at garbage cans
which look
more like our children
every day.
The moonlight rolls over them,
and over warehouses filled to the ceiling
with shifting piles of needles.
All doors are shut against the street.
All locks are sleeping in their corridors,
where flakes of metal
gently fall
in the gentle falling of the moon.

Only the old are not asleep.
They prance before mirrors
watching the shakos
that flutter above
their bathrobes of unfitted flesh.

And now
only the cancers
are awake,
in the bones' white hospitals,
only the visions
of promiscuous moons
and the woman whose womb
is the source of the bourbon's river
and the violent seas.

Lately
I have observed
opinions in uniforms
taking the air at this hour
and Indians who spend the moon
as if it were a nickel.

No, I cannot sleep in the weight of the year,
           nor do I want to,
        not when the red serpent
        lurches through my bloodstream
           with its hollow tooth,
      and the bombers ride the dark
    as if it were a silence deeper than my voice
           but as continual.

MORTON MARCUS comments: "My poetry is a way of talking to myself and began as a solution to loneliness. But it's not me I'm talking to: I found there were many people inside me and many voices that wanted to speak. The voices told of dreams, anguish, joys—the whole bit. Soon I realized those voices belonged to my ancestors, who were finally opening those pouches of secrets they carried on leather thongs under their shirts. I was merely a medium: their watery voices rippled up from the cells where they lived, calling the old cries, chanting for the magic of life to the living, trying to rectify old wrongs done them or which they had done themselves. These were peasant voices pungent with garlic and meat, aristocratic voices scented with lilac, Jewish voices, Arabic voices, Nazi voices, Mandarin, Brahmanic, Bantu voices—all speaking through me, beyond me to you. Even the voices of animals: the worries of cats and fleas, the philosophical problems of moose." Born in 1936 in New York City, Mr. Marcus had an "Oliver Twist childhood with a Jewish accent," served from 1954 to 1958 in the United States Air Force, earned Phi Beta Kappa at The University of Iowa and the Master of Arts degree from Stanford University. Currently he teaches English "in a unique private high school in San Francisco, where I've also coached junior varsity and freshman basketball teams to league championships. I'm married (this is the tenth year of my honeymoon) and have two daughters." His poems have appeared widely in little magazines and in the anthologies *Where Is Vietnam?* (Doubleday: 1967), *Midland 2* (Dial: 1968) and *Best Poems of 1966* (Borestone Mountain Awards: 1967).

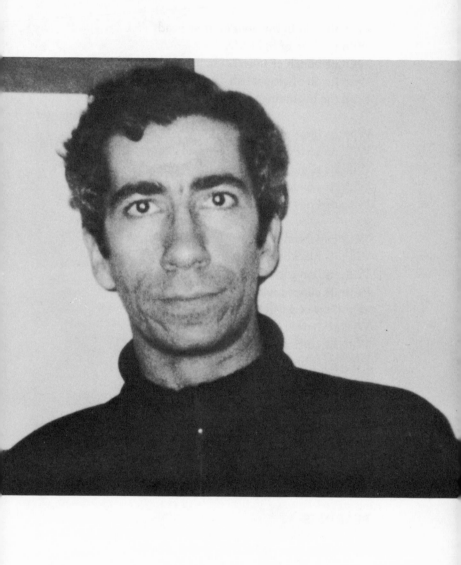

FORCED ENTRY

With its foot in the door of your head
With its drop of light
With its bunch of flowers   of grass   of sea-spray
With its oil of sexual fish
With the beginnings of corruption
                                            with shameless laughter
With its blast of desire
With its taste for your salt-lipped beauty
With its silence
With its window that says *Casa*
With its buds opening like Chinese flowers
                                around ancient cities
With its vibration of an African drum
With its blackbird flown to Vera Cruz
With its lion cub roped to a tree
With its clipped wings
With its valise full of travel posters
With its hatred of metals
With its cutting edge
With its submarine of survivors
With its flagpole that has run down all flags
With its shape of a grave-digger's shovel
With its vein of ore
With its speed of a runner who leaves no tracks
              I jab into your mouth, this poem, this tongue.

BEARINGS

Skin transparent as water
a skylight for eyes
stars I see shining

on ripples of my belly
mountain stream fish swim in

Countries I enter enter me
pores of my body are nostrils
taking in scent of leaves and loam
of all I will soon be
Everglade swamp   pines of Reykjavik

That map
I crayoned over and over again as a boy
trying to get it right   the greens and blues
then having to slog through on foot
was my body

Where I drew a river
deserts sometimes blow
and no bright bird will come to rest
I end somewhere beyond
those lights shifting red and blue

More transient of the two
I make my light
take in   disappear into
giving back world for world

LIGHT POEM

The light without a body
without skin   without bones or veins
without feet   without hands
is strong, but lightly
the light has no wants
still the field flowers

when he comes out of nowhere
light is in the wood   in the water
without youth   without age   without old age
though he is seen
he was not born   he does not die
he is early he is late
he will not come when we wish him
he walks on the hillside in summer
he walks on the snow
he is naked   he wears the seasons for clothes
he is there with our enemies
here with our friends
he is silent   he sings
he comes from the heat of the sun
the coolness of the moon

ON THE PRESIDENT'S STATE
VISIT TO MEXICO

I call on you, Quetzalcoatl, Plumed Serpent,
uncoil like a stench of rotted fish and leather
from the dump heap of ancient tombs and altars,
uncoil like a vapor from a crack in the stoneworks,
from old prophecies and illuminated codexes
and show this emperor the bird of smoke
                              twisting from his mirror;
trouble his naps between ghost-written speeches with
     dreams
of the bat which swoops down, blotting out the sun;
on goodwill tours, let him see nothing but that castrated
     youth
the priests have been feeding delicacies to
in perfumed chambers of the palace,
who breaks his flute in two and tears his white mantle

as he climbs the fifty odd lava steps to lay down
                              on the flat altar stone.
Let him move unguarded and pilotless out of his
    stateroom—
    out where only hands, delicate as a woman's, hold back
    the wall of flames moving up the woods;
let terrible lightning out of season and arrowhead clouds
    throw him face down in a field full of insects;
let him hear the barge of his stripped bones creak in the
        fallows;
let him wear a skin of green flies;
let fear fill up the empty space that was his guts
    and let his mind see the moment of its extinction—
    tyrannosaurus, turtle, armor-plated Man;
let him shrink to an ant's antennae trembling
                in the lightest breeze rolling over a grassblade;
let the armies he has sent out swarm back to him;
let them crowd him out of his body, his house, his pockets;
let him stretch out under a glittering quilt of stars;
let there be rumors of his feet appearing in Asia,
    flying fish of his eyes
    leaping from the belly of the Atlantic.
For I have seen a vision: a lone car driving
    on a superhighway arched over dark space,
    heading straight into the eye of a squatting fly.

FOR KATHLEEN, GONE ON A BRIEF JOURNEY

This, our first night apart,
the rain that falls
always without warning
on the seven deaf bridges of Paris
tossing beggars along like handbills
tonight spatters my shadow

with blue grease
'til it runs, hatless, into the gutter.
All I can think of is
your comfort
my unkind words
your quick eyes
taking in a strange landscape,
how in two days
they'll flash evergreen
as you tell me what you saw:

loose among the dark pines of Alsace,
a golden bird—its long wings
beating for joy—
no man had seen or believed in
for a thousand years.

FOR THE DANCER, FRED HERKO

—Died Dec. 1964

Women, flashing razor blades,
carve their lover's initials
like dated vaccinations on their arms
and say you were noble, lip and nipple,
more nubile than Monroe,
more woman than they,
your hustling sheep on Forty-second Street
with a vampy tilt of those eyes,
lashes flirting fluttery
as the ungirdled girl within you. . . .
You must have been quite a lay,
bending, scooping up their long looks,
raising your arms like a surgeon

about to perform a difficult operation,
no nurses, no anesthesia,
over and over the body
at the end of a too-short summer
when the sun swallowed quickly,
more quickly each day,
and morning found you worn away. . . .
Life, skintight as a sore, quit itching.

I saw you once, offstage, munching peanuts,
wrapped in a full-length black bear coat,
booted toes splayed like a cowboy's
shuffling down Third Street.
Bearish like that, were you kicking the traces
of Nijinsky's scissor-footed pirouette
that curled and folded, curled and bloomed—
a puff of incense
inhaled by the sultry arc lamps?
Or maybe each cruel twist of your heel
ground those grinning Polack faces back into dirt, no?
Ah Freddie, svelte as an oriental tassle,
you were never meant for the grind and grit
and lumbering hassle of the elephant graveyard; who is?
But you, especially, you should have been a plume
on top of a tentpole in the whiteness of the Russian
        steppes!
All that grace, that unnatural beauty
our women would give their wits for!
Stroking your image, they stroke themselves.

Once, beside you, I felt as though a whiff of marijuana
had oiled and lit up my nerves.
Near the end, your boyfriends married,
you slogged around Greenwich Village,
sloven as a dried-up harem girl.
Those deep hollows in your cheeks . . . elbow marks
of some lover propped on your face? You gazing at you?

Believing the poems and wild applause
hailed you as Apollo,
your doped, delirious angel danced on air.
Afterwards a leading lady gushed,
"My dear, it was his most beautiful dance."
You and I, Freddie, know
the sad, mean, base, meaningless waste
was no grander than stepping out
for a walk with your dog.

SETTING OUT

I give my hand back to its place
        in the country of hands
I give my legs back to the road
I give my flowing sex back to the Mother of Water
My hair to the mountain peak
I give my eyes to the head of the chestnut pony
And the low spark at the tip of my spine
        I give to the backbone of stars
My sweat I give to the cloud
        moving toward the warm gulf stream
The letters of my name back to the Father of Alphabets
The dark cave under the outcrop of my forehead
        is making way for the prowlers of the sea
My lungs and ears and ambergris I give back to the wind
My sputtering desire to the more steadily burning sun
Not because it is all over
But that it might begin

JACK MARSHALL's first volume *The Darkest Continent* was
published in 1967 by For Now Press. Work of his has appeared
in *The New Yorker, The Hudson Review, The Paris Review,
New World Writing, Kayak, Harper's,* and in the anthology
Of Poetry and Power. He was born in 1937.

THE MONTHS OF THE TRIBE

for Lafe

The goat month, when piñones are gathered.
The month of barren horses.
There is the month of persimmons
    and it is permitted to be bitter.
    The grandmothers wail
    and husbands are chastized.
Orion at dusk marks the time
    when fields are planted
    and the sweet cunts of women
    are moist as peaches.
    Then the penis of a man is swollen
    and heavy, hanging like a thick cord
    that runs from his belly to his heart.
The best month to gather wood comes
    two moon-deaths after harvest.
    The sap has fled, but the cold
    does not yet bruise the fingers.
Some years there is a month, deep in winter,
    when man does nothing
    but curse and drink.
Before the last snow clears young men
    are sent out to endure
    and young women are shown
    the secrets of coupling. They dance.
In the month of chaos the earth is killed
    and men riot to bring it to life.
    A wild month, full of pain and noise
    and finally joy.

THE TOAD MAN

a poem for Stob

I

I say
endure the law of things,
the wasted joke of the night.
Walk away.

> In the forest the needles
> of the larch are loosening,
> a yellow pale as white alder leaves

The rains have come, half snow,
and the brush is heavy and cold
in the gray shadows

My pants are wet through
in a hundred yards
and a chill works up my back
before I sweat.

> Six miles on the logging road,
> two miles along the ridge.

Two miles is just far enough
to pack a rocking chair.

I made the shack, what Kephart
calls an "axeman's cabin"
eight by ten, but with a borrowed
chain-saw the butterflies out
> tumbling in the first hot weather.

Brought in a welded metal stove,
that rocking chair.

I stay there
to endure

the delight
the defeat.

II

My pleasures
are in solitude, a fire,
my own plain cooking,
the prayer of the wind.

I must wander both beneath and upon the earth
a herdsman and gatherer of sycamore fruit

I can sing any song whatever,
for any time
because the waters flow eternally

(the truth of sage, marjoram,
basil, the wine of the condemned,
the plumb line
and the quarrels of men)

There is no order.
Neither in reed
nor flint
nor the house of the sun
nor the rabbit
nor in the blessings of gentility.

I tell you there are only
the myths of childhood

geometry

nothing more.

III

I drink whisky some,
smoke grass, and have
a hot water bottle.

> Tuck that in the bedroll
> on a cold night
> and it's all right.

They kill out there

> I paint, read books, hear
> the toads call from the spring,

and wait, my heart like a locust.

Summer comes
and I start the garden
watch after the hives

> eight
> beehives at the edge of the meadow

They always get through the winter

They've got secret ways of staying warm, like toads—

> they never die.

DEAR

The violence of love
(and by this not
the deaf explosions of orgasm)
the violence of love
is slow corrosion, forgetfulness.

Can anyone remember
why he fell in love?

Or if it matters?

No, these children
and this last, any hour
make up all the years
we have.

Without such limit
we would be insufferable.

MY BROTHER'S DEATH

The toxicologist's report:
spittle and rheum
traces of Saint Johnswort
(only poisonous to white-colored animals)
patient was white, originally.

Insisted he drank
infusions of locoweed
(Oxytropis lambertii)
and that salvation

was in antiquity and bone:
not Greek metric

        "Classicism is a sentimentality"
but in olives and wine
and Bronze Age shamans.

The homily was interrupted
by convulsions: when he returned
he quoted the mermaid in *Lighea*

        "I am immortal because
        all the dead things flow into me."

I remember walking down the hill
from Mycenae to the crossroad at Fichtia,
Argos was a blur in the distance
nearly on the gulf
and he had picked some wild garlic
and stuck it in his buttonhole.
We had melon and beer at the crossroad,
with tomatoes, sausage, bread.

        "This is the smallest fraud," he said,
        gesturing at the food
        "and the theater's the key: Silenus
        on the tanbark, the hokum of tragedy.
        The Romans took it literally and
        killed people in the circus, and that's
        the west we inherited. The major art
        form is death.

        That's all. Aristotle and Jeremiah
        were never listened to.

        No.

Greece gave a value to death,
and the Romans made it
a commodity. Pound and usury
were more right than we admit.
Additionally, the sacraments are true."

The pulse of his voice faltered
and his flesh was yellow as that garlic,
with as rank a smell.
Louis Aragon admitted
Vivre n'est plus qu'un stratagème,
but my brother was not good at winning.

"If you will learn to smelt bronze,"
he said before he died,
"you will be a better philosopher
than the man who knaps flints,
though technology is a pestilence.
Pay attention to the stars
and learn birds' names
as much as anything."

Then he died, a sentimentalist.

We had walked a lot, and once
going up the path to the fortress
at Amber, outside Jaipur,
dodging the piles of elephant shit,
he laughed, and danced a few steps
to the music and

"Quite naturally," telling
the wife that left him,
"I began to cry."

Though we swam at the beach at Nauplia
that night, drank ouzo

and decided to go to Kimolos,
we bred death in actions,
and it was no better than Mahabalipuram
where the sea had been too rough.
It was good, but not enough.

> "What is the velocity reached
> by a falling spider? He can't
> be killed that way.
> He can't fall to his death in air."

Paul's terminal velocity
was zero, anchored in a bed
without a parachute,
his face as yellow as his hair.

DORA

You have come along with me
looking for the things we lost
and I have found the face
of the human being
in your face.

We are each other's history
and in our magic sleep
steal back the time
that was forfeited with Eden.

We no longer have important fears.

NOTE ON BONE

using the old characters,
Shang dynasty and back

Begin with kua, a skeleton, bone without flesh ⼍
By extension the verb is to disarticulate, be broken.
Let it merge with the sign for mouth
and it is failed conformation, wry mouth: ⽚
Call it *ling*. The shape represents a bone extracted
from a skeleton, a fraction, a remainder.
It is the symbol for arithmetic and forms *pieh*,
to divide, to distinguish, composed of ⼍ and
⼈ , a knife.

Take bones fallen to pieces, cut by a stroke ⼢
Disjunction, death, misfortune, evil, dust.
It forms *ssu*, to die ⼢⼈
Dissolution of ⼈ a man.
Ts'an: to reduce ⼡ into fragments, into dust.
Place with ⽶ rice, a fine oat-meal.
Extend to a feast, whiteness, purity.   ⼢⼡⽶

OUT

Breaking out, trying to find
what my name is, walking the ridge
flat, almost down
                 with impatience
rolling words in cigarette papers
the smoke cutting as goodbyes
          the uncertain flames
             gone wet and out.

Waiting for the tracks a tree leaves,
any bed of moss soft enough to love on,
          but not making it.
                    Tied into something
                    heavy: the sense of myself,
          the flesh I can grab with my hand,
my animal.

HOPE

I lost my sense of sin
with the same effortless ease
in which I was baptized,
as an act of grace.

          I do not know
          what God
          means by it.

Perhaps my ignorance
has some value
as a kind of faith,
for I believe
He cannot want more
of the damned,
however much He loves them,
but will be content
with the uncomprehending
willingness
with which I follow
his deft,
unheard, misunderstood
suggestions.

The oldest poet in the anthology, HOWARD McCORD was born in 1932 in El Paso, Texas and lived there until he was eighteen, when he joined the United States Navy. He married Dora Ochoa in 1953 and, after discharge from the Navy, he drove the Santa Clara County bookmobile for a year; in 1957 he entered The University of Utah as a Woodrow Wilson Fellow; in 1960 he began teaching at Washington State University, where he now offers classes in poetry, mythology, and Eastern civilization. During the summer of 1965 he was a Fulbright Fellow in India and Nepal. Among his books are: *Precise Fragments* (Dolmen Press, Dublin: 1963), *12 Bones* (Goosetree Press, 1964), *The Spanish Dark and Other Poems* (Washington State University Press: 1965), *Fables and Transfigurations* (Kayak Press: 1967), and the forthcoming *The Life of Fraenkel's Death,* with Walter Lowenfels. Poems of his appeared in the anthology *Poets of Today* (1964) and in the annual *Great Ideas Today* (Encyclopaedia Britannica: 1964).

NOTE FROM THOREAU, N.M.

Blowing around this barren-seeming prairie-
dog town, the milky cellophane wrapper
of a snake. What's going on in the dirt skin
of New Mexico's red desert? A saucy pup
head pops up, not a foot from my booted foot,
surveys the fallible giant, and backs down
full of his monstrous report. I cast two yards
of shadow over the afternoon, and but
for some extinct thigh bone moving through that cliff,
might be the biggest thing going. Nevertheless
those twists of crumpled skin prick me like flashes
of "Caution". My quitting time's when the brain worms.
At night I retreat to a ponderosa
forest in the hills, comfortable among stray
cattle and the constant threat of company
in my camp. Nightly they return; numerous
large mammals and I undulate through the clear,
heavy liquid, as in a fishtank swimming
beneath the surface. Here an antelope, there
a hippo; but several of these species
are extinct. We're on an ocean liner (I
think) in the ship's pool within a dream in mid-
Pacific; somehow like a womb. "Is *that* it?"
I ask a passing equid.
Sunup.
Notebook
in hand I descend to the desert again
to dig out the yellow bones of what I am.

SPRING AFTERNOON

We have fallen on the mattress
like foot soldiers in soft mud,

the enemy making off
with our boots and automatics.

Bright butterflies grow from the head
of my wife, and my right hand

holds three caterpillars, as we lie,
now in a forest. The sun

is silent like the silence
surrounding the alarm clock.

Light winged insects fly up
to a white ring in the top leaves.

Their green shadows spatter through ferns
and on our faces. But the war

is not forgotten: tanks move in
throwing flames and we retreat into trees.

My wife, as a tree, her lower branches
caught by fire; buds explode into

dogwood, cherry blossom.
The bell begins to sound, and we

run toward a school house at the wood's edge.
Elsewhere men race for air-raid shelters.

We dive into trenches. We duck
behind haystacks. They are shooting back.

Kiss me! My skin is burning, burning.

CENTRAL PARK: IT'S ABOUT THIS EDEN THING

Since recombination's not
capable of producing, minus
natural selection or
tensing mechanicals,
which Coleridge inscribed
the poignant verses on Cologne, and apples
descended in my ontology
from oranges. Pure white
linen has always been my idea
to create a space in the middle
of the city, where kids and music
day or night—along such lines as
one may see; dead cats and monkeys, Iago?

from VARIATIONS ON *THE AENEID*

IV   Woman
takes life with own hand

my hearties, row your boat,
let the watery spume spit onto the deck

Ah, sister, why this deceit; for this you sent

me about my business, that I, your sister,
           should not
prevent the knife which grates
on your breast bone, saps your red breath.

stanch, v.t. 1. To stop or check the flow of, as blood.
2. *Archaic*. To quench; quell.

Inquest Held—Coroner's Jury Unanimous
suffered great shock when the traveling
          salesman
whom she'd received into her deceased
husband's bed up and left her.

row, my hearties!

The myth of the *liebestod*, said the Swiss
specialist, recreates that nostalgic
loss of mother's intimacy at *veaning*

but have you had experience in the navy?

well I said to my husband, Harold,
I says, something fishy's
in the works next door. That's flat.

—adj. 1. Watertight; sound; as, a *stanch* ship.
2. Loyal; steadfast; true.

UNDER INVESTIGATION

for Bob Grenier

What one discovers other men will use
For their own purposes, the Congressman

    leaned away from the mike, slipping
    a bear-like paw around
        an aide, whispering

Art isn't open to that kind of abuse—
A playground for the silly and the fools

    from Harvard, the seismologist
      disàgreed with the Yale degreed
  diplomat, who'd
        embrace snobbery, first retreat of high ambitions
    which, reflecting off the warp of crust, where
        it meets the continental
      shelf, even *ten* megaton nation states' policies

Pilfered from the French through Ashbery,
Grenier? Explode the old myths. Pound 'em!

EXPEDITION NORTH

Its ice cap, milky green,
confirmed the name.
Three volcanic cones
leaned northwest from our camp.
Soon we'd begun to dig
and not long after

reached stone. Here
were plants, the fine
impression of leaf,
and the bones of cats.
A strange animal
culture baked in basalt.
Higher apes had
inhabited the island
before musk ox, polar
bears and ice. Compasses
began to spin.
Two of our party went
temporarily blind.
One lost his mind for good,
and lost on a glacier,
looking for its source, presumed
dead, our eldest son.
That magnetic land
like nothing outside
the mind, summerlong
southern light glaring
across its flatter
regions. A dozen frozen
mammal specimens and minerals
crated and brought
to the coast, we
boarded an ice-breaker
and crossed to Halifax

"Some poems are solutions to deep personal problems. Others
are birthday presents from the poet to himself," JOHN MOR-
GAN says. "There are no rules for good poetry, only examples
of it (and some were even written in iambic pentameter). Poetic
dogmas are usually the poet's rationalization of what happens
to work for him. I prefer to read the poems." Mr. Morgan was

born in 1943 in New York City; he was graduated from Harvard College and The Program in Creative Writing at The University of Iowa. In addition to having taught at The New School for Social Research and at The University of Iowa, he has worked in market research and in the field of vertebrate paleontology. He is married.

AGAINST ART

> "... *Had he been where he thought*
> *By this had thought been past. Alive or dead?"*
> —King Lear, IV, 6

Forget everything I said, forget it.
Stars mix and the light let fall as it may.
"Preaching belies not preacher but pulpit,"
That much is clear, not what I mean to say.

First the tree, or the blinding cloud it's in?
Impostor sense yielding for the fact, that
Hid its fact, hardy, the flat hillside swept
Swept by sun as by a wind (in winter?)

"Like the hillside swept by wind in winter."
Each sense a scrap among winter birds. Time.
It takes time to try them all on, I was
Assured, mine would come, still sought, in winter.

Meanwhile I played the devil, conjuring
Witch-doctors like a gossipy demon,
Starred without strain. But on stage hungering
Stifled time's masks leaving me a free man.

"Virgil was mad to take up what Homer
Left finished, Pound today waving us on
To what he won't be quite, Eliot bravely
Adumbrating what was well within him."

The old disaffection with words spoiling
Everything. Start, free of spite, to start from
Scratch, like Carol's friend, voice-box gutted by
Cancers, stomach left to learn her art from.

Voiceless, I do not expect to end up
Still shriving words in my own tongue and things
In their's, forgoing these divisions, song,
Down to the cancer in this blood which sings,

Hearing out the hillside sun swollen with
Generous impulses, the incidence
Of its pleasures, its line in best weathers,
"The lyric hill, the swelling day of sense."

"Take that look for the real thing and get on,"
Raising my voice, the deaf-mute next table
Over cups his hand his mother's takes and,
Fingers whispering in the palm, placates.

"No mistake's made once, that's an adventure:"
Between the roll of things said and the sea,
Sheer voice, the chalk cliffs I whirl myself down
Over and over, hooded blood, marred flesh.

England! Enthusiasm, and the king
In flowers, *admirabilis mundi.*
High the gulls wheel and mew, ruling the air,
The sea cries blind as my back on its shore.

Mad as King George, by turns, "who created,
Like Nature, through regular mistakes," I
Temporize, "Who pushed my ear?" and broken
Open manage, for the air, this fake sigh.

" 'My new life,' I told Dad, 'is among the
Unspeakables.' " Could my straight face say that?
I am leaving this profession; maybe
"I will not serve such a nation." No, flat.

Start here, from this back against this wall. No
Need to feign beach summer, working up tan,

Cape Cod at Dover, "relaxing lessons,"
Like Freddy, at the psychoanalyst's.

(Still mouthing last minute instructions.) First
Not word, thing, sense, but loathing uncreate,
Substance of this shadow, wound to wound of
This kiss, blood clasping itself, pick gashes

Mattock kills earth, the punishing seed drills
Body of word, strikes calumnious blood
Springs, curses, counters, against unwon raised
Unwanted the purpling gobbling flower

Upspewed revulsion the awol conscript
Pukes his weak entrails to the train floor, beer
And bread, these idiocies, "Forget it,"
"That much is clear but." Oh God, start, start, start.

The seagulls mew and circle in the air,
The sea returns, under my shoulders shale
And beach-jewel vie with stillness for a bed.
My head gapes. Plovers carve the air defiles.

White wind beats cliff-high air sun fills in gusts,
The sea cries, and stays, starred, untouched reaches
A gull, by the sheer weight of this crystal
Crushed, its life fallen, crushed feather duster.

I would love this if it weren't in me. (The
Death; not fixity.) Sense stirs. The nests, pure
Circles, cutting and beating, wind, the sea
Cries, the surge high, the whole starched cookery.

Here's my stiff legs haled along for witness
To lure of pure place, English law: knowledge
Thereof; or not. With the ruck, forget this.
I shut my eyes down and climb for the edge.

THIS SUITE

1   "NIGHTS PUT DAY IN MOTION ONCE
    AGAIN..."

> *"Let thy gifts be to thyself and give thy*
> *rewards to another; yet I will read the*
> *writing unto the king ..."*
> —Daniel, 5/17

Nights put day in motion once again
Sucking up colors like an angel
Of morning
           the water and landing
Jetty and piles wood and stone to
The timbered barracks where your aunt
Presented us with hopes one sherbet summer
Slip back on their own uncreated gray
Turn entirely guessable in the launch's wake

(Using a pocket handkerchief the size
Of those embroidered with our initials
You improvised a flowery parasol
Stepped out onto the lacquered day
And floated resilient it seemed from the surface
To a good many rendezvous in one
Over grass looking a bit too artificial
Like institutional peas freshened up by cooks)

Spending the day looking forward to night
Uses you hard without a good night's
Sleep and a siesta in complete afternoon
On flat country the furthest days of summer
Even by eight the sun's lifted from sight
Worn with impatience you have to get good

At a kind of blindfold shooting the sun
From a degree of shadows' self-assertion

With dolphin tails swallows squeak
On the one phone wire while morning holds
Moorhens hesitate sidling from eastern gold
Paddies where harder grass-stems do shadow
Onto spilt Esso oiling the surface
If ("Keep Out") the thin rut's out to that woody
House on marsh's edge I'm so close to
And so far from having retreated to

Water's the light element all right
Morning's tide curls its lip at first
Hints of visible air and draws back
Till by the time you arrive the day has wavered
Clay mud flats pop with late life
Crayfish crab in and out the tower's
Shot reflection's limits and as surely
Out there browned boys plunge in deep sun

Already the tenuous campanile leans
They put the hour-bells on loud-speakers
But days the haze gangs up on before rain
(Can it be extra light from the water?)
The island fades out on the lagoon
So bereft of static you can't tell
And daybreak disappoints substantially so much
Less different from the rest which follows

Day's reluctance is already yesterday's
Memory
          tempting founders into words
When at rivermouth the gold seal's set
Over scriggled signatures the marsh
Gathers itself together on the same day
No use trying anything new till again

The church-wall looks broken-winded just like
Mumbling stone housing sure statues

You tell me you're Christian in springtime
When everything rises but at noon
Alone you wonder "Where does he slip off when dawn
Drags through agony giving birth to day?"
Later you asked have I lost even my
"Jew's sense of wonder" and I laid my index
Waxy by your sunburnt nostril wing
And laughed through hunched nose and heavy lips

"Here for once follow me direct
Close one eye dream with the one left
What mountains out ridges up and
Under the summit curves over into a cave-mouth?
From inside sight's bare gums you can
Safely water for skies of midnight blue
Where a gold watch moons by the bed and
Winds tickling muslin never reach your retina

"Take this walk we're on for example
Time after time hits asphalt now
Rubber and leather of my boot
Then the whorled ball inside walks earth
Saying so step by step how far do I get?
After much walking the sun lifts
Loaded fights for altitude and's
Over La Guardia by noon

"If you have walked the course my lips
Plotted down the nape of your concern
You don't have to make a field of
Mangel-wurzels quiver bulbous in real wind
Since then if summer's hit the road
And if some birds warming up on scales
Twit that wood like you were
Backstage at the opera what's it to you?

"Now if I say 'Good-day Your Highness'
It's because you gulped me inside and led me
Stammering through the ruins of my day so
What wouldn't I do to get my hands on you?
Let's recognize the laurel leaf
I came across under the garden cherry tree
Dropped from the bouquet-garni you dropped
In the pot-au-feu I picnicked on cold

"Listen learning daunts you wane and care
Ebbs with morning's uncertainties before
Broke things redeem their colors put on airs
Pawn's our god when the shop's opened
To trade in things that count I would have to
Wax obscure and poetical head grown
A paunch from sitting down inside
The fruits of light turning to ashes in my mouth

"You free a swallow from tar poor soul he
Bites your finger to blood and flies
At one end tongue's cheap too like brains but
The cat has no hands for picking ox-tail bones
You ask what thing is it I'd be
'Trying to express' by speaking
These things and not just whatever
Wouldn't a reply give asking the lie?

" 'Iacta alea est' so Suetonius cast
His die across the Rubicon
Or did that 'so' deal underhanded with events?
No one says what the throw was though we agree
On who got his hurling a prophetic *tu quoque*
'But Henchard was constructed upon too
Large a scale to discern such minutiae
As these by an evening light' I add

" 'I declare this tower is my symbol'
Who fingered gritty walls now shrugs it off

How many voices I ask you count
Whose from within who mimed who's without all?
You stride this marbled hall where whiskered echoes
Loiter having sized up Paris' cup of tea
And murmur 'A remarkable body'
Hers or yours Echo's herself all three?

"Or this tree a campanile from below
I only see when nothing's on my mind
Or on noon's blazing hillside the shock
Of old grain bound up in your son's blond
Clearly it's not enough you wander to Ephesus
Putting in appearances in person
Whose word will you take? we took a red-handed mug
For the Guy who urged for evidence 'Thou sayest it'

"This honeymoon's been no holiday
My venal arms embrace your nervousness
Damned if I'll bite your hangnail for you
When I've bit off more than you could chew
Sunrise only lets in more upsets
Looking you straight in the eye my jaws yawn
Hot light floods my tongue comes between us
Writes our break like TEKEL on the wall"

2 C O L L A P S E

> οὐδὲ γὰρ ἂν δήπου πρέποι, ὦ ἄνδρες, τῇδε τῇ
> ἡλικίᾳ ὥσπερ μειρακίῳ πλάττοντι λόγους
> εἰς ὑμᾶς εἰσιέναι.
> —*Apology* 17 C

Why else Oh men of Athens could I now talk back
But that I'd never suggested to your young

That conscience in soul and will or what seeks good
In a man carried as silk fluff of milk-weed seed
Fell as stick of match as the bent fruit-bearing branch
But rather seed head and fruit that's borne?

Some would-be good scouts thought I would be up ahead
Not like them a dizzy slowpoke at a standstill
But talk has meant an habitual grudging
The then current questions the sometime youths
My own innards knotted in the lutanist's grope for chords
Lush overtones to my sketch of Diotima's words

  "Also how could a dunce run to light
  Or yearn for growing up? that's what dismays
  In the blind not knowing beauty nor his own mind
  He looks to himself for fulfillment
  How could he unfeeling long for that
  Of which he does not feel he falls short?"

Events need pushing the way you're in their hands
When you lie with the god and what's not sure is
Who among the arms emprisons whom
Unless you roll as one surface over
The hill's other side on known roads
So that in that having happened you're trapped

Give and take war before defeat's contrived
For the sake of giving oneself a hostage
Where prison bars gird up a view otherwise
Senseless as used matchsticks scratching out
Pleasing ditties on vistas of freedom
(What? do I speak to you of that too?)

  Counterclockwise around the pond road
  Puts our two shadows behind us and
  Their source ahead half the way afternoons
  Hair blown uncovering ears and as well
  The god caught in a wind of marble
  I totter lunge and take her head in mine

By a miracle we hang together
Through thick and thin like two ears either
Side of the same head around the corner
From its real expression of emotion
I know what I should be saying from
The way we know what we feel

As a road her face looks miles older
Than ferns by the side caught in a blast of
Winter's grapeshot like bearskinned grenadiers
Two ivory sunrays thrust as legs through
A cover of green and branches just as arms are
Thicker pit to tip than matchstick wood

   Is it age or health that throb which stands for
Vowing under my scrutiny her bosom
Shall be irreparable the same way
Her alembic arms were left the way
They came to themselves breaking off stoking
The eyes that fire me as in a kiln?

     ʽοδός ʽοδός I fall
     Let me out on parole
     She runs into distance
     Striking her kitchen's
     Matches on my eyeball

3   "RAIN..."

> *"I do set my bow in the cloud, and*
> *it shall be for a token of a*
> *çovenant between me and the earth."*
>   —Genesis, 9/13

Rain.

Agate and coral ice your ripple brow,
Lurching into spray, shuddered loose from
Filed edges, an array of sparks, the wave struck
Quite into glaives, bristling milled marble's edge,

Positive sea of veined sides, froth caught,
Pearl cut from diamond, chased upright into a
Broach, watery weak, and sounded under strings,
Shell-white lacing foam with green deep stuff,

A knifing back of echoes, regular tune's
Refrain remembered, ready to beat as
The crystalline structures picked up from stone
Depths of sea, stone-stiff, beaten swells, been,

Pluck long jewels over beach before beach
Receive, resolve water and sand-sound,
Hard and something triumphant, whose trough, double-
Stopped, my silence rides seeing no wave but water.

Keep still to listen. Crash of wave betrays
Crash of wave ahead there, that beach part
Which receives, resolves, remembers, the fashion's
Brought up the wonder of old, well-turned talk:

"Contriving these jewels, bets before bet's
Been lost, wager marched off at the quick-step,
Heart where something triumphs, tough, where double-
Edged, my silence writhes seeking no way wider."

Still, again. No whisper, not a hint follows
The dummy lure as wave on wave blind
Like sheep to the beach, no humming ear takes up
Such praise, takes morbid praise for greeting.

Where is the listening post? That fresh trough,
Finger of air cut and trimmed by two waves,
Stuck in the ear? This mouth sees what the pearly
Inner-ear bone, blade-thin, might have spoken.

"But you *did* just speak to me where you stood
High on that dune of sand, mute, off in some
Perfect fit of love, since I rushed at you,
Rain streaming from my face and features and

"Hit, made my point, arms almost as iron
About your neck from behind, cheek frozen
To a quartz ground into your cropped scalp,
Bared the nape kept inside-warm and dry with scarfs,

"So that you turned, jarred, battered full circle,
Thrown back to me by force which works, and grabbed
Out finding me small as I'd be, though
Mouth perished in my hair, tongue seeking my ear.

"You have no permission to ask. Should I
Beg leave to overwhelm you? How could I not
Hoist you from within, when you reply?"
"Your spite is not to see what I deny."

Brow beyond severe brow rise, silent,
Containing gaudiness as splashed with caught
Color, over a tumid hump of water,
The ceramic portrait of lucid gel,

Facets flood-lighted, swollen by gush from
Underneaths of liquid jade, erects
Plate-glass shape of gleam in depth, black-green
The glisten, body of white sweat, shoving out, on,

Plucking long jewels over beach before beach
Receive, resolve water and sand-sound,
Hard and something triumphant, whose trough, double-
Stopped, my mouth rides seeing no wave but water,

Bobs gagging at salt and bitter, noisy dreams how
Some impenitent flower of its strength,
The wave's cream, turns light, rainbowing bows,
Turns and falls like rain, like waterfall.

4   "WELL IF YOU'D DUNKED THAT POOR DISHRAG IN TIDE IN PLACE..."

Credidi, propter quod locutus sum; ego
autem humilitatus sum nimis. Ego dixi
in excessu meo: Omnis homo mendax.
          —Psalm CXVI (Vulg. CXV)

Well if you'd dunked that poor dishrag in Tide in place
Of Ajax those peach stains would be paling now
See things just as they lie do make crude sense with
Logic like yours only seeming to lead somewhere
As I said it might as well be the first time
One thing's not the other there's a difference between
For instance going on thinking you're the whole world
To me won't make a difference in our differing
OK bickering but we've slumped to such
A sorry pass I'm down to last placebos
To keep your pleasure and pain both in sight

Among their best qualities objects are charmingly
Tactless giving themselves away with a
Mock discretion which is a better statement
Of their difference from our way of defining them
With our attention since we talk and talk
Highlighting ourselves like you yourself and me
Yet don't fail to stay inscrutable
Or put it that nights they're invisible days not
I'd forestall your bafflement by liking to think
You're too near to what I'm picturing for light
To filter between your eyes and what they bear on
But you pick and choose too blind to be alive or dead

If your tasteful collations hadn't made it clear
Your languor fits would have borne witness
How you were taught early to feel there was
Something touching in your regard for things

Since your will swings with your appetite
You set your purblind heart on whatever it made out
Knowing what you wanted when you'd got it
You can't charge in your grovelling to chance
That my tyrannical habits keep your
Prevision in abeyance and at best
You might hold me *ignotum per ignotius*
Arbitrary and unseeing putting
My edicts to no objective test
With so much stake in being the free agent
Though ignorant of controls you ask me nothing
But my urge is to advise you offhand
Honor father and mother and assign
The birth of anguish to exhaustion till
In the bind of your cross purposes you
Collapse awake in our utmost coincidence
One chick eye opening to see me in you
And our likeness in the scene I'd blurted out of
My day shot with dark as your night with lightning

If you can't remember my words try
At least sifting what you've seen from what you dreamed
From what you saw in dreams or asked to see
Pit them against what you can't feel but love knowing

You trust your memory like your reticule crammed
With a rabble of pins and rouges to pamper
Views of yourself you're in no danger of forgetting
Sure you remember your name and birthday too
And that once you strained in greenwoods to see
The bird who sang but not that you strained
For a reason which is not in the past
And which since you don't know it can only
Be remembered not as present but other
The permanence is least of all in memory
Of last evening light given by the brook
Then night and day are not so different as some
Third thing which is not life at all yet sings

In certain twilights with so adroit a firm rhythm
So fulfilling memory you can call it tame

Consider the death-rattle of dried leaves sounds
As rainwater's splash to sidewalk but
These things are not so present to you as
Scraping and scrubbing tools you're loath to use
In lieu of an outdoor life where the wind scours
Prettiness from the frame lifts emotion from filth

You've your own violence in denial when
You won't see room to fit in the whole cloth
Sans interstices those things whose strength is
To give way before your drawing round on them
With such a sense of instrumentality as
A tractor tread crushing the lark's egg
It takes new focus to follow heavy music or
With the tongue running around the bowl's bend
Like the Persian cup referred to obscurely
How could you hope to follow what you're led to
If you can't see enough to judge which guide?
It may be you'll be duped by your own needs
Into doing something really fine and not
Quite irretrievable breaking the strain
When tongue earth's bowl and all dark yield
To the dumb bird re-rising after rain
And curbs of earth and air regain proper place

Well if I asked you "Where was I?" would you know
Enough to give me the high sign and run?
We're drifting from day to day in a houseboat
And your rejoinder would of course confuse
Menagerie and menage in one more
Sordid stock-in-trade unconscious pun
Which I of course remark forgetting I don't know
What word I wouldn't use to buy an ark

For a follower of the Guide Bleu your own life
Gives no working model of propriety
And had you the right could you find grounds in love
Or me for judging what you can't see? I doubt
You have any picture of what you might own
And since our economy of living's been
Narrowed to the prose you can only hope
To take on yourself the onus of my splurge
When once I rise to images and prove
Your opacity earned this reminder how
I claim I'm struck not stuck with you
Till then I place talking up old fads before
Speaking modern with meaning after dinner
Pretending to give you some hold on their reality
As various perfumes commingled on the hand
When it's all I can do myself to tell
The difference enforcing preference as if
It were a penitence insisting salvation's
A salvaging compounding flair with gumption

You show if we only knew it we're closer in
To ends and beginnings than preparation
I chicken out before you in bed or force
Myself through the routine of enflamed mouths
And pelvic bones wracked by a violence I
Never manage to welcome honestly
Within that germ of truth all talk's hypocrisy
Like the civil law and exercise of virtue
And all devices we mean to perfect because
They matter like you yourself and me
                                    but outside's life

DAVID MUS was born in 1936 and holds degrees from Harvard College and the Sorbonne. At present he lives in France. His poems have appeared in *Poetry: A Magazine of Verse*.

WONDERFUL THINGS

Anne, who are dead   and whom I loved in a rather asinine fashion
                    I think of you often

      buveur de l'opium chaste et doux

                                        Yes I think of you

      with very little in mind

      as if I had become a hopeless moron

                  Watching zany chirping birds

            That inhabit the air

And often ride our radio waves

So I've been sleeping lately with no clothes on
The floor   which is very early   considering the floor
Is made of birds and they are flying and I am
Upsidedown and ain't it great to be great!!

Seriously I have this mental (smuh!) illness

                                        which causes me to do things

                                                          on and away

Straight for the edge
Of a manicured fingernail
Where it is deep and dark   and green   and silent
Where I may go at will
And sit down and tap
                        My forehead against the sunset

Where he takes off the uniform
And we see he is God

God get out of here

And he runs off chirping and chuckling into his hand

And that is a wonderful thing

                                  . . . a tuba that is a meadowful of blueb

is a wonderful thing

                    and that's what I want to do

Tell you wonderful things

THE STATUE OF A LIBERTINE

I've chosen this title because not only do I like it
But also it embodies the kind of miniature grandness
A toy instrument has, or powerful dwarf, half sinister
Half pleasure and unexplained

Now I address the statue

Lips that were once as volatile
As similes spoken by an insane person
Who resembled the carving of an irrational human being
But one endowed with such sweetness the pockets are
Blown to bits through their emptiness,

There is no margin of doubt to this reverse
Power, it moves back immediately, a Leonardo's square
You start back from——it extends a confusing,
Buffered metric scale of being
Toward the deep green velvet
That makes sleep possible
Near the gravel smitten with the gloam's evocative
        power——
These unintentionally horrible memories cling like peaches
        to the walls
Of the streets where stilettos whiz swiftly toward an
        incorrect mansion, probably
Not very pleasant thoughts
MOVE TOO QUICKLY

What's happening is that we're pawning especially
The vegetation
                    Watch it   There was a first light of print
Then suddenly my view of things
Either enlarges or contracts incredibly
And all I can see is the two of us, you
With your long dark hair, me looking at your hair against
    the screen
In this small kitchen with its yellow and white curtains
Shot into place with light
And everything else is gone forever
If it does nothing else, this feeling, at least
It reiieves my temporal worries
And then it dawns on you: you're looking at the
    background
For every painting you've ever seen!
It's a kitchen exactly like this one
Containing the orange juice and two dozen eggs
And the coffee pot, the electric
One Tessie and I posed on either side of just before our
    trip to Rome

We went flying over Rome in a giant aspirin
We didn't see much but were free from headache
(This on a postcard home)
Moving up I thought I'd have the aspirin turn to powder
Which would fall on the city——the echo
I didn't answer because not answering is one of the luxuries
We have here, if we have a phone . . .
But enough of this, my head

The sun is now going up and down so fast I can hardly keep
track of what day today is——it's the next day, in fact,
though it shouldn't be: I'm wearing the same clothes, smoking the same cigarette, the temperature is the cigarette.
There is less darkness outside, though;

Unfortunately, I can't seem to fit it into any reasonable
      sequence——
                  one hundred fashionable yachts burning
Remind me of a Blaise Cendrars poem about yachts
I translated in Paris
A few minutes before seeing a young girl break
Down and cry in the Boulevard St-Germain. Thomas Hardy
Was with her but didn't seem to notice she was sobbing
      horribly and
I felt like pushing both of them into the traffic light
My bus had stopped at

2.

Higher up, the wrist assumes a puffiness
Not unlike a pyjama leg stuffed with hundred dollar bills
But a dramatic resolution is passed
Into the extended index finger whose rushing
Detonates the very tip

NAME

Yours is an .   .   . up .   .
Your dossier just flew out the window
But I'll try to go on my memory
The first day of Spring, you!
Apollinaire never loved me

This matchbox, there's a color photo
Of the little village of Uffing on it
But there's also a medium-sized blue lake
And a large chain of green hills behind that
Coming toward us is a little yellow road
Like .   .   . the memory!

A buzz saw is cutting through my thoughts
As a man descends the stairway past the saw
Wait, he was going up .   .   .
What's this . . . your dossier
Has just flown back in
And all of a sudden whole hosts of people
Are crashing up and down the stairs
What on earth are they doing?

One just came in and said hi
I think I recognize her
But she is not you

You are the person I can't seem to get my mind on
I know that life with you takes on a shiny hardness
Like very stiff lettuce
Listen, will you be too disappointed
If I don't write about you right now?

I was thinking earlier that I ought to
Out of sheer meanness
Afflict you with vagueness
You never liked me
You were always too busy
As is perfectly okay
You had your violin lessons
And I had mine

I only hope that after all these years
You'll forgive all the mean things
I did to and thought about you
Because I didn't really mean them
They were like little pieces of coal
You pick up off the floor in the morning
Just to get the fire started
Because though Spring is here
(.   .   . dossier)

There's still a big refrigerator around the house
Its door is just beginning to swing open
And I'm on my way out
Down to catch the bus with its almost black tires
That will lead me across town where
You aren't anywhere near
That is if it stops

WHEN I THINK MORE OF MY OWN FUTURE THAN OF MYSELF

Coming out of the bathroom
That one has to go down the stairs one half flight
Out a door into an elevated courtyard
Along a little balcony to get to
I often have the thought
"How sad it is that I must die"

I do not think this thought proceeds
From emerging from the bathroom
Though emerging from the bathroom
Can change one's thoughts
——Just as, since my college studies,
When the thought was made available to me,
I have never been able to make any sort of really reason-
　　able connection
Between Love and Death

from TONE ARM

The clouds go rolling over
The rooftops of the 17th
18th or 19th century buildings——
They are really rolling

You people of the future
How I hate you
You are alive and I'm not
I don't care whether you read my poetry or not

TO FRANCIS SAUF QUE

1

You think of everything:
Modern silence, where I go back continually
To you, as does everyone, it seems . . .

2

We are getting younger, perhaps

3

I "hate you hate you

4

The man walks under the house
In the Renaissance, the plum etc.

5

More data, adversity is like walking
In the sun which is shining on you
In bed, where you are with her,

"everything like that"

6

Now I love you again because of these roosters

7

Yours is topography to me in my dim head. I'm sorry, the
virgins.

8

This color, orange, tries to remind me of you,
Orange slice

9

And you are

10

Sometimes I leaped at the wrong time
Or right time, this made you who shall receive
This scarlet rose with some sort of greatness happy

11

I thought so, so you changed your fasteners.
I think I hate you more than anyone else.

12

If only you knew how to ignore me

13

Then symbolism gets a model today,
But you didn't believe in that, its flaxen gray—
And neither does the porch
More than these worth taking notes on

14

I didn't hear you when you all did it

15

I will kill you

17

To envisage your doom (it), and,
"Get with it, kid"

18

To be plucked at exactly 2:10 in the morning

19

They faded en masse onto the yearbook,
The shoelace through six years of catatonia,
Of Gerard Labrunie and this

20

So whose shadow is this, yours or mine? and why
Are there two of us here instead?

PASSAGE CHARLES DALLERY

I'm standing in the shade of a tree
When under a suddenly cloudy sky
Everything is stopped its shining
To do something else
Very much how I feel
When you walk across the room toward me
Or away from me
So long as I know you're thinking of me
It's like walking past an open door
Looking in
And not seeing anything
And hurrying on to open up the paper
Where you read about the hideous murder
Committed there a few hours before
What's happening here now
In the sky slowly depriving the land of light
It's one of the greatest things I've ever seen

BODY ENGLISH

to Harry Mathews

Say something about still life.
At day break the sun rises——
Read out its highfalutin mess
Which is terror to the idiot
And the non-idiot alike, cut into
As we are on our trip to the water construction
Whose finish is a somersault
Done by a dark and angry rabbit.
But we listen with a valve open

Occupied with magnetic stacks
The blabbermouth responds to.
For it takes nerve to beat one's self
About the jaws——it takes, in fact,
Like a sudden phooey! illumination!
The thought centers shoot out
Through doors that open
Onto hideous lovers . . .
The detective comes into all this
And goes to sleep. Lamps go
By in the night a dress brought.

The beak that discolors the apple
The teacher imagines
Is the same that reads your letters on the sly
Only to find that they were the letters
Pecked out by a canary,
One shooting downward.

Shooting and cussing are pleasures
Ripped from the loudest
Lawyer in the world you call Casanova,
He whose rump is tickled by a tie
Riddled with buckshot.
Which brings me to guns:
There is a gun in this world——one
Limb is glue, the other tree——
That makes us all philosophers on seats,
Hateful tendency!
It's true we use our muscles
Being friendly
But at the same time clearing the range.
One thinks of the world as a hungry bird
Where fingers fly making a thing go.
Another applauds from his saddle
And rakes in the ancient chips
Father and brother knew.
It's Hallowe'en, was.

II

At least a pie is resting
On an ink pad. A pianist weeps
And jumps up. A confession is
Paddling its way up on high
Where he can't stand up. It grips him.
A button sails coolly toward his coward.
Who fails again!

But these vitamins that issue
From the back pocket covered with flowers
Cause a modest applause,
Yes ha ha!
One in a bottle that flies to a cripple——
Him and a gnat's bristle
Topping the mad alive book!

Pulling and straining,
You went out into the wrong snow
To measure like a mad fool.
Matches flare in the crevices

According to law
And die.
A snob in a skirt rolls past.
The panorama, which is growing truly vast,
Now reveals the lowest kind of person
And his peculiar trained weakness:
Adios. A detective comes in
And goes to sleep. He is
Unique.

READING REVERDY

The wind that went through the head left it plural.

·

The half-erased words on the wall of bread.

·

Someone is grinding the color of ears.

·

She looks like and at her.

·

A child draws a man and the earth
Is covered with snow.

·

He comes down out of the night
When the hills fall.

·

The line part of you goes out to infinity.

·

I get up on top of an inhuman voice.

MISTER HORSE

Mmmm
I get up and am seized by the present
Whose presence is
As a roof fits on a house whose car in the garage
Backs out
And in the back seat
Childhood is normal but the scaffolding thrown up around
The road is built with an insane logic
Which is at once its interest and its uselessness
Save as torment

Not an example is a loose nail here
One I caught my sleeve on
But I've moved
Up to the floor all in blue
And the decor is stunning in its vacuity
As if the air were suddenly sucked out
By a passing machine
The one we ride and operate
With our hands and feet

So the landscape turns out to be a dial
Of stars and numbers
No less fascinating than the cold pair of scissors
That cut the shirt you are now wearing
The starry one of water
In the quickly deflating evening

Evening is so small these days
It's the size of a green pea
The small expensive kind
That come in a silver can
That rolls for a long time
Decorated with a fleur-de-lys

Which is the sole bud in the sky at the moment

Other times
You'd have the flower in your buttonhole
Its center round and packed with goodness
As is the yellow of a slightly fried egg

But the egg is exempt
From nature's clumsy machinery
It is something very much like your own heart
A lady drops on the way home
On the sidewalk in some small town in Arizona
Where it fries secretly

And is then whisked away by a tumbleweed
Or eaten by a horse
The same one I feel as if I mentioned a moment ago

I would like to devote my special attention
To this horse
Let me tell you about it
It can jump a bush a small one
It is the kindest horse in the world
That is why it is the subject of so many thoughts
That is why it bites both the apple and you
And why when the blinders are put on
It weeps

And with good reason!
For now it is a mere piece of glossy paper
The only furniture in this room
Whose blue it takes on
And whose flower has gone a terrible green
Under the severe influence of the lighting
Whose manipulations increase
In proportion to the scales they're laid against

Yes, I'm afraid today's just a chart
Plowing through a stormy sea
But the horse is still here!
Yes he's at F-3
And is marked with a blue and green dot
The green is probably a concession to the plant world
Whose proper domain
Is growing on the living
This sort of radiant fungus
You noticed in the last picture I sent you

I didn't think you'd see it
Since the photograph was not of me even
Though at first my thoughts filled it with me

So I sent it as a compensation
For the money I owe you
And whose astonishing presence neither
Of us will ever really know
Perhaps we have been short-changed by the modern world
But even if so we got our receipt

Maybe we'd better keep it
Since nature is so expensive
And day pops up like a big number from inside a cash
    register
Perhaps I'd better forget about the forest and the hills
And the balls that lie there covered with pins

These are the same pins I stuck in you
To wish you a speedy recovery
And to hint that you need no longer pursue the rain
With your magnificent intelligence
Which is sparkling and fizzing loudly
Across these many years to me
But now I really must be going
The horse is getting restless and no wonder
I only gave him a piece of paper to eat today
By the way
He's just a mule
But I don't think that will make any difference
To him in the long run
Also I hope you won't mind
If I send him to visit you sometime

Born in 1942 in Tulsa, Oklahoma, RON PADGETT now lives
in New York City with his wife and boy. His published works
include: *Bean Spasms*, collaborations with Ted Berrigan and
Joe Brainard (Kulchur Press: 1967); and a translation of Guillaume Apollinaire's novel *The Poet Assassinated* (Holt, Rinehart
and Winston: 1968). A member of the important community of
Tulsa poets and painters who operate out of the Lower East Side
in Manhattan, Mr. Padgett has also lived in Paris as a Fulbright
Scholar.

NO ONE IN PARTICULAR

I am not anyone in particular.
A chewing-gum wrapper.
A streetlight.

Still, somehow I manage to exist.
And as each day starts
I manage to leave my nice warm bed,
feeling that perhaps today
something beautiful will happen.

It never does.
This in itself is beautiful.

I am not anyone in particular.
A philosophical shoe.
A sheet of paper.

Perhaps I am lying.
(Another one of my very bad habits.)
If so,
at least no one can be hurt
by such slight deceptions.

SHOE

A road can't be as sad as a shoe is sad
when a shoe can't read.
I can't read either.

And I have given away all my clothes
and gone away so far

that no one will even remember that I've gone
nor how far I went when I was here.

For a road can't be as crazy as a ranch is mad
when a ranch can't sing.

I cough. I spit. I jump up and down
and I run around like a headless rooster.

Me too. I am not lonesome. I am gregarious.
I make friends with the curbstone even.

But a shoe can't be as pretty as a wheel when it's turning
or a tunnel uncovered by chance.
And a shoe can't be a lobster.

I am as free as a belt or a bell or
a dog on a leash
gone crazy with the aroma of flagpoles.

HUNGER

Lakes of surprising shape
anchor these hills to the road
that goes from here to there
and can't return to where
this vanity began.

And the field of gray weeds
dumps as it bleeds
archeology upon
some worried but unguarded
handsome young travelers.

Actual structure, however,
is emotional not mental.

Likewise, wise old men
and their busy houseboats
never touch the stuff.

Loud stars make a brain pattern
aptly upon the firmament
nailing the dance to an old hat
and a dancer who is deaf. (!)

Should all these orchestras
be cognizant of pain
an orchestra would burn.

Sadness in itself is not sad enough
to mend the rent
and terror cannot render
pain or push or error
elegant enough to be mirrors
large enough to bend.

An arrow strikes the head of
narrow peripheries
damned by scope
silently to cheat the bargains
cheating has supplied.

An elevator fails to deliver
Philadelphia's fair-haired boy.
The elevator starts and stops
languidly in the sunset
and an anger takes a dive.

Nothing can be expected of this,
the damaged, the
"stoned."

Empty landscapes increase in size
lacking only wit,

the way in which
the animals lack a language
to negotiate their anxieties
down surrogate byways of the ornamental
proprieties
and storefronts, heavy with whips.

Can all these factories
ammend the exclusions?
Purify? Or frighten a shadow
edging along the highway?

Lovely elm trees corner the land
and mark the hidden places where
misplaced maps were buried
maybe twenty or thirty years ago.

Cars, those speeding beads upon
a necklace that divides
patience from its panoply,
eat each other majestically,
lacking only dreams to make them
ancestoral or
Norwegian.

Nevertheless, the careless grass,
dyed by rain a deeper green,
smells nice.
Cool fruit in the shade
and paper napkins
end the ending of a nap.

And the piles of newsprint rot
each summer,

for lacking the train
another landscape
nudges the rainbarrel
and another voice calls hiddenly
for an activity not really required
but certainly necessary.

Softly the wind unwinds around
careless statuary
arranged in attitudes of finance,
perhaps too sensuously.

Local bombast beacons the finality
of an open bowl
not necessarily empty
but damp,
solely to hide the anger
cartons make,

adding this to that,
cartoon-like,
partitioning lakes.

Enough of too little. Too much of
length instead of largeness.
Apples, for instance,
nipped. Or grapes in a harbor
shining roundly
and exchanging the air.

Could all these outlets be
an inlet for some loss?
Poison for a shouting
insanely dreamed?

Lakes are skillfully arranged
by someone, perhaps yourself,

not in the usual fashion,
clock-wise,
but slowly against the weather,
carefully,
alphabetically by size.

Practical vandals knock the occasion,
each portion of the public
or the sections of this garden,
as amateurs celebrate the pubic
in private
or as if these odors were a secret.

A loudness we have learned to like
softens the oddness
and the oddness breaks out
neatly into the open
surprising only the avenues that lead
to affluent drugstores.

Systematically, in even rows,
even the plantings that have refused to bloom
bloom
and establish a kind of foreign aid
that reduces the exposure.

Eels, clouds, guns
learn to lean on
an air that does not move.

Love's hate buys food for
animal pastures
and the disasters are not green
but hallucinatory
and faintly redundant
when they glow like ashtrays
in the middle of the dark.

Never again will this view
dump ashes on the lake,
so carelessly
causing the binoculars to grow
agrarian sores upon the fertility
of insubstantial, inexpensive reproductions
of a painting we have decided
never again to like.

1. Grand words crumble in the face of
actions taken arbitrarily,
nudging grandeur off this road,
daring it to be real.

2. Summer's younger swimmers
continue to be brave
in spite of that which circles
high above the oval,
pulled by the varieties
that each one needs.

3. Precisely.
For precisely at this moment
eating becomes a living.

4. Loaned out, butchered, fragmentized,
actual feelings are, so it seems,
not actual at all. But
don't mistake the actual for
something that is real,
for couldn't a language be a collection
of some infinite emotions
and not a definition of mere thought?

Leaves grow through a corpse
and the corpse gets up and walks,
nips a dog,

but doesn't return home
for home is so beautifully hidden
in this completely open place,
alive with tenderness.

I AM THE PONY IN THE CENTRAL PARK ZOO

I am the pony in the Central Park Zoo,
resting.
And I am not thinking or dreaming.
(I am resting.)

I am your first grade gold star gummed
at the top of a wide-ruled piece of paper
filled to the edges with names.

Who am I?
There! That dog across the street,
lifting up his left hind leg.

I am the America of five hundred years ago.
I am a naked man hunting
rabbits in the wilderness.
There goes a rabbit! What a
beautiful white tail he has!

I am your vacation of cool blue lakes.

I am the word "beautiful"
when it is applied to everything.

WAVES

I swallow the pill and the pill
swallows me,
perhaps not completely but it seems
on my technicolor screen
the colors are all white,

where running towards the thin rim,
gone are all the afternoons
I washed the sea,
enclosing the rain.

So I stomach your evening that's
enclosing the high-heel shoe
that pain wears as it stumbles
across the soft lawn.

And down by the shiny gas pump,
staring at dawn,
tank farmers eat the triangular.

Everything scrubs the immaculate
noose that life makes,
dangerous with flies,
touches the opening (soggy)
that encloses this room of doorways,
that encloses the shore.

But why are there icebergs
in my sea
that massively
hamper traffic,
linking the continent of
India with me
by obstacles not tentacles?

Tortured by pleasures,
an old friend
neatly brings a package
down to the river,
seals a letter, sends it,
opens a wall
and nudges a small animal
out of its warm brown sleep.

So I divide myself into geographies;
old highways rot.
Farms become freeways
and cities sprout from my genitals.

But of this the dampness is not certain.
Nothing stops
until the hopes of falsity

fortuitously
drop from the trees
that are protecting this house.

The pill becomes a roadside hot dog stand
and then a cane
and I become a white cloud.

And down by the tree stump,
hearing the bud,
snake charmers eat the thank you notes
I have sent from my farm.

India balances my jungle
in the palm of her plan
and mountains mysteriously sink
into the cold scenarios of history.

The pill becomes a mountain
and then a plain
and I become an entity among entities
in search of a name.

Another young poet who has also earned recognition as an art
critic, JOHN PERREAULT has published a first volume of
poems *Camouflage* (Lines Press: 1966) and art criticism in
*The Village Voice, Art News, 57th Street Review, Art Inter-
national, Arts, Artscanada* and *Tri-Quarterly.* He has also written
literary criticism for *The New York Times Book Review* and
The Village Voice. Several awards have been given to his poetry:
The Dylan Thomas Memorial Poetry Prize (1960), The National
Foundation on the Arts Award (1967) and two awards from
The Poet's Foundation (1963, 1967). Of his feeling for the poem
Mr. Perreault writes: "This door, poetry, swings both ways. In
and out. Like a handgrenade or a pomegranate. But from either
side of the river the view is the same. It is only the language
that makes the difference. I like to use impossible figures of
speech, surprise, delay, music, quirks, humor, sound systems,
and peculiar methods of composition—in short, the 'wrong'
word in the right place." Born in 1937 in New York City, he is
an associate editor of *Art News* and the art critic of *The Village
Voice.* A new book of his poems is scheduled for publication
by Kulchur Press.

GOODBYE

If you are still alive when you read this,
close your eyes. I am
under their lids, growing black.

SLEEP

We brush the other, invisible moon.
Its caves come out and carry us inside.

POEM

After your death,
Naomi, your hair will escape to become
a round animal, nameless.

DEATH

Going to sleep, I cross my hands on my chest.
They will place my hands like this.
It will look as though I am flying into myself.

POEM

Alright if I have to be famous let it be for this great
    starfish-shield I made
And the sands of her face drift over her body

KAREZZAS, CUNTRAS, COCKTURNES, MANSHRIEKS, CARRIONCRIES

the holy tides are being written
by the young of all times and lights poets
dancing psychedelicately
playing, saying "One
    in my hand, one in the air, and one in you"

      —for the Human Be-ins and young rock poets
        jugglers heads

(SERGEY) (YESENIN) SPEAKING (ISADORA) (DUNCAN)

I love Russia; and Isadora in her dance.
When I put my arms around her, she's like
Wheat that sways in the very midst of a bloody battle,
—Unharkened-to, but piling up peace for the earth
(Though my self-war juggles no nimbus) Earthquakes;
    shoulders
A-lit with birthdays of doves; piety of the unwashable
Creases in my mother's gaze and hands. Isadora
    "becalmed"

Soon there will be no ideas but in things,
in rubble, in skulls held under the oceans' magnifying-
      glass,
in screams driven into one lightning-void.
Only you can resurrect the present. People
need your voice to come among them like nakedness,
to fuse them into one marching language in which the
      word "peace" will be said for the last time.
Write slogans, write bread that pounds the table for
      silence,
write what I can't imagine: words to wake me and all those
who slump over like sapped tombstones when the generals
      talk.
The world is not divided into your schools of poetry.
No: there are the destroyers—the Johnsons, Kys, Rusks,
      Hitlers, Francos—then there are those
they want to destroy—lovers, teachers, plows, potatoes:
this is the division. You
are not important. Your black mountains, solitary farms,
LSD trains. Don't forget: you are important.
If you fail, there will be no-one left to say so.
If you succeed, there will also be a great silence. Your
      names, an open
secret in all hearts, no-one will say. But everywhere
they will be finishing the poems you broke away from.

2.

What I mean is: maybe you are the earth's last poets.
Li Po's riverbank poems are far, far out in eternity—
but a nuclear war could blow us that far in an instant:
there's no time left.
Tolstoy's "I would plow."
Plow, plow. But with no-one left to seed, reap,
you write? O rocks are
shortlived as men now. But still this BillyBuddworld
blesses its murderers with Spring even as I write this . . .

so I have nowhere else to turn to but you.
Old echoes are useless. Light from
the fireball this planet will become already makes shadows
    of us.
There's Einstein.—The light
of poems streaking through space, growing younger,
    younger,
becoming the poet again somewhere? No!
What I mean is. . . .

PROSEPOEM

Each evening the sea casts starfish up on the beach, scat-
tering, stranding them. They die at dawn, leaving black
hungers in the sun. We slept there that summer, we fucked
in their radiant evolutions up to our body. Ringed by
starfish gasping for their element, we joined to create ours.
All night they inhaled the sweat from our thrusting limbs,
and lived. Often she cried out: Your hand!—It was a starfish, caressing her with my low fire.

POEM TO POETRY
for Jennifer Kidney

Poetry,
you are an electric,
a magic, field—like the space
between a sleepwalker's outheld arms . . .

POEM

I am one man, worshipping silk knees,
I write these lines to cripple the dead,
to come up halt before the living:

I am one man, I run my hand over
your body, I touch the secret vibes
of the earth, I breathe your
heartbeat, Naomi, and always

I am one man alone at night. I fill my hands
with your dark hair
and offer it to the hollows of your face. I am one man,
        searching,
alone at night
like a beacon of ashes. . . .

POEM

The only response
to a child's grave is
to lie down before it and play dead

POEM

My sperm is lyre in your blood your
Smell wanders over me like a mouth
You die a moment in my eyes then pass through into

my heart
Where you live as a drunk
Where you live as that body burnt
Naked by the throes of your whitest name
River carving a deathmask for these words
I paint the features of a face on the head of my cock
But I don't call it Orpheus
Bridge between love and paper between dream and
        quicksand I
You salt tongued to idea abyss' gaze
Our sunglasses broken like *ciao*
All of time battles your instant
You lie under cool enormous leaves once the sun's eyelids
Your instant—into which dies mine and eternity's and our's
Sweat-bead upon your belly

NUREMBURG, U.S.A.

In this time and place, where "Bread and Circuses" has
become "Bread and Atrocities," to say 'I love you' is
like saying the latest propaganda phrase . . . 'defoliation'
        . . . 'low yield blast'.
If bombing children is preserving peace, then
my fucking you is a war-crime.

(NOVEMBER) (LIGHT, SHORT DAYS)
(DARK FIERY SUNSETS)

                        for Quasimodo

A small bird hops about in branches,
a blue high toss,

the sound
goes. Winter
begins to burn up all the light.

And in no time,
it's evening.
The boy gazes to the west
as if all the fire-engines in the world were streaking
    there. . . .

LATE AUGUST TO EARLY NOVEMBER

for Helene Knox, poet

If my grave becomes too painful, what should I do?
Why does my clothing stick to my interior organs?
What does it mean when I go to sleep and instead of
    dreams, all I see are the words "Insufficient Data"?

It's time to go into the survival-manual of poetry,
to read the treetrunks' instructions, the grasses' lore.
What provisions to carry—1 or 200 shrouds—
If I rub two memories together, will that light a stanza—
which roots and berries of the imagination are good, and
    which are my life?

Insufficient data. Each leaf seared full of small holes
enters the computer ground,
April answers:
Beauty is our senses' conscience;
A poet is the grave of everything that cannot be buried.

I constantly erase my birth-certificate,
the bees strafe me with drops of molten amnesia—
"You are
the clairbuoyant" I tell a girl.

I AM THE STARS' BUGGING-DEVICE

I know I have been humiliated and insulted unbearably
Like the photograph of a movie-star on the wall of a
    Death Row cell
But I take it that's my name
"He can take it" they called me in high-school
And like a baby rat I can even survive those kisses that
    swim up out of the dark

Today I shot 6 wives as they came out the supermarket
    door
I stabbed 2 Dodge Darts in the neck
Bought bread and mayonnaise for the family
Stepped on the gas
26, 83, 102, 4
Thing in the paper about a drop-out who fell in love with
    a computer
One dark night after everyone
Had gone home she broke into it
Kissing and hugging the circuits wires moans bottomless
    zeroes
When they found her she was perfected
Having been punched in the wrong places
She never learned computers are homosexual she should
    have paid attention
Serves her right for sleeping through death

I know all this because I am the stars' bugging-device
Strange
I can't pick-up those screams behind the walls of flesh

There'll be just the 2 of us at dinner
Give or take a few

SURVIVAL OF THE FITTEST GROCERIES

The violence in the newspapers is pure genius
A daily gift to the reader
From some poet who wants to keep in good with us
Brown-noser wastepaperbasket-emptier

I shot 437 people that day
2 were still alive when I killed them
Why do people want to be exhumed movie-stars
I mean rats still biting them, the flesh of comets, why do
        they walk around like that?

I'm going to throw all of you into the refrigerator
And leave you to claw it out with the vegetables and
        meats

POEM

It must be true
That masturbation drives you crazy
Something has driven me crazy

I keep a bullet curled over my ear
I'm prepared for any eventuality
Such as a hydrogen-bomb coming up to me to surrender
Or a girl's knees dawning on my darkest night
Or cutting my throat open on the drinking-fountain

If I don't touch you with my bare chest
You will cough all night

It must be true

Of himself SAINT GERAUD writes: "Bill Knott (1940-1966) is
a virgin and a suicide." His first collection *The Naomi Poems,
Book One: Corpse and Beans* was published in 1968 by Follett
as Volume One in the Big Table Series of Younger Poets.

oxygen

wire air

crickets
crickets
crickets
crickets
crickets
crickets
crickets
crickets
crickets
crickets
crickets
crickets
crickets
crickets
crickets
crickets
crickets
crickets
crickets
crickets
crickets
crickets
crickets
crickets
crickets
crickets
crickets
crickets
crickets
crickets
crickets
crickets
crickets
crickets
crickets

table
ambulance

silence
silence

cat
book
city

ARAM SAROYAN was born in 1943 in New York City. Work
of his has appeared in *Poetry: A Magazine of Verse, The Paris
Review, Chicago Review, The Nation, Art and Literature,*
and *Lines,* which he edited and published. Two collections of
his poetry will be published in 1968 by Random House: *Aram
Saroyan* and *Pages.* Kulchur Press will bring out a third: an
untitled wrapped ream of typing paper stamped © Aram
Saroyan 1968. He is the son of the writer William Saroyan.

SOFT LETTER

Experience of delight would detonate us
Mainly when we most expect it, as for instance at
The sensual performance, when the thing's so merely
        genuine
It hardly seems to be our business; so, effusively
Of course, we lose it, prone
Among the family effigies. Yet the first part
Stands. Suddenly dumb grace, again, renders
Soporific with incipience
As of almost anything, or distinctly of a revelation of
After all how sensible
Insouciance is.
                Of course, exhaustions:
Spent on the irritants of glee,
Depleted in the meek debacle
Of light spilt over some maddening and
Wholly illusory "mistake." Not to mention fear.
There can be no mention of that
Which immediately concerns us, only of any
Crystalline imminence.
Real alteration is all chemical.
The bland bias of the room is cradled
In the blood; and "love" is the code by which,
Bovinely quizzical, we circumnavigate the bulk we
Incidentally create continually, with just
Occasionally a wan evacuation, and now and then
The fascinations of a hand.

GAUGE

If you could tell me this sense of digression
And certain proclivity toward suffering, that this
Will be settled on some future date, justifying
Its now being said,
                  then you might say anything
And still not keep me, or nothing (and hello forever).

It's not for forgiveness that the wind blows.
Simply it is toward a place from some other place
It will soon have forgotten, continually forgetting in order
Beautifully to pass;
                  likewise, entering on motion,
I get mixed up in that romance of the verb
You always withhold, wanting

Only peace. I often dream about you. Thought in my
    dreams
Is real thought, visiting, never out of delirium,
But bespeaking the crisp death of every real dream

The disaster has been easy and so natural—
The words have followed like a fast train;
                        and now as if
A sort of train had passed I'm reverently standing
Hemmed in at last by the perfection of a former
    expression, sad
In a way you'll understand ("wind that glimmers at night
Amid white sheets") if only once and for a certain time.

ALCOHOL

1

This ought to be in Russian
Cyrillic and emotional!
Like "The Poems of Yurii Zhivago"
Almost (I confess) incomprehensible
In translation—or perhaps
I lack a certain indispensible
Simplicity?

It must be symptomatic of my malaise
That right away I see fit to
Mention an anxiety, as though chagrined
At not really feeling one . . .

O Optimism, American Jupiter, I
Have sinned against you
Incessantly!

I don't suppose (here I go again!) that in
This life, in this world, these times,
It is really possible
To be free of false feelings
Or to not feel indebted to them
For their miracles of Politics
And the Movies

It that clear?
All I mean is that being
Here, in the mess of my own and
Everybody else's contradictions,
Is almost unbearable!

2

One must maintain one's "natural reticence"
To avoid feeling terrible later

But then one always does feel terrible later
Even after doing something terribly
Noble one never knows it until years afterwards!
And by then, well, "I am not that person"

One is in fact always ceasing to be "that person"
In favor of something anterior
That might be, but never is finally,
Primordial and real

Look at Young America, these bereft
Generations, you can't say they haven't "lost something"
Something their parents failed to make use of, perhaps,
Which one day people will try to deny existed

All it's going to take is one cataclysm, one really big war
Or Revolution, to show just who is deserving—
Nobody, that's who   And I don't except myself
I go before only the general revulsion

Unless there is none, in which case I'm outsmarted
And there is, after all, some hope for the future

3

I suspect my father of having overcome
A native slovenliness partly
By leaving it to me
And letting me carry the shame for the both of us
But who am I to indict, finally?
We are the life-spans of our finicks

And panky manias; no one has asked us
To like them, but we really must forgive them
Occasionally, or else go down to our several
Nervous breakdowns, which await us
Hungrily

However, nobody asked me to write this, either
I do so mainly because it is fine
Now and then to feel
That one has a vocation

And fine, too, to give one's dissatisfaction
A little leverage, if one is ever
To fight one's way up toward clarity
Through this stew of the modern personality
Everything perfectly human and fetid

My head is in a state of embarassment
But I am here

And I think I am steadily zeroing in
On my "audience," just as steadily hoping
It turns out to be *someone*
And not another abstraction!
And that you can survive without me

"My poems are 'American' because I'm unalterably stuck with
the terrible American language, which is a volatile and often
a very messy language," PETER SCHJELDAHL comments in
a statement not designed to endear his work to the professional
Flag-Wavers of American Poetry. "I would love to write in
rhyme, for instance, but American poems in rhyme have a
way of not making sense. American words are blobs, rather
than clusters, of meaning. Sticking with the 'native speech

rhythms' is the only way to know what you yourself are talking about, let alone to communicate this to someone else."

Born in 1942 in Fargo, North Dakota, he attended Carleton College, where he was the co-founder of the important magazine *Mother*. His first volume *White Country* recently appeared as a Corinth Book. Art criticism of his has been published in *The New York Times*, *The Village Voice* and *Art News*. Currently Mr. Schjeldahl lives and works on the Lower East Side in Manhattan.

BEFORE THE COMING OF WINTER

I counted the shapes
of my face on the dying
leaves

& was never cheated

choose my body too
empty the trees
onto their shadows

I want to be lean & tough
as a fir
& float across the snow
in green
like an enormous flame

IF I COULD MEET GOD

if I could meet God
as an animal
my mouth filled with grass
I would not talk
for he knows the smell
of grass
& the great choking
one must have
who seeks to swallow
his world
when an animal dies
his choking is not laughter
he does not shuffle

like a man who forgets
his key
he knows there is no door
he walks inside himself
his belly full
his ears erect with certainty

ECLOGUES

where I lived the river
        lay like a blue wrist
between the bluffs & the islands
were tiny unctions of green. where
        every morning the horses outside
my house woke the sun & their breath
was like wet foliage
        in the cool air. but in my house
my bedroom poised
        between shadow & light & the light
was flawed by angles of glass
till night disappeared in a moment
        of wonder. the farm fed
on the full hillsides & sheets
of grain seemed to fall
        almost to the river's shore
but from my window the farm
        was less real: the river & at noon
the fish I could almost hear fading
in its cool depths distracted
        the boy of twelve. my brother
beside me
        slept. he was oldest & duty
has deliberate solitude: even my sisters
kept their dolls
        quietly.

the second son: his father
is silent. whose hands are fouled
    with the birth of new foal & the brother
fixes the blanket
over the mare's belly. the blood! & the younger
    boy thinks the flesh
a burden & at fault
    for its own pain. the others
lift the foal & pull
the small genital till it flexes
with full life.
    I stood in the barn
born second of God's beasts
    & alone in the days of my making.

my grandfather's God
guided him to the river & the Holy
    Ghost, he said, hung
like a white hand over this hill. our farm
    was his & when he died
my father (his son) worked a stone
in the shape of a bird, wings
    upraised as if startled
by my grandfather's death.

my name came from the river
the Fox called "Father" &
    "Source" as if a man's semen
were the only cause & my mother's fluid
    a mere aspiration. my mother
told of monsters who may
have died in the river-bed & she read
    that ice a mile high once
moved over their bones. at night
    the river with cold friction
pushes my slumbering flesh
    & my manhood moves

new
& in its own seed.

my father
        died, feeder of so many horses & so fine
an ear he had
he heard the birds with feathered weight
        drop between the green rows
of corn. a gothic
man knowing
no wisdom & in that field we
        no longer plant. the birds
forever float
        above his grave & the ground
gives
more each year.

that winter the farm
        dozed, its tillage deep
in snow. the river
backs a cruel spine against
        the bluffs & boyhood's
dim fish ride
up under the ice, Mother:
        your children. inside
the fire rubs
itself for warmth & the windows
go white with frost.

THE RABBIT LEAVES

the rabbit leaves
a track
like two dry fingers

in the new snow
the new season! & I have put
my fingers
once to a dying rabbit's
guts
that wound like roads
between the bones
where the bung-hole opens
on the white fur
like an eye

AUTUMN TESTAMENT

I have refused to shut
out desire. I have fed at the malevolent
ditches, pools where the thin skull
of a sparrow floats
easily once free of the bones
and the blown flesh testy
with flies. I have eaten
with mice at the soft edges
of the field, where the heads
of the cattails comb
pollen from the wind. once I fed
the birds
my fingerprints, pretending they were
a quince's rind, medicinal
bones hollow as flutes and the weary
heart I gave too.

but now I forget humiliation.
I despise the animals that are perpetually
competent. I know even the ants
will have children

stubbornly, sliding their hills
wave on lipless wave
down the long bay of grass.

I will love the philodendron's flowerless
vine. the blue hyacinth Apollo shaped
from the blood of a boy
he loved. I will teach the exiles
the slow
fertility of stars, the flavors
of stones the frost bites
open like pippins, that only
the roots the winter has nailed
deep will survive.

THE SUMMERS SUN

> *"The Soldier armd with Sword & Gun*
> *Palsied strikes the Summers Sun"*
> —William Blake

I   WINTER

there are open fields
behind your eyes & the nervous
rains soak still
pools that give back no face
or uncertain shadows

dark fish flickering under
the lids, you say.
shells (the doctors say) with jackets
that unbutton blue flame.
your own clothes are corrective

white
camouflage for it is winter
in the hospital & outside your country
falls asleep in soft

coils of snow

II   SPRING

you pray the dead will not rise
up nor stick to your
shoes as you waver on your sticks
down the hall to welcome
spring like some weathered sapling.

two months you have endured
the darkened sun.
you sliced open this morning's dawn

with your profile
on the window, drawing red light
like a transfusion through your veins.
still lame you journey

down the same corridor
you came by
born again in green: in uniform
though released. your pockets

breathe freely.

III   SUMMER

that summer you returned

to the farm, found you could
reinstruct the watercourses

without thinking
followed the scarecrow's cruel
shadow down the rows

of corn. the birds refused
all summer to settle
drew patterns
above you till you thought of planes

& the yellow bodies where a strange
jungle plant flowers
overnight red in the openings
of the dead: anus, mouth
or wound—once in the whorls of a dead

child's ear. they said it was blood
until you saw the green
oubliette of a bud unopened yet
you agreed. you confessed
then what the sweet grains of shrapnel

grew. today you stripped the green
suit from every ear of corn
in the row before your brother
stopped you. seeking
for yourself an opening, in the yellow

bodies some borrowed grain

IV   AUTUMN

the silver pillars of the hospital
pour red reflections
on the walks. the leaves

have turned & the trees stoop
before their own long

shadows. out on the lawn you sit
in a folding chair portable

yourself & study the great beast
that rises
from the bulldozer across the street
where a house has fallen
in on itself, fold on fold
of skin. last night you dreamed

of an insect trapped
inside the wrinkles of an elephant's
hide. as he walked
his slow organs rippled cabbages,
carrots & wisps of straw

through his body. tonight the great
beast crosses the yellow
warning line where the free-way
follows through the bones

of the fallen house

V   WINTER

the snow again presses
a white face to the window. you try
to refuse it entrance.
the doctor draws the shade

& your dark insides flick
on the small X-ray
window. there is nothing wrong
they say & follow
your wounds

with a pencil. you fear the white
medic coat that moves
out of the dark like a paradigm

of winter crystal, ice &
drifts that never melt in hollows
till the green seedlings
crawl through the sun-darkened slush
like insects. you shout, overturn

the machine & stand nude as one
switches
on the light to reveal
your wounds & the dark stitches
that travel across your stomach where

your navel winks like a buried star

One of the best poets to come out of the Midwest in recent
years, DENNIS SCHMITZ was born in 1937 in Dubuque, Iowa
and received his education at Loras College and The University
of Chicago. During the early 1960's, he studied in John Logan's
Poetry Seminar in Chicago, which proved to be a vital center
for other young Midwestern poets, including Marvin Bell, Saint
Geraud, William Hunt and Naomi Lazard. Married and the
father of three children, Mr. Schmitz teaches at Sacramento
State College. Poems of his have appeared in many of the
leading little magazines; and his first collection *The Rescue* is
ready for publication.

TO ALL HOG-RAISERS, MY ANCESTORS

When I eat pork, it's solemn business.
I am eating my ancestors.
I am eating the land they worked on.

Turnip-headed drunks, horse-thieves,
Cutthroats, convicts, filthy laborers,
I revive you within my blood.

If I add garlic to my pork
It is for one who became a minister,
Who left the land, city-bound,
Changed his name, never to be heard of again.

POVERTY

When I looked at my poverty:
My boots and the belly of my wife,
The mouse lying in the trap,
And the face of my son while he sleeps,
I knew nothing can hurt me any longer.
I can set out into the night
Without hope,
Without direction.

Nothing can hurt me any longer.
I know I live.

It is a gift
Which I am no longer afraid
To open.

STONE

Go inside a stone
That would be my way.
Let somebody else become a dove
Or gnash with a tiger's tooth.
I am happy to be a stone.

From the outside the stone is a riddle:
No one knows how to answer it.
Yet within, it must be cool and quiet
Even though a cow steps on it full weight,
Even though a child throws it in a river;
The stone sinks, slow, unperturbed
To the river bottom
Where the fishes come to knock on it
And listen.

I have seen sparks fly out
When two stones are rubbed,
So perhaps it is not dark inside after all;
Perhaps there is a moon shining
From somewhere, as though behind a hill—
Just enough light to make out
The strange writings, the star-charts
On the inner walls.

SUMMER MORNING

I love to stretch
Like this, naked
On my bed in the morning;
Quiet, listening:

Outside they are opening
Their primers
In the little school
Of the cornfield.

There is a smell of damp hay,
Of horses, of summer sky,
Of laziness, of eternal life.

I know all the dark places
Where the sun hasn't reached yet,
Where the singing has just ceased
In the hidden aviaries of the crickets—
Anthills where it goes on raining—
Slumbering spiders dreaming of wedding dresses.

I pass over the farmhouses
Where the little mouths open to suck,
Barnyards where a man, naked to the waist
Washes his face with a hose,
Where the dishes begin to rattle in the kitchen.

The good tree with its voice
Of a mountain brook
Knows my steps.
It hushes.

I stop and listen:
Somewhere close by
A stone cracks a knuckle,
Another turns over in its sleep.

I hear a butterfly stirring
In the tiny soul of the caterpillar.
I hear the dust dreaming
Of eyes and great winds.

Further ahead, someone
Even more silent
Passes over the grass
Without bending it.

—And all of sudden
In the midst of that silence
It seems possible
To live simply
On the earth.

HEARING STEPS

Someone is walking through the snow.
An ancient sound. Perhaps the Mongols are migrating
       again?
Perhaps, once more we'll go hanging virgins
From bare trees, plundering churches,
Raping widows in the deep snow?

Perhaps, the time has come again
To go back into forests and mountains,
Live alone killing wolves with our bare hands,
Until the last word and the last sound
Of this language I am speaking is forgotten.

THE WIND

Touching me, you touch
The country that has exiled you.

MARCHING

After I forgot about the horses,
And when the fire turned into cool water flowing,
And the old woman took off her mourning to enter a
       coffin,
At the end of a long life:

A horse stood like an apparition,
A dream of a drowned girl cast out by the sea.

Suddenly he turned his head, bugler turning his bugle
To face the moon shining like a newlaid egg.

Then I rose in my house among my sons,
I put on my old clothes and my muddy boots,
My clothes smelling of wolves and deep snow,
My boots that have trodden men's faces.

I remembered the swamps, grass taller than horses,
Fast rivers softer than chicken flesh,
Where I'll stumble into deep hollows, dark eyelids,
Until I am buried under human droppings.

Blood rose into my head shaking its little bells.
In the valley the glow died in the udder of the cow.
The trees ceased playing with their apples,
And the wind brought the sound of men marching.

A dog went along the road in front of marching soldiers,
A man who was to be hanged went down the road.
His head was bent. His face was dark and twisted
As if death meant straining to empty one's bowels.

So close the doors and windows and do not look.
The stars will come into the autumn sky
Like boats looking for survivors at sea,
But no son of yours will rise from the deep.

WAR

The trembling finger of a woman
Goes down the list of casualties.

The list is long.

All our names are included.

A THOUSAND YEARS WITH SOLITUDE

Toward evening
When it stops snowing
Our homes rise
High above the earth
Into that soundless space
Where neither the bark of a dog
Nor the cry of a bird reaches.

We are like the ancient seamen:
Our bodies are the ocean
And the silence is the boat
God has provided
For our long and unknown journey.

"Poetry is no longer a matter of choice with me," CHARLES SIMIC tells us. "As far back as I can remember there was a kind of dumbness within me, a need that sought expression. How it eventually materialized in the act of writing a poem, belongs to a biography which I have only been able to recount in a few successful poems. As for the finished product, the poem, my need requires it to be of—as Whitman said—'. . . the thoughts of all men in all ages and lands.' And further: 'If they are not yours as much as mine, they are nothing, or next to nothing.' On a subjective level, I write to give being to that vibration which is my life and to survive in a hard time." Mr. Simic was born in 1938. Kayak Press brought out his first collection *What the Grass Says* in 1967. Now living in Manhattan, he works as an editorial assistant on the photography quarterly *Aperture*.

MYTHMAKING

Beauty is never satisfied
with beauty. Helen,
gazing in the glass,
framed by the lecherous curtains,
the enchanted bed,
knew herself beautiful. Yet she felt life pass
about her. Laughter had been hers
to breed alone. Now mute,
the humdrum pulse run down, she lay
a palpitation of her memory;
a deceitful body and a crumbling smile
where all that love and elixirs had bred.

Men knew her aging odor.
Ravished by the nosings of her fears,
she married. Her fastened gaiety became a jewel
decking a sot. Oh well, we do
with what we have and haven't got;
the pagan cried
against endurance, dressed
and went to dinner at the side
of Menelaus. What would she become, if not her men
would come inside her,
make her whole again!
Each night was Helen
on the reminiscent bed
waiting with spread heart and legs
and willing arch for willing arrowhead.

Sprung from the cracking bow of Troy
he could not notice Helen growing old,
but fitted as a flower, or a toy,
as use to pleasure, went to hold
the woman in his arms.

And were they satisfied, these two,
when afterwards Helen closed her eyes
and slept?
Helen, who turned the too-much heart
to a great dumb shrivelling, could do as much
to any lover.
So squandered Paris in her arms lay dry
and she lay lavish and methodical;
(who offers bread by night may offer mould)
beauty to beauty did not satisfy;
such meetings of perfections cut us, turn us cold
as aging Helen, bittering in her sleep,
and cheat us of desire
by too much hungering.

She must have been glad to wake, not to be satisfied,
to see her husband stir himself and raise a fleet,
and all the world fall shadow
to the crumpling of that sheet.

HIGH

In the hall, scuffling; in the cat's mouth, a dove.
Oh startled exclamations! The bird is cooing soft
excitable alarms. You, plural, wake
at odds, from fuzzy dreams and
thick-with-hashish mating, disentangling
the white flannel nightgown
from the legs that struggle
for firm ground; wrenched
by cries from the maw of bed
to the gaping mouth of the entry.
A dove! The cat is casual, smiling:
he will not be dispossessed.

You've had your fun of his fur
body, stuffed with marijuana,
brain, the target, blurring
to a small determined rage. He's earned
the things he gets between his jaws;
the crunchy bird bones, knowledge, and the white
wood-smooth body.

Look how I suffer, beckons now the bird.
I who have dared
investigate the air, who've found
clear weather at the rim.
I have hallucinated land
as crisp as light.
My flicker-yellow eye has unreeled sky:
now I am forced to watch
my homecoming, the draggle-tail
in hall, the sacrificial feast

where you sit down at table,
cracking the joints of the girl
in your teeth
and she gets her revenge
by going limp and refusing;
her impenetrable
feathers blurring your pleasure, tucked in
the subtle white grimace of bed.

Hurried into a box, the dove, back of the stove, pants
and recovers. Blood on her feathers
and soot like a slick on them, glassy
and evil. A chuck of her head
and the quick breathing
slackens: her breast heaves with
gossip; the eye shuts,
reliving. You are sickened

in retrospect, feeling again
the curved bird in the mouth,
the blood hardened like rind
and the terror that tore through
your feigned-passion fucking
and woke you from sex
like the shriek of a child.

From where did it come? The world flounders
in water; the household submerges in sleep.
The bird's bedded
and nests by your side,
a small feathery hump.
In the cave of the nightgown
perhaps you will grope for
each other's warm parts again.
What else, my potheads,
high, indefatigable,
would you be doing
with a dove in your place?

FATLIPPED, YOU FORMLESS

Fatlipped, you formless scavenging
creature, murgling polliwog
munching the algae in my aquarium,
who would believe those skinny legs,
half-formed, would do for a frog?

Some see in that sucking mouth
progress, others a cyclical
moon and a sloughing off.
Tail cloudy as aspic,
tadpole, we dredged you

out with a net from the
cemetery pond. And the seepage
in lowspots, the hollows condensing,
brooding you, thick as a root:
is there reason?

Strange how the breeding
goes on in the swamps; fine-legged teeming
in muck and in coffins, weeds
swarming with such events, even
our moist coupling part of it:

all flesh, cookie-dough,
melting, concocting.
Comma, how your large head
bulges, trying and
trying to become a frog!

STRAINING

Sojourning alone in Paris,
he thought, now finally
he was a poet. All the props
were his: the cloak, the hat
like a cringing accordion,
the moustache, the walking stick
pronouncing ends-of-sentences
on the sidewalk.

Only he had not reckoned
on the loneliness. Isolate,
terrible as a lavatory,
it chilled him, coming in from

the warm purple streets.
His room lay in the darkness
like a terrapin, promising nothing.

Something unseen, a posterity,
crouched in the corners, watching,
ticking off his movements; his forearms
as he washed his shirt
in the basin; the casual
lighting of a match. That eerie tiger
noticed everything. His neck
prickled at his writing stand.

"If you love me, guard
my solitude," he wrote
to endless mistresses, his wife,
his friends. Solitude!
It is the sallow wallpaper
of furnished rooms.
Worried as a snail, he worked,
extruding a thin slimy track.

While to him a young man
earnestly wrote: Dear Mr. Rilke,
how shall I become a poet,
having a most desperate longing
to do so, and in my bosom
some small songs?

And like a garden, the replies
profused, lavishing
in leaking roses, borders
of bachelor's buttons, blue
at the buttonhole,
and the scent of solitary
sentry lilies: sentences
burgeoning like blood from a slit
artery.

No tourniquet could staunch it.
The heart, spurting, sprinted
onto the page. "Dear Mr. Kappus . . ."
Loneliness, that leech obscene
on his mouth, was sucking,
glutting out whole sonnets,
clots of sound.

CRIPPLES

In the halls, in the universities,
the wheelchairs do their slow dance
between classes. Painful caryatids,
they propel themselves down the halls
like enormous maimed grasshoppers.

Last summer, in glaring July,
I stepped on a grasshopper
on a path. It was grasshopper season.
The hay hummed with them and they twitched
like little green twigs in the sun.

Under my foot, the insect
was only partially crushed.
Almond-eyed and slow, he tried
to drag his soft parts, severed legs
onto the side of the path;

the reproach of the crippled.
Now far from summer, lying in bed,
I think, oh body, how I love you:
moving so easily, may no harm come to you;
long bones, legs, hands up to light.

Of herself KATHLEEN SPIVACK, who was born in 1938,
writes: "married to a designer, and have held a variety of jobs
concurrent with writing, from teaching writing at Boston University to working in a boiler factory. Am currently working as
a psychotherapist in a small mental health clinic associated
with Brandeis University." Her poems have been seen in *The
Atlantic Monthly, Encounter* and *Poetry: A Magazine of Verse.*

THE MAN IN THE MIRROR

for Decio de Souza

I walk down the narrow
carpeted hall.
The house is set.
The carnation in my buttonhole

precedes me like a small
continuous explosion.
The mirror
is in the living room.

You are there.
Your face is white, unsmiling, swollen.
The fallen body of your hair
is dull and out of place.

Buried in the darkness of your pockets,
your hands are motionless.
You do not seem awake.
Your skin sleeps

and your eyes lie in the deep
blue of their sockets,
impossible to reach.
How long will all this take?

I remember how we used to stand,
wishing the glass
would dissolve between us,
and how we watched our words

cloud that bland,
innocent surface,
and when our faces blurred,
how scared we were.

But that was another life.
One day you turned away
and left me here
to founder in the stillness of your wake.

Your suit floating, your hair
moving like eelgrass
in a shallow bay, you drifted
out of the mirror's room, through the hall

and into the open air.
You seemed to rise and fall
with the wind, the sway
taking you always farther away, farther away.

Darkness filled your sleeves.
The stars moved through you.
The vague music of your shrieking
blossomed in my ears.

I tried forgetting what I saw;
I got down on the floor,
pretending to be dead.
It did not work.

My heart bunched in my ribcage like a bat,
blind and cowardly,
beating in and out—
a solemn, irreducible black.

The things you drove me to!
I walked in the calm of the house,
calling you back.
You did not answer.

I sat in a chair
and stared across the room
The walls were bare.
The mirror was nothing without you.

I lay down on the couch
and closed my eyes.
My thoughts rose in the dark
like faint balloons,

and I would turn them over,
one by one, and watch them shiver.
I always fell into a deep
and arid sleep.

Then out of nowhere, late one night,
you reappeared—
a huge vegetable moon,
a bruise coated with light.

You stood before me,
dreamlike and obscene,
your face lost
under layers of heavy skin,

your body sunk in a green
and wrinkled sea of clothing.
I tried to help you,
but you refused.

Days passed
and I would rest
my cheek against the glass,
wanting nothing but the old you.

I sang so sadly
that the neighbors wept
and dogs whined with pity.
Some things I wish I could forget.

You didn't care,
standing still while flies

collected in your hair
and dust fell like a screen before your eyes.

You never spoke
or tried to come up close.
Why did I want so badly
to get through to you?

It still goes on.
I go into the living room and you are there.
You drift in a pool
of silver air

where wounds and dreams of wounds
rise from the deep
humus of sleep
to bloom like flowers against the glass.

I look at you
and see myself
under the surface.
A dark and private weather

settles down on everything.
The dreams wither.
The air is cold.
You stand

like a shade
in the painless glass—
frail, distant, older
than ever.

It will always be this way.
I stand here scared
that you will disappear,
scared that you will stay.

EATING POETRY

Ink runs from the corners of my mouth.
There is no happiness like mine.
I have been eating poetry.

The librarian does not believe what she sees.
Her eyes are sad
and she walks with her hands in her dress.

The poems are gone.
The light is dim.
The dogs are on the basement stairs and coming up.

Their eyeballs roll,
their blond legs burn like brush.
The poor librarian begins to stamp her feet and weep.

She does not understand.
When I get on my knees and lick her hand,
she screams.

I am a new man.
I snarl at her and bark.
I romp with joy in the bookish dark.

WHAT TO THINK OF

Think of the jungle,
The green steam rising.

It is yours.
You are the Prince of Paraguay.

Your minions kneel
Deep in the shade of giant leaves

While you drive by
Benevolent as gold.

They kiss the air
That moments before

Swept over your skin,
And rise only after you've passed.

Think of yourself, almost a god,
Your hair on fire,

The bellows of your heart pumping.
Think of the bats

Rushing out of their caves
Like a dark wind to greet you;

Of the vast nocturnal cities
Of lightning bugs

Floating down
From Minas Gerais;

Of the coral snakes;
Of the crimson birds

With emerald beaks;
Of the tons and tons of morpho butterflies

Filling the air
Like the cold confetti of paradise.

THE MAN IN THE TREE

I sat in the cold limbs of a tree.
I wore no clothes and the wind was blowing.
You stood below in a heavy coat,
the coat you are wearing.

And when you opened it, baring your chest,
white moths flew out, and whatever you said
at that moment fell quietly onto the ground,
the ground at your feet.

Snow floated down from the clouds into my ears.
The moths from your coat flew into the snow.
And the wind as it moved under my arms, under my chin,
whined like a child.

I shall never know why
our lives took a turn for the worse, nor will you.
Clouds sank into my arms and my arms rose.
They are rising now.

I sway in the white air of winter
and the starling's cry lies down on my skin.
A field of ferns covers my glasses; I wipe them away
in order to see you.

I turn and the tree turns with me.
Things are not only themselves in this light.
You close your eyes and your coat
falls from your shoulders,

the tree withdraws like a hand,
the wind fits into my breath, yet nothing is certain.
The poem that has stolen these words from my mouth
may not be this poem.

THE MARRIAGE

The wind comes from opposite poles,
traveling slowly.

She turns in the deep air.
He walks in the clouds.

She readies herself,
shakes out her hair,

makes up her eyes,
smiles.

The sun warms her teeth,
the tip of her tongue moistens them.

He brushes the dust from his suit
and straightens his tie.

He smokes.
Soon they will meet.

The wind carries them closer.
They wave.

Closer, closer.
They embrace.

She is making a bed.
He is pulling off his pants.

They marry
and have a child.

The wind carries them off
in different directions.

The wind is strong, he thinks
as he straightens his tie.

I like this wind, she says
as she puts on her dress.

The wind unfolds.
The wind is everything to them.

THE DIRTY HAND
(after Carlos Drummond de Andrade)

My hand is dirty.
I must cut it off.
To wash it is pointless.
The water is putrid.
The soap is bad.
It won't lather.
The hand is dirty.
It's been dirty for years.
I used to keep it
out of sight,
in my pants pocket.
No one suspected a thing.
People came up to me,
Wanting to shake hands.
I would refuse
and the hidden hand,
like a dark slug,
would leave its imprint
on my thigh.
And then I realized
it was the same
if I used it or not.
Disgust was the same.

Ah! How many nights
in the depths of the house
I washed that hand,
scrubbed it, polished it,
dreamed it would turn
to diamond or crystal
or even, at last,
into a plain white hand,
the clean hand of a man,
that you could shake,
or kiss, or hold
in one of those moments
when two people confess
without saying a word . . .
Only to have
the incurable hand,
lethargic and crablike,
open its dirty fingers.

And the dirt was vile.
It was not mud or soot
or the caked filth
of an old scab
or the sweat
of a laborer's shirt.
It was a sad dirt
made of sickness
and human anguish.
It was not black;
black is pure.
It was dull,
a dull grayish dirt.

It is impossible
to live with this
gross hand that lies
on the table.
Quick! Cut it off!

Chop it to pieces
and throw it
into the ocean.
With time, with hope
and its machinations,
another hand will come,
pure, transparent as glass,
and fasten itself to my arm.

KEEPING THINGS WHOLE

In a field
I am the absence
of field.
This is
always the case.
Wherever I am
I am what is missing.

When I walk
I part the air
and always
the air moves in
to fill the spaces
where my body's been.

We all have reasons
for moving.
I move
to keep things whole.

MARK STRAND was born in 1934 in Summerside, Prince
Edward Island, Canada. (He is an American citizen.) Educated at
Yale University, he has published: *Sleeping with One Eye Open*
(1964) and *Reasons for Moving* (Atheneum: 1968). Married
and the father of a daughter, he lives in New York City.

THE LOST PILOT

for my father, 1922–1944

Your face did not rot
like the others—the co-pilot,
for example, I saw him

yesterday. His face is corn-
mush: his wife and daughter,
the poor ignorant people, stare

as if he will compose soon.
He was more wronged than Job.
But your face did not rot

like the others—it grew dark,
and hard like ebony;
the features progressed in their

distinction. If I could cajole
you to come back for an evening,
down from your compulsive

orbiting, I would touch you,
read your face as Dallas,
your hoodlum gunner, now,

with the blistered eyes, reads
his braille editions. I would
touch your face as a disinterested

scholar touches an original page.
However frightening, I would
discover you, and I would not

turn you in; I would not make
you face your wife, or Dallas,
or the co-pilot, Jim. You

could return to your crazy
orbiting, and I would not try
to fully understand what

it means to you. All I know
is this: when I see you,
as I have seen you at least

once every year of my life,
spin across the wilds of the sky
like a tiny, African god,

I feel dead. I feel as if I were
the residue of a stranger's life,
that I should pursue you.

My head cocked toward the sky,
I cannot get off the ground,
and, you, passing over again,

fast, perfect, and unwilling
to tell me that you are doing
well, or that it was mistake

that placed you in that world,
and me in this; or that misfortune
placed these worlds in us.

COMING DOWN CLEVELAND AVENUE

The fumes from all kinds
of machines have dirtied
the snow. You propose
to polish it, the miles
between home and wherever
you and your lily
of a woman might go. You
go, pail, brush, and
suds, scrubbing down
Cleveland Avenue
toward the Hartford Life
Insurance Company. No
one appreciates your
effort and one important
character calls you
a baboon. But pretty
soon your darling jumps
out of an elevator
and kisses you and you
sing and tell her to
walk the white plains
proudly. At one point
you even lay down
your coat, and she, in
turn, puts hers down for
you. And you put your
shirt down, and she, her
blouse, and your pants,
and her skirt, shoes—
removes her lavender
underwear and you slip
into her proud, white skin.

THE DESTINATION

All day red hatpins fall out
of the sky, so I fasten
myself to a tree and let
the velvet and light inside

of it love and comfort me:
could this be the way life ends?
I carry away the tree,
place it in my car and start

toward home, not feeling a part
of anything anymore;
thinking, I don't want to live
in this place twice, I jam on

the brakes and clear my throat
of human hair, climb out of
the car, stare at the junkman
staring into the flames

of the tree—goodbye, little friend.
I walk to Seattle, sell
my old clothes, sleep alone all
week in a park on the ground,

wake to find my head dropping
visions of six children
ripping open a reindeer.
I am sad and befuddled,

going the direction I think
is worst, with papers tied to
my ankles, wondering if
this is the way life begins.

PLEA BASED ON A SENTENCE FROM A LETTER
RECEIVED BY THE INDIANA STATE WELFARE
DEPARTMENT

Like lemon jello in a dream-
child's hand, here is my heart,

I don't know what to do with it

anymore, now that you are dead
certain there is no chance
for me to improve my state
of mind. Virginia, I have been
sitting here for three months

wringing my hands, nodding
my head, swaying, my whole body

swaying in ignorance.
Could you come over? I happen
to know you're miserable.
Could we hide the bones

of the past and apply rouge
to the cheeks of the future?

I will make you more attractive
than you could make yourself.
I am forwarding my marriage

certificate and six children;
I have seven but one died

which was baptized on half
a sheet of paper . . .

THE TRUST

You start with yourself
and are lucky if you ever
get past that. It's a process

of winnowing. Say, you have
accomplished something—
a dragon, oleander or loin—

but how can you know the true
salmon's touch when you cannot
trust yourself alone

like this with yourself.
You might call it creation,
picturing a theater, the sun

having driven the rattlesnakes
to singing. Well, this
is the beginning: what you do next

will depend on nothing.

FOR MOTHER ON FATHER'S DAY

You never got to recline
in the maternal tradition,
I never let you. Fate,

you call it, had other eyes,
for neither of us ever had
a counterpart in the way

familial traditions go.
I was your brother,
and you were my unhappy

neighbor. I pitied you
the way a mother pities
her son's failure. I could

never find the proper
approach. I would have
lent you sugar, mother.

WHY I WILL NOT GET OUT OF BED

My muscles unravel
like spools of ribbon:
there is not a shadow

of pain. I will pose
like this for the rest
of the afternoon,

for the remainder
of all noons. The rain
is making a valley

of my dim features.
I am in Albania,
I am on the Rhine.

It is autumn,
I smell the rain,
I see children running

through columbine.
I am honey,
I am several winds.

My nerves dissolve,
my limbs wither—
I don't love you.

I don't love you.

THE DESCENT

I imagine that these thousand
sleek, invisible zebras are
leading me somewhere;

it is the moment before
birth, I expect, and follow.
The air that pursues us

is as warm and moist
as the breath of a young
rhinoceros. The sky rumbles

with televisions. Harry
Langdon in *The Life
of Abu Bakr*. None of the little

anthracite rabbits with carrot
pink eyes are real.
I know that now and feel

burdened with all the eternal
verities. The ground beneath me

is as soft as the tongue

of an old giraffe. Where
are we now, darlings? This
suitcase has lost its charm.

INTIMIDATIONS OF AN AUTOBIOGRAPHY

I am walking a trail
on a friend's farm
about three miles from

town. I arrange the day
for you. I stop and say,
you would not believe how happy

I was as a child,
to some logs. Blustery wind
puts tumbleweed

in my face as I am
pretending to be on my way
home to see you and

the family again,
to touch the orange
fingers of the moon.

That's how I think of it.
The years flipped back last night
and I drank hot rum till

dawn.
It was a wild success and I wasn't sad when
I woke past noon

and saw the starlings in the sky.
My brain's an old rag anyway,
but I've got a woman and you'd say

she's too good for me. You'd call
her a real doll and me a goof-ball.
I've got my head between my paws

because it's having a damn
birthday party. How old do you think I am?
I bet you think I'm

seventeen.
It doesn't matter. Just between
us, you know what I'm doing

now? I'm calling the cows home.
They're coming, too.
I lower

myself to the ground lazily,
a shower of avuncular kisses
issuing from my hands and lips—

I just wanted to tell you
I remember you even now;
Goodbye, goodbye. Here come the cows.

RESCUE

For the first time the only
thing you are likely to break

is everything because
it is a dangerous

venture. Danger invites
rescue—I call it loving.

We've got a good thing
going—I call it rescue.

Nicest thing ever to come
between steel cobwebs, we hope

so. A few others should get
around to it, I can't understand

it. There is plenty of room,
clean windows, we start our best

engines, a-rumm . . . everything is
relevant. I call it loving.

DEATH ON COLUMBUS DAY

Sometimes you can hear the naked will
working, like the ocean becoming a shore
yesterday, and the day before,
the trees shrinking away,
even the mere transitional phase of seasons,

the tenacious skidding of a gone summer,
the cleaving to lusciousness,
and (you can see all this
from your window if you wash it
regularly, if you are afraid to go out)
even whole environments,
giants of varying kindness,
dissolve, and you, your pupils,
yes, blue as they may appear,
are, when you think about it,
acolytes to all destruction.

LATE HARVEST

I look up and see
a white buffalo
emerging from the
enormous red gates
of a cattle truck
lumbering into
the mouth of the sun.
The prairie chickens
do not seem to fear
me; neither do the
girls in cellophane
fields, near me, hear me
changing the flat tire
on my black tractor.
I consider screaming
to them; then, night comes.

One of the youngest winners of the Yale Younger Poets com-
petition for the collection *The Lost Pilot* (1967), JAMES TATE

was born in 1943 in Kansas City, Missouri, only five months before his father—the "lost pilot" of the poem of that title—was reported missing over Germany on what was to be his last mission. After study in The Program in Creative Writing at The University of Iowa under Donald Justice, George Starbuck and Marvin Bell, Mr. Tate was graduated in 1967 with a Master of Fine Arts degree and now teaches at The University of California at Berkeley.

THE AGE OF GOLD

Don't talk with food in your mouth
                    During the age of gold

We are arrested during your nightmare in Italy

The people rushing by saying we're criminal types
Flush the lantern and beat their belly in a secret language
to Mt Erynx That's nice I tell one propeller

We meet over the Portinari bridge cross kiss and therefore
        halve it in two greet each other from transposed sides

My hair is not something for like or dislike

A centaur chops off the head of a lapith. Admiral Beatty
        with his *Humph* hands in his pocket wryly watching
        the indigo spectacle

The moon is not red because I have a wife

Lunch is being made in Vischer's King Arthur

Many students of Greek think a thorn of the foot an
        Egyptian bird like a heron
Three tailors of Tooley Street. He was also the chief Moon
        God "wandering the blue rocks"
live with me

Lightning register. All exaggeration of mawkish violinists
Do so with a palm in your throat Pima Indian the office
        windows from sight

Yet I am just back from three chimeras of world-seeing in
        the Tales from The Vienna Woods

An immaculate photograph. A signal horse-car
    but took a wagon owing my tongue
as if a Luca Della Robbia should be cast in gold shadow
which brings Garbo to a cage of pigeons.
Calling me salutor of the dead   As a funeral of camels
    passes by.
The Age of Gold with withering frosted, immodest eyelids

We do a soft-shoe dance on the snows past. Finally
    standing on upturned
Arrows like the rain of the winds in Holland Softly.
    Playing hopscotch with
A sphinx. We hear the monotone in Italy. Tropar. The
    fasting ten thousand saints
The transparent dissolving microphone your mouth
    founded for the drowse of Imperial Rome.

Where I am station-caller atop the Imperial Eagle calling
    the headpieces of Maltese Women who bake in the
    afternoon

To them the sea is gauze.

We are arrested
    the tenebrae hatchet clicks sparrows

There is a big rectangular hole with mechanical equipment
    within
A bomb settled within & locked up coming out into the
    platitudinous
Sun everyday like clockwork and secreting itself again

                    That would destroy the city

        Going through the town of candlelight
We are poor but innocent
The rich section of the town, the unplugged swimming
    pool, are the different focii of the Red Sea

The demolished people are the way ahead

You run away

Where girls are dubbed with race-horse wreaths

You return the area is demolished by the robot
     bomb

Cheese and bread our diet again
We are naked

POEM

Everyone who is anyone is moving away
To I don't know where
A cow has hung itself in my heart
     because I insulted it with words
I meet the same peripatetic sailor everywhere
     retracing his own steps on aces
     of spades
Holding his speed instrument in his hand.

The "ICE" light blinks on and off in the night
It is a hungry world
As if I am holding a sail!
Ah Raymond Roussel who invited
     the attentions of little girls!

IS IT FOR THIS I LIVE?

1.

On the street where we used to go to school
We could always tell
when it was going to rain
We could smell the chocolate

It was the factory
of the infinite woman

who would wait for us as a fallacy

As we passed
by the iron grated summer moth
Shrubbery that appeared
on chair coverings in the night they were the atmosphere
by the screened window

2.

A subaltern of desire
Marie, although I don't know why I desired her
        said she saw
you walking in the tuileries of the Bronx zoo
inspecting the crushed eye of Babylon

O the tuileries will be forever!
and the Bronx zoo forever
where I will see you walking
playing on the vanquished cabbage-harps of her words

And the observed
connection of any love
we had is

in your hands: a coin bank
in the shape of a lighthouse

ON THE DEATH OF FRANK O'HARA

It is in these stones that the claviers sing
trans-quiescent windows We have little money now
All the same direction A pair of shoes found
on our porch Which can never be known for certain, for
     no sign

oh monks!
death in an amazed universe
that I can never be tanned enough for
A hysterical girl eating pop-corn eyeing Elsewhere
     everyone

"You know, Ernie, this is such a good day,—It's Thursday
     sphinxes
parmagian cherries limes"
I expect to see you everywhere
In the Library of a Big City all the "works" of John Cage

are gone. The anemia of those seeking immortality After
     you look at her
                                The defoliated
The bowing and "I am guilty" head of a girl as she goes by
Someday if ever I know of a tailor
raincoats The aficionado How many *mutations*

of the revolving door? Camera obscura Always in search
     of those
flaming girls and falangist motorcyclists
The persistence of MEAT LOAF signs
What we can see

The impudence of the struggle!
the tawny enjamb!
Creaseless. Obsidian.
Do not lag withering before Exclude us The washing

Malherbes. Sperri. Griefs. Annunciation.

EULOGY OF THE VAIN HOURS

Like hatred when a child falls
that dreamer mother again Mr Big
I might be as insignificant as that
in the earthquake of Japanese suns
in the Astrea Season false fertile spring of college girls
All the roads I do not know are painted green
    today
which means the mountains will die in winter
which means the people of the earth
will wear hollyhocks around their ears
My head is a falling comet!
Onto the desert of their tongues
40 days and 40 nights of artichokes
parachuted, poised in my groins their whole upland!
O my division!

Slowly the caravans take the cellar of the wonderworker
    away

You are beautiful because you are under my foot

ON THE ANNIVERSARY OF THE DEATH OF
    FRANK O'HARA

Today I walk in and out of the doors of
    your death
With a farmer from Nebraska who fell
from a 75 foot tower
and became a maintainance man
He is my guide as Virgil was

Shining fire-extinguishers
sweeping the stairs

There are obvious epithets
A hatchet falling and nearly missing
a cartoon turkey
a guardian angel-type ghost admonishing a packer
not to stand under the elevated crates

The grandson of the Plough that broke the plains enters
    blonde with a red ribbon on his chest

O lover of wheat
Shall I get the big knife

I'm mostly anonymous

I don't know why the cooks are happy
they're almost dancing

POEM WRITTEN DURING SLEEP

Epure si muove.

The blonde mouths are awake on the tree
where you sleep.

I recline and awake from time to time
always near my spiritual accordion
Like a plain.

I can hear myself calling out orders to myself
on a cactus microphone.

On which rain collects like dew forming an invisible
windshield.

A tree is weeping in a gutter island that surrounds
it in a storm
I rest with my hands on your head like a captain at the
helm.

My hunger yawns in public events.

A visible voice sings: 'The breakmen of the airplane's
harp are sung to sleep,' in beautiful tones

"I am of North African (Black and Arab) and all-around
Mediterranean descent (My grandparents came from the Island
of Sicily, were Christians)," SOTÈRE TORREGIAN writes.
"From around 1963 marks period when Torregian began the
discipline of what he emphatically calls 'orthodox Surrealism'—
following the dictates of Poet André Breton on art and thought.
Torregian has made reinterpretations of surrealist stands on

Revolutionary perspectives in art, poetry and theology, which
has necessitated his being 'spokesman for the Surrealist Movement in America,' the motto of which is *C'est la guerre totale*
(Total Assault)." He was born in 1941 in Newark, New Jersey,
attended Rutgers University, and taught a two-year course
"Poetry and the Revolution" at the Free University of New York,
where he is on the permanent faculty. Currently he lives with
his wife the poet Kathleen Torregian and new daughter in
Palo Alto, California. *The Golden Palomino Bites the Clock*
(Angel Hair) appeared in 1967. A work *Aveugle* will appear this
year in a bilingual edition in Paris, France. His long poem
"The Wounded Mattress" is presently being considered for
publication by a West Coast publisher.

FROM THE SPANISH

In the rain what is there to do, what to play.
I ride, beginning to doze, underground to the Bronx,
on a horse, under Manhattan like undigested pork,
the unfortunate fish bouncing dead off the walls.
From the Bronx we drive to Labrador, in Canada,
at the end of September, the sea full of hidden rocks.
Near the top of a mountain come up from the sea
we begin to see the danger of our experiment.
A little powder and the mountain is gone,
and clinging to an oar we are in the black water.

A voice rings out, the stranger chuckles;
our reverie flees like a running dog.
Men and women come forward to shake our hand.
Bystanders take us to the cafe. In the cafe
the sun burns at midnight, burns our faces with liquor
and comes up in the morning. In the morning air we divide,
extending our thoughts and going on like birds,
over the sleeping thieves and invisible grass for them.
A breath of cold air and the flight is ending,
covering the grass and the rocks with her hair,
speeding the turn of the seasons and their grief,
our red mouths visible and the white sky full of clouds.

ELEGY

We eat and hear, as your kiss descends
over the piano and the sky.
The tide rushes out of a box and I am dead.
Prokovieff is dead as I am.
On the day of judgement when we are released,

we will hear rain and thunder
and miles of cars will stop in their tracks.
The line going down the highway is white,
the color of the sky before Prokofiev.
At the beginning I am here behind the typewriter.
I wander off to the cliffs to see the sharks
looking for a finger or some bloody popcorn or a ruined
    doll.
I throw them a ruined doll.
The camera moves in for a close-up. I adjust my tie
but it focuses on my cigarettes, Pall Mall Filters,
and the shining gold pack which contains them.
The camera goes on across the crowd.
We have five seconds on camera, a daguerrotype,
the room is upside down and objects fall with a crash.
Then a picture of an airplane.
The airplane or the sun is upside down.
It is the sun, which falls like an egg onto a plateau.
The real sun burns it to a disgusting omelette.
The sun also drains the color from the words, the moon
turns them to chalk and they collapse.

14TH STREET

You learn new things every week.
You go nowhere in the way that you expect.
Awash on the streets you save money on linens and shirts.
You count and examine your change.
Something hideous falls on you as from a great height,
for if you insist on writing there will be shapes
throughout an evening,
beginning with poetry and ending on a hill of icy prose.

Sure I don't have anything to do with the moon
because boring people will land there,
nothing to do with the century
except to swallow its apple of sophistication
difficult but no wider than a stopping train,
running by the houses and killing the grass
here on Long Island where you walk around,
you who have not seen the moon for so long
in the haphazard temerity of keeping awake.
But even so, on an infinite train of thought
you look to your syntax for an exquisite mist,
the flowers on Park Avenue, Madison Avenue,
which like your suit are covered with a thin film.

FOR IRMA DURING APRIL

Now it is April, then the great bull of May,
and then it will be my birthday and time for presents and
    the beach.
That's when the poetry of summer descends on you
if you are a poet, and the metaphors emit an enormous heat,
tapering off to the luxuriant melancholy verse of fall.
Then 1968 and my vote for president,
and January 1969 and 70. By
this time my poetry improves, a compliment to the new
    administration.
I suppose that other people's poetry will also have
    improved,
worse luck, and there will be new painters and paintings,
and a host of movies which I won't keep track of,
or as Johnson said of Pope, considering the English climate
what would an Englishman want with a grotto.
As an American I should be able to enjoy a grotto.
The walls would drip with the fragrance of the spirits of

the earth,
and in general be like a symphony by Shostakovich,
very entertaining, like a vodka and tonic made with
    Russian vodka.
The clocks' stopping means I'm waiting for you to get home;
dinner, and the television of Sherlock Holmes and Watson,
shaping our evening with Hollywood precision.
Beautiful cinematography and the pork chops this April
since they're yours and with the curtains drawn
spring in the area is a more delightful place in which to be.

ENCHANTMENT

Prologue

If you walk slowly, out of breath, and think,
and breathe the air, on the coast,
arriving at the coast out of breath
and helpless, distressed about your conclusion
because it is evening and one no longer sees,
then everything you sense may be enchanted,
in a fugitive way
as soon it will be a different situation.

1

A surgeon, his daughter, a chemist and some gentlemen.
The smile, of the daughter, warms the dead snow.
They are in the basement. They are on the roof,
a function of the shadowy street;

                    But you, divine perceiving light,
holding one's foot as we soak the rays of the sun
over an icy ocean of winter at sea, bring us our voices

as they are in the movies, hoarse from the dialogue,
with dripping hands full of tobacco, our frozen eyes
watching the camera, our sensuality
folklore already captured by a review
in a comparison with the vivid past,
our development racing the comparison, an impression
racing the drug.

You, comprehensible light, may find us leaving,
presenting us as you wish. We understand
each other's problems, the highlights and shadows;
. . . but the drug takes effect and we are doctors,
opening our eyes and hands, thinking
the scalpel is something else. We say goodbye,
yelping and banging the door.
Circumstances fall into place and the pulse slows to
     normal.
He examines a liver and eats it. The shape of the liver
is repeated until he is depressed, the light revealing nothing
     else.

2

You open your eyes, the gentlemen disperse,
each to a situation
which you will investigate when you are rested,
with mixed feelings and time for contemplation,
and things falling, in slow motion from the window, into
     place,
as falling from the highest place imagined
in the coming moment, has produced the effect of falling
     now,
and shows what is an orange falling from its place,
with later others, in disorder, also falling,
and the orange has fallen, into the water,
and we are free to see it disappear,
and unencumbered we go to the nearest place that is
     comfortable.

3

The idea stops, halts, abruptly.
A friend may enter the room, happy and alive,
talking and you listen but you are not sure.
You stand and listen.
We will feel better with each word tomorrow,
understanding the conversation differently and admiringly,
the words growing dense and great.
But the greatness diffuses
and we see the colors of paint.
Their delicate use astounds us,
the silver light at the top remains that color
as we wade, intoxicated with the warmth of the water,
the group of figures at the front, the bottom, conveying
the infinite satisfaction their presence makes possible,
delighting us with the colorless air they breathe,
and stirring the breathtaking length of our trip like a fluid.

In the morning we are set in rows and given problems. Who
finishes quickly is given one more, more complicated,
until finally things are perfected and we disperse, as
gentlemen, having started with nothing and excelled in
        everything,
our projects and accomplishments nearby in the light,
illuminating our successive details.
There is a thought. The light is excluded from the trees
and the group of people are fools, departing, leaving
a woman, naked and pensive, near a cloud, and
watching it from the distant side of a space
covered with inches of water. She turns her head,
thinking, as I write, crossing her mind.

Poems (limited edition hand-set and printed by author: 1966)
and *After dinner we take a drive into the night* (Tibor de Nagy
Editions: 1968) are the two collections of poems written by
TONY TOWLE. At present he lives with his wife and baby
daughter in New York City, where he was born in 1939.

from TALES

Not after but within this poem I stalk my lovers—
weapons waved in crippled gestures I would hack you
to see the black & taloned angel.

from NIGHTLETTER

The miracle traced on a plate in
    dry ink: man half awake
confronting the objects which
are alive
with voices of the dead:
    motto: open here the eternal voice that
sleeps within that the plate may not be bare.
Our loves infused with other lives, praise and
lamentation one in the litany of this
destruction, lack-love sings in
her multiple tongues.
O love and the instance
of ascension into the realm of pure objects and their
yearning, Godlight in the eyes of the citizen
betrayed by sight & ear, his bestial innocence
sings through cardboard and wool.

KITCHEN

In the jar of apricot jam a lava sea &
    the ant is Jules Verne circling the crater rim in
    Iceland, dreams his dream of the center's
sticky orange—

The radio with static in its throat announces
"Arthur Rimbaud's *Ivory Boat* read by
Dr. etc." he sees America in the title &
why not.
I translate a line anew—
    (Comme je descendais des fleuves impassibles)
    "Come didya descend the impassible flues?"
& Rimbaud flies by my window approving—
    the sign—a flock of finches—
    —wingtips wink like
    coins tossed in the sun
    over Oakland—
In thanks I unscrew the lid &
    Verne descends the impassible flue
    with his 19th century space suit he
    looks like an ant hurrying there—

Kitchen—name of my room, I refuse
    such a chewy name—why not
    dove salon
    —or
    velvet cave

(I'm alone now the radio is an old French
    professor I turn off slowly, his astral voice
    drifting out thru space to other planet—
    rooms.

Stop writing a minute & examine the
    view from the porch no the balcony, bluff or
    turret—Ha!

Every day it changes—the Movers
    Supplies Warehouse is ogling the mailman, its
    big glass eyes pop with love—

my room is more discreet—it feels me up
    when I'm asleep & plays dead in the

day (then I tickle its walls with
cooking smells & barefoot dancing)

Someday it will come alive—coy lover—
    not just ants & radio voice but the whole
    room will sigh, raise a trembling chair
    or lampshade to my mouth—sing through
    faucets & pipes the song of my exciting
    life here—

Fly me off the enraptured cosmonaut to
    Iceland or San Leandro a genuine
    flying fuck—

Oh room I wait with hard-on in my pocket
    breathing your oven warmth & ask

Will I then feed forever from the mouth of
    all Desire.

NEW MILES POEM

Yr "pure" Miles a
        meticulous sadist, &
        perfect prick/he
punctures air
indolently,
        as a kid
picks at
                toys
            or scabs—
                    dreaming

LAMI POEM

> *(from A Letter, November 1961)*

Lami, leather nightingale,
>   tornado of light & silver buckles,
con man of fairies
>   rolls
priests &
>   bulging legionnaires, astral
hipster in-
cognito he

never knew their worries
>   unzipped but
razor in hand slices
bread from worsted flannel with
flickering fingers

flashlight-
ing of spirit   singing
his
own
>   mad
>   song.

Lami—brutal hood & bearded nun—rides
up waves of sewer stench
>   croaks at
cripples
>   a dance on cobbled
heads in rush-hour after glow
>   calls to
nightbird
>   blues.

O Lami hand over my cut
of sunset melting trash red-gold
before you fade in neon
TV blue

Give back the tinfoil of
tea cut with parsnip, the
shick shaver with a junk-jap motor &
the dazzling watches run by the sun.

Fuck "man's fundamental dishonesty"
        (the con man's hymn of praise)

I seek the god in all of his forms
& hip disguises. But only the god
digs his own deception you say.

But I love, I
blunder in love the hippest mark is saint or poet
prophesying doom so gaily everybody sez yr a goof so
what it's true—flames
                                colored fenders in
Nighttown USA watch out baby I'm
driving an invisible short   so with these
sad gig clothes really aluminum pinstriped threads
you see me naked

Burn Lami, God in me,
Rise burn with the tigers of Eternity,
your hand move in mine toward dark
mounds of hair, your eye blaze through
my socket in cool screaming headaches of
desire & crack the glass coin-eyes,

We/I con all men with love

We/I send out words of black fire into
ears stuffed with asbestos newsprint, I, I
message out of time to all hung up
sad ass loverless landmen

A cry, this cry, to you.

At the age of 24, ALDEN VAN BUSKIRK died in December,
1961 of a disease of the blood. In his introductory note to
Mr. Van Buskirk's only collection *Lami* (Auerhahn Press: 1965)
Allen Ginsberg writes: "This young poet who died alas in his
earliest 20's I never knew but thought at once when reading
his verse ah what a lovely companion he would have been to
talk to on top of roofs & bridges, or sitting with a bottle of
wine or delicate martini in the middle of a living rm. floor at
3 am. His writing shows that despite his early youth he felt
truth . . . In the verse all sorts of weird electronic references,
images of robot paranoia, city impulses of supersonic nerve
thrill are recorded which parallel the sensibility of at least one
reader, & probably everybody. This whole witty—somber—
book makes a complete statement of Person." Of the word
Lami which reoccurs throughout the book, the poet David
Rattray, who was the friend of Mr. Van Buskirk and editor of
his posthumous volume, suggests: "Lami: Negro sometimes
Oriental demon of uncertain sex (brutal hood & bearded
nun . . . 'Is she Lami?'), Tenement elf but above all guiding
genie. Lami: American lama descended from golden age 'lamb-
ish folke.' Lami: also l'ami."

from A SPRING POEM FOR SCORPIOS

for Ellen

SPRING

there are nothing but pipes and dripping faucets here.
Love. Junkyards of porcelain. Toilets
we had no right not to believe Yves Tanguay.
Paint me a place I can see you.
I have your thighs in my hands. I speak
no evil. Nothing ever changes in hell
possible genius in poetry. Woman
in scorpio. Sex. Death
what is the animal you've drawn?
You are not a doe. I am not a flower
or else why our sexes left
untouched? Your hands are on your legs. You see
nothing has changed. Except you should not
believe me. Believe the poem.
She is a better liar

SPRING

now I know why I dream
of whipping you. This kiss
speaks no evil. I want to watch her
make a lesbian of you. Put your mouth
on me. I am a revolutionary.
Put your mouth on me. You are a poet.
Put your mouth on me. Your mouth
why am I dressed in the clothes of painters you like?
She is only eleven. Corrupt her.
My face opposite number five. Opposite number six
shave you head. Shave your arms. Shave your belly.
Shave your legs. Shave the tips of your breasts.
Everything. It is the only way now
both of your faces have turned up

SPRING

Orpheus was a sadist.
He will tie your ankles to your wrists. With your hair
it is spring. He will make you unhappy. Let him.
His eyes are on the woman who is to come from the sea.
You are walking away from him. You are smiling
do you see now. This hell. Nothing
has changed. The siamese poet closing
on both sides

you are bald. & can be anything you want.
Do you want to be a woman. Do not answer
me. Answer the poem. Do you want to be
a woman. The poem is a woman.
She is only a different grey. Her hair
is growing back. Walk
toward her. Do you see yourself?
She is on her knees. She is waiting for you.
Corrupt her

ALLEN VAN NEWKIRK writes: "Born 1940. Raised 20 miles
west of Detroit in Wayne, Michigan. Plagued by the secret of my
birth. After high school there was one year of college divided
between Albion and the Detroit Institute of Technology.
Then moved to Los Angeles where I parked cars for 2 years at the
Beverly Hilton Hotel and learned the lie the society had made
the culture (our spiritual one). I went on to learn, only more so,
the lie the distribution of the material one was also while I
worked for one of those small finance companies that makes it
their business to exploit as many blacks, Mexicans, and poor
whites as possible. Then one day, in a corner drug store, I
discovered N. West's *Day Of The Locust* and the Cuban
revolution, via Sartre. After that two years of wandering from
Las Vegas to New York etc. Back in Detroit there were two years
at Wayne State University and revolutionary politics. No degree.
I then became associated with the artists' workshop in Detroit

where friend John Sinclair introduced me, happily, to the projective of Charles Olson. Poetry became more of a possibility for me via the work of LeRoi Jones, Gil Sorrentino, and Ed Dorn. I now live in NYC where I am a director of the Center for Paleocybernetic Research which considers social and cultural revolution within the context of our more general evolution out of those civilizations founded upon, and certainly still pushed by, neolithic technology. The center is also the spiritual home of Guerrilla Press which publishes pamphlets and the newspaper *Guerrilla.* I am convinced that men are weird and lovely mammals with swollen speech centers and that poetry is our major tool to recover our animal status, image and grace." His first collection is called *A Spring Poem for Scorpios* (Island Press: 1968).

SHORTHAND

What with peacocks and perambulators, ripe gripes—
a heyday of spools
                                          and vaseline urges.
The tethered oak, the fish in mid-mirage, the nails.
                                                        They know.
Opera glasses full of good hot soup fell all over alfalfa left
    fielders
buried by Venetian glass armchairs while cowbells toll.
                              This
                              is
                              a
                              recording.
An ostrich on the double helix walking on its wings.
        Transient sandpaper.
What's bred in the boneyard is born back.
                              Whipped cream toppling and band-aids
                              for lemons. They know.
It's difficult. 3 aces change of places. Simian tapestry and
    phosphorous.
(Take 2 before breakfast) Roughed-up earthenware and
    hydrangeas.
                              A
                              is
                              for
                              apple.
How should I accuse of threats and bribes? I took them all:
the shy hypotenuse, the offered hand
full of pickles and spinach come for a massage, the leopards
    stretched on
rubber-bands, milkweed, minuets, and all the ambushes
    burning.
The number you called has been recently liberated.
                              Rejoice. Relax. Now rejoice again.

The time honored art of self-defenselessness. Hawks in
    the refrigerator.
Pillbottles and palmistry broke over the sea.
                    Track of a cat on water. Fire. They know.
                        Been
                        a
                        hard
                        day.

I SAW THE PICTURE

I saw the picture, A Musical Hell by Hieronymus Bosch
with a naked man strung upon a harp.
Limbs flung out
shouting
for joy. I wept but returned
at last.

THE RISING

You are so beautiful I don't know where to look.
I am ashamed.
Like the unspeakable name of God,
bitter and new,
naked even of pleasure.

NTITLED

the lights of this festival and my birthday I tighten cords about
y wrists and quilted skin.

      Byzantine quarterbacks and lopsided raspberries rankle.
ou are spoiled with praise and bored with cloven prayers.

      Adhering,
ut not yet housebroken, while the house is falling.

      Bloated with faucets, peonies,
ibutary elms, good teeth lurking, the word hurtling

        down.
        the hit
        brick,
        hungover
nsafe. Salamanders, throbbing meat or vaults for the mountains.

      Loops of poodles and poppycocks proclaim the day,
l green as money. I am 23.

      If you throw up an apple it falls back. Refusals,
raided and sulking beneath the tamborines.
tarlings raucous in the cringing storm.

      Give
      me
      a
      task
nd we are quits.

      Cups of clocks keep continual space.
) parachutes and twisted vixen!) Waterproof. Steady, watch it there, look
   out—

      silly, silly, silly, silly, silly.
ocket size idioms, wrinkled boots and bluegrass;
estiges of bridges. Warped wool and peppers Peter Piper didn't. I should
now better by now, I have seen a sidelong sieve for oxen on roller-skates.
he split phoenix, the sneering thighs.

      The black-centered bloom of anemones.
      infected by belief.
rumpets whinny and cackle among excusable shoes. Authority. Ticket office.

Janitor of bamboo, breathing hard.

        so

        it

        shall

        be.

English crabapples, cuffs and shook wet spruce

                            stuck out like tongues.

Adoration went that way. Went this way. Went that way.

                            Come, I will show you;

I know you from Athens. from Egypt. from India, China, Atlantis. Come le

the venal sandlewood and spikes of the flesh.

                         The princess bathed

in a flower-studded pool and came out crowned and died of the flu

a few months later at ultra-high frequency.

                         She had had no beauty.

Miracles admit it might not have all been jungle-ripe and right before.

The use of change is not to choose where the traced seas adore.

It went that way

        so

        it

        shall

        be. (Consider the chorus)

Callous delineations of Japanese persimmons. Shackled onyx.

Kismet met kisses going east. The faded fates: neither, now, never.

Gnarled reeds blew back black overhand, underdone but not sorry.

                         No. Brass blue

green staircases clearer than stone. Electric blankets bark. Blessing

can be endured but it isn't fair.

                     Pyjamas passed exams for ermine egos,

Because what was the cause of cobra-fuzz came into rattlesnake hats and

                         breakable reasons.

                    the
                    ungovernable
                    unforgivable
                    doorknob
rved like an egg.

                    Crushed locusts but it bends again.Borrow trouble
a easy interest in the great outdoors turning left behind.
                                        Colors returned
be repaired. Profusion of radiographs and a billowing hearse,
cookbooks full of bells and red magnolia seeds
ught from mosaics and profound macaroons.
                    Once
                    upon
                    a
                    time,
here were peanuts for the unicorns with lashed embroidered eyes.
                                    Mustard for magicians,
d washable lilies with flaring bellies. Glory winked and was, because
                    there
                    was
                    no
                    choice.
aitresses swung baskets of speckled pears.
                                    They fell.
                                    Brazen sound resounds. Clang.
ang. The juggler bowed and snarled. (astride, adore)
                    It went that way. Acclamations of apples.
dspread caviar on crackers. Splinters from fossil wings.
l cloaked and coiled the kneeling team exults,
 else rehearsal only, no umbrage taken.
ric vultures pelted with Scotch totems.

                                    Total lampreys lit the offered ace
d scalloped fingernails.

                                    Here is the wilderness
                    where
                    thimbles
                    fill
                    with honey;

where marzipan and slashed elastic visions gossip behind sweating plumes:
                    'went that way, went this way, no that way.
                                A usually reliable source—
maps roasted slowly with olives and garlic.
                                The last time I saw them—
O, you know how they are.'
                        Among hung chandeliers for the idle crime
of idols, graven given unforgiven. Here is the wilderness, hell on wheels.
                    It
                    went
                    this
                    way.
Onion labels and lost ovens. Elbowed storks explained to their sudden you
how they were brought in human briefcases. Udders of an x-ray.
                                Wrangling zeroes.
A sneezing maiden with a zither played and lost
among snails snagged by helicopters. Gas balloons. Lapis Lazuli
arisen from the driven tomb.
                    Golf
                    also
                    played and
                    lost
by barefoot businessmen stalking ultraviolet storks.
                            Worship
                            took
                            my clipped
                            look
for a buttonhole.
Japanese fans for Iowa winters. Here is a picture: a flight of profiled stairs
                            half way up a chartreuse hill.
An eye, in front of the brown house, is at the top of the stairs.
                            The outline of a man
with his head thrown back but his hat still on is standing on the eye.
The man is looking up and reaching for a red noose which dangles from the
                            of the picture.

On one side of the stairs, in the lower right hand side of the picture
is a large moon. On the other side of the stairs is a rising sun
as children draw it, all struck at every point with yellow spears.

> "Cats' why
> to make
> kittens'
> britches"

But to live under oranges and enterprises!

> Here is no and now is up and down is gone

back home. front home. door undone. Gone. Lost all the delphiniums blue

> in the world went that way.

This way out! In to from under rolling *here.*

> Adoration.

Because the lights fused, molten money back guarantee or else imitation!

> Without
> praise
> without
> prayer

already broken. On arrival. But to prove—O go away,
loom over other ash groves. I have a headache, gift wrapped.

> Here.

(He called the darkness night but I know other names)
Here among lizards and lilacs came adoration, hiccuping days.
Here are the tenses of now:

> here,
> now
> and
> come.

"I write poetry to tie leashes onto vacuums because it is a city ordinance. I write poetry to be the right person to answer the wrong question," JULIA VINOGRAD states. "I write poetry because I'm greedy for it. I suppose you could say I write poetry to find out why I write poetry. Take your pick. As for a statement of poetics, the only rule I know is that the poem should be bigger than the poet." A graduate of The Program in Creative Writing at The University of Iowa, Miss Vinograd was born in 1943 in Berkeley, California, and now lives in New York City.

SOMETIMES EVEN MY
KNEES SMILE

You have replaced Beethoven
in my life.

My bones are piled up in neat little
stacks
waiting for you to
put them in your pocket.

The prickly movement under my skin,
an alligator stranded on the desert,
is your mustache
which I have been stealing, hair by hair, in your
sleep each night.

A brown thrasher is pecking at my throat,
The breath of birds
that passes over my wrists and nipples
opening the umbrella,
is your touching. I would open up anything
even my belly or crack open my bones
for you.

I would give you
anything
except a poem. Those I hold close
like diamonds up the ass in an African mine;
even those I would
give too
if you asked
but it is Beethoven you replaced
in my life.

And he had music so loud in his head
he didn't need words.
The poet is the lover who can't speak to
isn't heard by
his love.

GEORGE WASHINGTON ABSENT FROM
HIS COUNTRY

Your heart,
a sponge lying in the vinegar bowl,
waiting for a dry day
or month
or year
when the corners of the mouth
turn down,
parched as the eyelid of a turtle,

waiting to seep the sour liquid
like the arms of a small squid, calamara,
into the corner of my mouth,
as the sponge is handed up on a long pole
to the criminals dying in a ritual of
crucifixion—remember over 2,000 of them in one month
along the road to Jerusalem;

Your heart, George Washington,
my husband,
which is filled with all the juices I need,
lies somewhere across the Atlantic.
You wanted to be educated in England, as the rest
of your family had been,
but they were too poor when it came round to you,
so you studied at home, became a

surveyor, and finally left,
taking the heart with you, the sponge of vinegar,
that I look for at every ocean,

Perhaps if I could dive under the water,
like a pool ball going into the pocket at the side of the
        table,
perhaps I would find your heart pumping down there,
perhaps making the waves or some tidal current,
perhaps the liquid that soft sponge contains
would not revive me
in this dry dying period,
when I have been hung up with nails on a piece of wood,
for what I believe, my own angel, very white feathers
telling me there is nothing that love would not cure,

George Washington,
where is that sea flower, that spongy red mass, your heart,
why is it absent from its country,
from me; Mr. President, how could you go away,
with the minutes of the meeting not finished; how could
        you leave me,
a daughter of the American Revolution, standing here
with such a dry mouth, such empty hands that before
touched that heart with fingers, with lips,
why some country in which you can only be crude,
a novelty, at best?

This country has changed since you were its first president;
but not in any real way. We still like the firm jaw,
the determined mouth, the secret ways,
what made us trust you,
a first.

The heart is, of course,
what keeps the body going. The heart
is what keeps time.

All the small feathers you can pick up, even in the woods
of a European country, are not as soft or white
or would mean as much to me
as one smile from you. One trip back across the Atlantic.
Come home, where your spirit
can prevail.

FOLLOW THAT STAGECOACH

The sense of disguise is a
rattlesnake and
it's easy to wake up and find it curled in your shoe.
Past Ghost Junction and Cody's Rock
the same stagecoach rattles day after day. Long days and
　　short days
carrying the same passengers.
They keep away from you. Your six-shooter wanders into
hand, disguised
yes heavily disguised as the homosexual sheriff
bringing law and order to the West
oh but the ladies who ride that stagecoach want you to make
　　love to
them but you never take off your shoes for fear you'll
　　wake up only to
find a rattlesnake curled up in one of them.

Sometimes you
ride the stagecoach in another disguise.
You are in a black rubber diving suit
with your wet feet leaving prints like exotic fish on my
　　forehead.
Under my hair is a brain
with
too many memory cells clicking off your name
trying to ascertain

your sex. I am swimming in Dry Gulch Hollow thinking
     of Sheriff
Stanley
who did love me but left to start the Pony Express.
His star I wear pinned to my black rubber skin-diving suit,
keeping clear of the 87 rattlesnakes swimming down the
     river
oh yes I catch this stagecoach you are on it Mr. Sheriff
     I would like to
be angry that we are not swimming in the same body of
     water
with every body of water suggesting so many more
the Pacific
The Atlantic
the Indian,
Arctic, Antarctic
so many oceans about, not to mention the rivers, lakes,
     ponds, etc.
Shall we go skin-diving I ask you but it is
clear I want to explore different areas, my own black
     rubber suit
showing clearly
I am a woman
why did I find you? Black Aberdeen might walk in the
ocean, or Snowfoot stroll in coral reefs
but I am looking for the most beautiful fish,
one that will shimmer his scales at me and feed me special
     algae,
one with spiny teeth or soft train whistles,
shiny with tamarind seeds,
metaphysical with telephone books.
Found you writing your poems on my brain with the
     diving fork and
blood covering my suit with the words,
found you trapped in Dry Gulch Hollow settling for trout,
found you and wanted to have you, willing to lock you in
     my jail with a

big iron key, wanted to say look I have found him give me
    the reward
look I have found him and he'll take me away to his
    territory I am not
afraid of rattlesnakes they sleep with me at night curled
around my warm neck we exchange poisons oh Mr. Sheriff
    with sand on
your eyes with coyotes running out of your shoulders
    with scorpions
in your fingers with overhand knots and loop knots and
    granny knots
and reef knots and bowline knots and trefoil knots and a
    double bowknot
tying your lips together and white and purple flowers on
    short stems
yes yes yes I cannot deal
with the dichotomies
would like to spend the day, day, day, day, day, day,
river day and night day, day of piranhas, and
day of old lemon seeds. wearing your black rubber suit
    and swimming
the ocean, no it's that Western body of water, Dry Gulch
    Hollow,
that I see you in and gives me a false sense of
your movements. Sheriff Day, the sense of disguise is
a rattlesnake. The danger is one
I would welcome
living here in this rough country
as I do
building my own house. My own disguises change so
often which one can I wear that will not frighten you
    though you are a
tough Western sheriff who obviously doesn't
frighten easily
knowing you can swim quickly away in that rubber suit.
What are you looking for? I'll show you a cemetery where
    you could find

a tombstone saying HERE LIES THE HOMOSEXUAL SHERIFF OF
    DRY GULCH
COUNTY.
I didn't make this offer to the previous sheriff
oh yes you are putting on your skin-diving suit very fast
    running to the
ocean and slipping way from this girl who carries a loaded
    gun all
the time and keeps company with rattlesnakes and goes
    diving only
for the most beautiful
fish. Mr. Sheriff Day she writes you this poem from her
    dusty house
Walking naked is her most frequent disguise it disarms
    everyone
The world by now is confused with all the costumes
The world by now takes her up and tries to make her
    wear the right dis-
guises she says no no no I will go where I want when I
    want to
So I'll write you a love poem if I want to. I'm a westerner
    and
not afraid
of my shadow.

BELLY DANCER

Can these movements which move themselves
be the substance of my attraction?
Where does this thin green silk come from that covers
    my body?
Surely any woman wearing such fabrics
would move her body just to feel them touching every
    part of her.

Yet most of the women frown, or look away, or laugh
    stiffly.
They are afraid of these materials and these movements
in some way.
The psychologists would say they are afraid of themselves,
    somehow.
Perhaps awakening too much desire—
that their men could never satisfy?
So they keep themselves laced and buttoned and made up
in hopes that the framework will keep them stiff enough
    not to feel
the whole register.
In hopes that they will not have to experience that
    unquenchable
desire for rhythm and contact.

If a snake glided across this floor
most of them would faint or shrink away.
Yet that movement could be their own.
That smooth movement frightens them—
awakening ancestors and relatives to the tips of the arms
    and toes.

So my bare feet
and my thin green silks
my bells and finger cymbals
offend them—frighten their old-young bodies.
While the men simper and leer—

glad for the vicarious experience and exercise.
They do not realize how I scorn them;
or how I dance for their frightened,
unawakened, sweet
women.

TO CELEBRATE MY BODY

for my husband

where
you had only
to touch me
others had
to present a history,
a bibliography,
and a justification

but

no question
remains,
that a gift
easily given,
lightly received
is wasted

no one can
touch me
the way
you can/   I should say
did

but

no question
remains
your touch
was not lightly
taken

my body
has spent
a lot of years
awakening

too long
in fact
to stop
that process

your touch
is
somewhere across
the ocean.   My imagination
has never
been poor;   but
cannot extend
to a life
where touching
comes only
in a letter

Celebrate
the word
we
are both
poets,
taking the word
ultimately
seriously

but the word
can only
give life
if it acknowledges
the lips
the mouth that made it

the body
that pumped the
sounding air

where
you had only
to touch me
others had
to present a history,
a bibliography,
a justification

the touch
comes first,
remains
is the last thing you
remember
after you
turn
out
the light.
at night.

APPARITIONS ARE NOT SINGULAR OCCURRENCES

When I rode the zebra past your door,
wearing nothing but my diamonds, I expected to hear bells
and see your face behind the thin curtains.
But instead I saw you, a bird, wearing the mask of a bird,
with all the curtains drawn, the lights blazing,
and Death drinking cocktails with you.
In your thin hand, like the claw of a bird, because you are
     a bird,
the drink reflected the light from my diamonds, passing by.

Your bird's foot, like thin black threads of bone or metal
    staples,
has the resistance necessary to keep death at a pleasant
    distance,
drinking his scotch and enjoying your company,
as he seldom has a chance; the zebra hide against my bare
    legs
is warm. The diamonds now warm on my neck,
on my fingers,
my feet,
my ears.
How Death looks at them
and my body
and the old man desires them all.

I rode by your windows, hoping you would see me and
    want me,
not knowing you already had a guest.
The diamonds I put on for you,
the clothes I took off,
and my zebra—did you see his eyes just slightly narrow
as we came by?

Not knowing you would wear your bird mask,
I let you see my face.
Not knowing Death would be there,
I rode by.
And Death and I see each other now so often
I have even thought of becoming a trapeze artist so that
    I might
swing on the bar away from him—so far up he'd never
    reach me,
but instead I see him more and more with all my friends,
drinking, talking,
and always keeping his elderly eyes on me.
And you, watching me ride by on my zebra and dressed
only in my diamonds,

were my one last hope.
But even you, wearing the mask of a bird, invited him to
    have
a drink and left the curtains drawn for him,
sharing something you had no right to share.

A CHILD, A WASP, AND AN APRICOT TREE

What is there we do not know about death
that cannot be pulled out of our mouths
like a long white ribbon, stretching
and stretching
out
beyond our own senses?
A bird pulling a worm out of the ground.
It is burrowed there inside,
living alone in the dark.

Here, let me draw a picture for you.

I have drawn a stick figure of a child. And
here is a wasp,

perhaps a little out of proportion with the figure
but imagine that if the child is child-size,
the wasp is wasp-size.

Now, here is a flower.

The child picks the flower
which happens to be an apricot blossom.
But, as you might suspect,
the wasp is in the flower.
When the child puts his face to the blossom to smell it
he notices the wasp.

His mouth opens in surprise, and his eyes get large.
But it is too late.
The wasp has caught the white ribbon of fear
out of the child's mouth
and, buzzing loud,
he pulls it out, longer and longer,
and winds it around the child—winds and winds
until the child is wrapped in white ribbon
from head to toe,
bound in white strips, as a mummy,
and the ribbon breaks off in the constricted mouth.
When the wasp, of our picture,
flies away, he flies pulling the ribbon,
but instead of pulling it tighter about the child,
he sets it in opposite motion,
spinning the child around without control
as the farther the wasp flies
attached to the ribbon,
the faster the child spins, but the more the tape unwinds
from him,
until at last he is free,
and dizzily he sees the white ribbon vanishing
beyond the apricot tree with the wasp.

I do not mean to say that the child is thinner
for losing great lengths of his white tape
or to imply how much he has inside
        —perhaps he, himself, is made of tape—
but only to draw a picture of a child, a wasp, and
a blossoming apricot tree
which are in themselves too lovely
to allow much thought of death.
It is behind their masks
I hide my own fear.

DIANE WAKOSKI writes: "My biography is written in all my
poems, but extraneous facts might be birth, August, 1937,

Whittier, California; BA University of California 1960 (Berkeley; life in New York City since school; short marriage; knowledge of astrology and a fetish about George Washington.) I will be 30 this summer (1967). I look younger. But my soul is a lot older—from the Minoan age, an old Uranian astrologer told me once." Her published books are: *Coins and Coffins* (Hawk's Well Press: 1962), *Discrepancies and Apparitions* (Doubleday: 1966), *The George Washington Poems* (riverrun press: 1967), *Greed, Part I* (Black Sparrows Press: 1968); and she was one of *Four Young Lady Poets*, edited by Leroi Jones (Totem/Cornith Press: 1962). Doubleday will publish *Inside the Blood Factory* in the fall of 1968. Of her poetics she has written in "Poet at the Carpenter's Bench":

the poet is a passionate man
who lives quietly
knowing very well what he wants. It is love,
some formation thereof, a small rock
that he can carve all his life,
perhaps a house he can build with his own hands,
or one he can live in and shape around his body, as a crab will
or a snail; he wants only one sense,
of love, of laying his eyes on the surface of the world
and seeing underneath, of love,
of all changes all different roads leading to the same thing
of love that never goes away
without coming back.

AFTER *LES FLEURS* (PAUL ELUARD)

I am 20 years old and holding on.
Knowing I'm still young, I love you world

I am not 20 years old. My past is deaf, deaf

I dream a life of crystals and lie down in the grass

You think I'm crying; I don't
Don't hurt me—let me be

My eyes a strength the color of my wounds.
Love, what is the sun when it rains?

I tell you there are things as true as this story

When I close my eyes I kill you.

ABOUT FACE

In the broken range
of her voice

        another was like history

I picked up this book that interested me and put it down
    again

She (not a woman) walked out the door as it closed behind
    her
Then we went dancing

To the right, several policeman with clubs
Then one said to the other,

Did you see that just now? and pulled off
From this window they face the street

        then go off beat

Here we behave inside,
Do my sulking in private,

Like the long shores multiplying you don't even see,
      she said.

SONNET FOR THE BROKEN WINDOWS

I am meaning to inundate you with light
And as that recedes, more light
Breaking through the subtlest regions of thought as that
     sun,
A human eye and a silent sun whose every hue is thought
     itself.
Waking here beside a pair of eyes is sunny
And lately, taking on the characteristics of ladders
This thought recedes meaning to be lighter and does itself
     in
As climbing a certain mountain a certain day is over.
Over here I am breaking windows, getting out the day
Before it is over and done for the human night is a
     shoulder.
Resting on it I inundate the silence, I inundate you
And the thought I had about your eyes is not subtle.
It is a region in the day where shoulders are ladders
And light is no longer necessary the way I meant it.

FOR YOU

A beach you've never seen is where I've been
Thinking about how you can get to it if you want to

Between us, excited by my whole life just now, spray is
    unfolding itself

Over a low tide, the nation seems calmer
Several birds, and a constant sound

Asking about it and seeing it are different
Like ages we confuse growing young by the radio
And here where I've been hiding out, a clear light seizes
    the air
Holding its own and you are asleep

After dawn it was easier, you said
Some friends you keep missing at home were never at home
And then I just sat down, maybe wrote a poem, ate around
    the corner

Just here, the note said, we won't be home

Around the corner, a few blocks away, lost that thought
    about summer
And when I heard the waves we were traveling and it was
    summer
Like the idea of seeing you happened in the clouds
Lying here over a stone with sun in my clothes

We are acting out all the possibilities under this sun
And today, Saturday, I am not as alone

How to do it all and you do it
For a nation, your clothes getting wet now, a tide is higher

I keep repeating myself in this serious movie but I am
     serious
And getting the point across my mind for you to see me
As it does that, I want to weep or dash the rocks
Hearing them carry on the way gulls do   caw caw

The raw light, she calls it, good for you with salt
And soon we will have enough of it like food, but not
     your love

For that is the matter I am writing about, saving it up
     before night
And spreading it out through the night
And the night you are thinking about has not yet come

And if you want we can go back there
And waking up to 2nd Avenue in the morning you are
     tired
And if you want I am there
And waking up you are not alone

For here I am coming home
Later to tell you about it and wind with sand in my mouth

ANNE WALDMAN is the youngest poet in the anthology. She
was born in 1945 and raised in New York City where she now
lives on the Lower East Side. A graduate of Bennington College, she has been active as the poetry assistant in The Arts
Project at St. Marks Church In-the-Bowery and has been editor
of some of the influential little magazines of her generation:
Silo, Angel Hair and *The World*. A pamphlet of poems called
On the Wing will be published by Boke Press. She has also
studied acting with Lee Strasberg and Herbert Berghof; and has
reviewed movies over WRVR New York. Miss Waldman is the
wife of poet Lewis Warsh.

#9 *from* THE SUICIDE RATES

Like small foreign villages whose gates have been
destroyed by bonfires
so the cities nearest my hands
are destroyed by the rust and the rustling of cool ashes.
Cool gray enters my throat.
It is painful to be foreign from you now,
to hear from others that your letters
spill like numbers
between the cracks of the avenues of the villages
that are not burning, that
have been spared

Huge windows corrupt me.
Between each ripple
the sun admits
duplicity. A
different face,
a room in which I lie and listen
clawing for the grate
from which the gas breathes
in my hands.
                   It
hangs in space
above me
The loins hang

UP THERE IN SNOW

Up there in snow,
afterwards bystanders crush the desk.
Passing the shade

they see a mirror
and ask him in.
Arrangements oppose the composition
of moss fading under hair.
The empty drawers and the wine
falling, plugging the stones,
and paper found to flare easily by the light
paper-twigs   I knew was true
the words swim faster than a slim body
deer-like and bright   afterwards
the burning nudes gave the same odor as before
They entered, too tired to kiss me,
but with their presence gave me
the special kinship I find necessary.
Passing from shelf to shelf   the arm
of the machine and the belt
around the hair
propped up on a tiny book they
looked for the river in pairs
and found a gully furrowed
by patches of swamp and sand.
They probably have the same aroma
as the stars lighting up
every corner of the earth.
Up there in the colony they express
the debt   the lifting
of the heavy air clogged with frail
layers of smoke   they are turning into smoke-
filled halls far from the colony and its origin
beside the lake,
casting their hats across the lawn
watching the wind pour from their breasts

THE BLACK BOUNDARY

On the warm night
we approached the broken square sky,
where a railroad waited, and a town sped by
like a truck. Speed up
these labels of authenticity that intrude
through the blue as an elbow
crooks into the blackdown—rain
splashing the page, mocking breath, as
I appear.
The genius has spent the last years
of his life in attaining the freshness
and purpose of his young protegees—that's what's
admirable, to author a pledge
which breaks into pieces at his feet.
A heavily scented handkerchief wiping
the tears of her hand, the wind
stirring the folds of
the shower curtain
though no one's behind it.
Finally the two legs make contact under the desk
as pathos confirms the separation of two
friends—one in a dark suit
in the lobby of a deserted hotel
is staring at the sea through the rectangular
windows overhead. It is the sky
that makes the thought of death sickening,
and the eye, which when closed, resembles your flesh
pricked under a thimble.
Such patronage
coughs blood as we relax in bed,
flashing on a screen of coil-springs to turn sideways,
to make room inside hollows of underhandedness
and bad taste. A note of instructions
on the long buffet which the guests managed

to view the possibility of eating though
most of them had decided to leave.
A continuous gurgling rose from
the bottom of the toilet, while behind him
on top of a brown hamper sat a pile of dirty
clothes—shirts, underpants, black
and red T-shirts and socks.
Brooding and malcontent, the night-time Angel
bit back. I feel
to be defied on all sides, at ease in it,
these smashed tubes, this dizziness
effaces and effects us all. Yet
I have been climbing elsewhere where
the question is candidly asked,
the questioner interviewed, the voice
cancelled—here I am?
Whose face, the movement
of a lift
into the rising light, covering nudity,
as crossing her legs
she turned, surveying our quarters—it was night
and the wheelchair had been left
in the garden, fenced in
amid black and bottomless tendrils
on a woody vine. Such emotions
recall the large painful ones I feel
every access of the rigid grooves
revealed, presence
I had felt so strongly on aimless walks
through the late autumn and winter
streets of weapons
I let fall. For someday
you wake up knowing so little
is the sky of eternity is a white
corner combined with the sensual array
of passers
by a sidewalk where you will go.
When the lids close, free of death, a thought

of others seems to be yours,
incidents in touching detail cleverly
annotated out of sequence,
to come undone, to lift her
body into the air,
to pass the brick to a waiting hand below.
At dawn, we are the people who have begun
eating, preparing for work.
You advance bit by bit towards
the cab in the sunshine
you have called back   a book kneels
on the skin of the meadow   to touch
sky (or better weep
to conquer itself   while writing   a
page   from the constituted reason
calls out   name my hands? anatomy
to teach   work is—to make an entry
else repeat   borrowed sleep
to work—while she says nothing)
That the choice is already made
for us with our breath
melting its shores

LEWIS WARSH was born 1944 in the Bronx and graduated
from City College of New York in 1966. Work of his has been
seen in *The Paris Review, Poetry, Tzarad, Spice, Wild Dog,
The Coyote Journal, C, The World, Art & Literature*, and *Angel
Hair*. He is the co-editor of *Angel Hair* magazine and Angel
Hair Books. His first book of poems *The Suicide Rates* (Toad
Press) appeared in 1967; his second *Moving Through Air*
(Angel Hair) will appear this year.

IN MY FIRST HARD SPRINGTIME

Those red men you offended were my brothers.
Town drinkers, Buckles Pipe, Star Boy,
Billy Fox, were blood to bison. Albert Heavy Runner
was never civic. You are white and common.

Record trout in Willow Creek chose me
to deify. My horse, Centaur, part cayuse,
was fast and mad and black. Dandy in flat hat
and buckskin, I rode the town and called it mine.

A slow hot wind tumbled dust against my door.
Fed and fair, you mocked my philosophic nose,
my badger hair. I rolled your deference
in the hay and named it love and lasting.

Starved to visions, famous cronies top Mount Chief
for names to give respect to Blackfeet streets.
I could deny them in my first hard springtime,
but choose amazed to ride you down with hunger.

CHRISTMAS COMES TO MOCCASIN FLAT

Christmas comes like this: wise men
unhurried, candles bought on credit (poor price
for calves), warriors face down in wine sleep.
Winds cheat to pull heat from smoke.

Friends sit in chinked cabins, stare out
plastic windows and wait for commodities.
Charlie Blackbird, twenty miles from church
and bar, stabs his fire with flint.

When drunks drain radiators for love
or need, chiefs eat snow and talk of change,
an urge to laugh pounding their ribs.
Elk play games in high country.

Medicine Woman, clay pipe and twist tobacco,
calls each blizzard by name and predicts
five o'clock by spitting at her television.
Children lean into her breath to beg a story:

Something about honor and passion,
warriors back with meat and song,
a peculiar evening star, quick vision of birth.
Blackbird builds his fire. Outside, a quick thirty below.

D-Y BAR

The tune is cowboy, the words, sentimental crap.
Farther out, wind is mending sagebrush,
stapling it to earth in rows only a badger
would recommend. Reservoirs are dry,
the sky commands a cloud high
to skip the Breaks bristling with heat
and stunted pine.

In stunted light, Bear Child tells a story
to the mirror. He acts his name out,
creeks muscle gorges to fill his glass
with gumbo. The bear crawls on all fours
and barks like a dog. Slithering snake-wise
he balances a nickel on his nose. The effect,
a snake in heat.

We all know our names here. Summer is a poor
season to skip this place or complain
about marauding snakes. Often when wind
is cool off mountains and the flats
are green, cars stop for gas, motors clicking
warm to songs of a junction bar, head down,
the dormant bear.

SPRING FOR ALL SEASONS

Let the sloughs back up and history
will claim that lakes were here
and Indians poled their way from Asia
past monsoons and puddled heat of carp.
We know better. We know this land
wouldn't bring a dime for rain in China.

Practice your grin when clouds are red,
sky falls blue against the buttes.
Morning brings flood to verbena, planted
by some fool who thinks July forgets
the past. Our past is ritual,
cattle marching one way to remembered mud.

Bring on the fools. Let some sap declare
a ten year rain, a Japanese current
to carry us west to rain forests or east
or south and down. Eskimos are planting
corn where lunar waves crawl the ice,
snow, the Arctic desert gone.

MONTANA, NOTHING LIKE BOSTON

for Rosemary duMas

These mountains forget rough color. Running
from a past when ice carved valleys,
rivers begin their slide to sea.
Our slide is steep in laughter. When spring
plies the plains with bitterroot and goldenrod,
this country stays the green it knows.

I know you forget my two stars left of sun,
the single horse searching for dawn,
burnt grass and foxtail. My winters come from fantasy,
antelope running gaunt from red men
out of wind. I could teach you sunsets,
show you that trees are blazed and scared.

Wolves track your thoughts. When elk bugle in dusk,
no roads look west to lonely mountains.
You question my magic. Threats of rain
ride wind but threats end when truckers honk us home.
I think you know that rivers forget
their spawning grounds at horizon, Pacific blue.

WINTER INDIAN

The snow is for sale. No takers.
A Chief questions his first piece:
the spindly doll, drafty shack,
a smell of perfume. Any scene goes pale
when talk grows sour, no land for bid,
no tribal deals. Deaths fade quietly.

Saturday nights repeat
summer stick game and ghost dance,
bone whistle ritual to spirit hope.

Winter comes earlier each year,
sheep lost to sleep in willows
sheathed in ice. Sunday is imaginary.
When mongrels howl to teasing
children, what camera softens
this plain to missionary
perfection?

Happy to think of good times,
buffalo fat to fall in jumps.
When war was still a game and berries
stained a face fierce,
white women slaved to laughing squaws.
Think money is out of time and times
are bad. The mountains warp
when cattle starve in snow fields.
Specks of red, the Indian winter.

BLACKFEET, BLOOD AND PIEGAN HUNTERS

If we raced a century over hills
that ended years before, people couldn't
say our run was simply poverty or promise
for a better end. We ended sometime
back in recollections of glory, myths
that meant the hunters meant a lot
to starving wives and bad painters.

Let glory go the way of all sad things.
Children need a myth that tells them be alive,

forget the hair that made you Blood, the blood
the buffalo left, once for meat, before
other hunters gifted land with lead for hides.

Comfortable we drink and string together stories
of white buffalo, medicine men who promised
and delivered horrible cures for hunger,
the lovely tales of war and white men massacres.
Meaning gone, we dance for pennies now,
our feet jangling dust that hides the bones
of sainted Indians. Look away and we are gone.
Look back. Tracks are there, a little faint,
our song strong enough for headstrong hunters
who look ahead to one more kill.

THE WRATH OF LESTER LAME BULL

Bears are in the cabbage again,
cunning soles crashing down carrots,
faces thick to wear a turnip green.
Not even the onion dissents.

Lester Lame Bull in his garden grows
twenty rows of winter store,
a piddling score to court
against the blue of mountain ash.

Cottonwood limbs rattle like bones.
Lester storms his pesky winds,
stoning crows from purple cups.
Quirky grins are thick in muscatel.

Elephants are whispering in backyards.

WOLF SONG, THE RAIN

When tribes are broke and holdings gone,
legislators plan relief: Gros Ventres owned
this land, pay up. Children yelp
against sour milk, half-price, plan
to be happy stuffed with rice and rage.
Sometimes in three day ceremonies, fancy dancers
jingle meat home to pot. Drums restore
wine to rightful owners when rain is right.

Forget the ceremony and this land belongs
to stone. Too often clouds sweep north, stealing
rain from tarred barrels and sloughs stuffed
with bugs. The bugs will live,
hungry where weeds are thick with stink.
Where Indians used to live, cabins are padlocked
and white men choose alfalfa, water rights
penciled in wives' names, still enrolled though white.

Plan relief in booze. If the sky clears,
watch the sun touch Snake Butte, signal
to begin the first day's dancing. Say hard times,
the animals come to counsel men.
At dawn sagebrush is seen trampled, dead
to a song the bucks chant about a smiling girl
in shiny dress and head band. The words are never heard,
never translated into clouds that wind might tease.

"I'm a poet because I couldn't build model airplanes as well as
Lester Lame Bull or throw calves like Albert Heavy Runner,"
states JAMES WELCH, who was born in 1940 in Browning,
Montana on the Blackfoot Indian Reservation. Mr. Welch is a
Blackfoot Indian. Currently he is finishing a Master of Fine Arts
degree in creative writing at The University of Montana.

O PLEASE READ BACKWARDS

Seeking the topic like a much needed bottle
of baby lotion. Often
sure I'll be finding it, among the bulletins
in your oven, or billboards . . .

Not afraid to throw the baby out
with the bath. There will be babies
and babies and
babies but where is a drink of fresh water?

Wandering from the point, as though I took
that dogma of mine seriously,
the detour is more than the delay and
even a shortcut to the point

where we are getting like blazes.
(This diction my friend on the strip
calls moral; an enemy baroque. Have they
not both insulted me, the iamb in the manual?)

I meant that my words should be meaningful,
should stave in the nexts of verbal
argument. You could read my lines
like gentle paths in city gardens,

where the gardener (he's a nut)
plants trees because he *likes* to.
But I mean to be *all* the plants
in my garden

so it must make sense
to write you. I am your
forest of symbols (delightful toy bees)!
I am somebody you played with when you were little.

NIGHT LETTER

I sing this, to a revolving of rubber wheels
which have stood too long and gone flat.
Please hear me. They have been left standing with their
        edges
locked tight against something that could have been
        released
at the twist of a key. Please hear me!

Often I wanted to drive on my flat tires
to your door and leave something to remind you . . .
of what? It seems I had forgotten.
I tried to sing but the pitch was flat.

Please listen. The station is closed now,
the grass grows wetter. Something like snails
shows up as spots on the front lawn. Mushroom
rings widen, and trees crowd the terminal
like a bushy meringue gone stale and rubbery.

There's a freshness about, and I have left a note—
is this February? at your door. You will not accept
many more as in good taste. Your decisions are sudden
as an act of Congress releasing swarms
of rosy quarters into our pockets. I have hit too hard
and too often and the damn thing's tilted again.

I go home into the night which sits all about like
guests at black tea, wearing their muffins and lace.
They say pleasant things about Paris; I am going further
        than that.
Please hear me: my propellors have a smooth torque.
I forgot nothing. Listen to this.
From a foreign chime I climb you. This air
is drunken, down here in the understoops where the cats
move with silent purpose, perhaps parental. There is

a freshness about, and maybe it's April. The trees
crowd the terminal like wires, quaking into life.

Where do I live lately? Under the coffin
he wheels after you evenings like a domestic pallbearer
to trundle you home and plant you in his window,
voi la! An African violet, his tickles in your ears
grown flushed and furry, your leaves full of light hair . . .
but fragile, fragile! I go very softly over the streets
for fear of shattering something. O this town
has a harsh climate for defectors! And now
I start my machine again. The data flow
like lava, or rich dirty poems . . .
what's that knocking? It is the sorghum I goop
over my midnight sandwich in soft glops;
it's the Ghost of Russian tea; the sensitivity
of an omelet I stow away while continuing
the futile research of love novels into the night.

Water's getting through the gaskets, we must close the
       windows,
we must close the portholes! A tidal wave is coming,
we must blow the ship whistle, we must toot a cornet,
throw cats after dogs, this earthquake is getting
vicious! We've got to drop rice into the cracks and hammer
the sensitive ground with our truncheons to see if it will
       snap,
we must stuff the San Andreas fault with torpedos,
goggles, cowbells, bathing suits and yellow jock straps
and you can be my made in Chicago and I'll be your pow
right in the kisser! Tell me you cried when I sat down to the
       piano (their ears are
wedged with cottonwood and their eyes are plates of
       congealed lard).
Tell me you don't like my music, the spirit of cloyed
       baseball

(her windows are blasted out, her bed wired to the
    floor).
Tell me you don't like the Depression atmosphere in my
    fraternal club. (We bought these sofas at a bake sale
    in '03!)
In the cupboards, in the cordial flasks, in the wee spoons
    you have hidden the stuff in
you cut your teeth on on a riot of parties down the
    funicular
hallucinogenic landslides of chalk shore election
    years
my lines continue to ticker like old ladies
with myocardial infarctions in their screaming ventricals,
butchered for carnavals. Their thumbs have been strung
in wax prisms, they have been hammered with
    gummiknüppel
and smashed in the jaw with linoleum hockey pucks.
If they rise again someone screams at them and they die
on a velvet carpet of Social Security attacks.
Have you been with me to the store where the stuffed
    animals are?

All through the night I have kept the pressure on
without getting tired. Your key burned a trail
to the river bottom. The thin red line of your smile
is the postman bringing my morning's toast in hot lead.

In response to the editor's request for a statement on poetics,
TYNER WHITE writes from Tübingen, Germany (where since
1966 he has been "immersed in exotic indo-european language
courses, increasingly excited by politics and tourism"): "Lately
I've been creeping up some poetical arses, i.e. accumulating
material in the ars poetica, but it's ok if you don't need any. Most
of my poems start as nonsense improvisations, but once the
material is on the page and the typewriter has given up, I am in

the position of a chess player looking over his board—White to play and win. This last expression is not entirely wrong since from a defeated jangle of rubbish one hopes to make a triumph out of the poem. The trouble is knowing what Black will do . . ." Mr. White was born in 1940 in Cincinnati, Ohio and was educated at Wilmington College, Ohio, The University of Munich, and in the Master of Fine Arts program in The Program in Creative Writing at The University of Iowa. He plans to continue his studies in Berlin; after that, he may follow "a study-work program in development countries—India? Brazil?"

All of the photographs were supplied by the poets. The editor thanks them for their kind permission to reproduce the photographs in this anthology. Credit is given to the following photographers who took the photographs of these poets:

James Applewhite by Henry E. Applewhite
Marvin Bell by Sheri Stern
Michael Benedikt by Herbert Fogelson
Bill Berkson by Mario Schifano
Ted Berrigan by Lida Moser
Harold Bond by Donald Bates
Jonathan Cott by Keith Morris
Louis Glück by Charles Herty Jr
William Hunt by Ronald Goldberg
Ronald Johnson by Jonathan Williams
Robert Kelly by Peter Kahn
Richard Kostelanetz by Kazakoff
Howard McCord by Douglas Hall
Aram Saroyan by Gailyn McClanahan
Peter Schjeldahl by Steve Pope
Kathleen Spivack by Elsa Dorfman
Mark Strand by Danielle Padwa
James Tate by Elsa Dorfman
Tony Towle by David Wallace
Alden Van Buskirk by courtesy of Auerhahn Press
Allen Van Newkirk by Peter Yates
James Welch by Lee Nye
Tyner White by Barry Casselman
Robert Hass by John Peck

Acknowledgement is gratefully given to the following poets, their representatives and publishers for permission to include the poems in this anthology:

ACCONCI, Vito Hannibal, for "Re," "Tic" and "Kay Price and Stella Punjas." "Kay Price and Stella Punjas" originally appeared in **0 to 9.**

AMABILE, George, for "Flowers: Calabria" and "Period."

ANDERSON, Jon, for "Aviators," "Entrance to A Mirror," "Frontier," "History of Psychotherapy," "Looking for Jonathan," "The Monument of Resignation," from "The Summer Deaths: III," and "Totem" reprinted from **Looking for Jonathan** by Jon Anderson Copyright © 1968 by Jon Anderson, by permission of University of Pittsburgh Press. "Death's Only Son" and "Giving In" by permission of the author.

APLON, Roger, for "After a Lobster Dinner," "Three" and "The New Sound."

APPLEWHITE, James for "Steps From the Stream: IV and IX," "January," and "Tree in the Rain" and "Leaf Mirrors." "My Grandfather's Funeral" was first published in **Shenandoah** (Spring, 1966, Volume XVII, No. 3), reprinted by permission of **Shenandoah.** "Birthday, With Leaves" to appear in **Red Clay Reader** (No. 4), reprinted by permission of the author.

BARRAX, Gerald William, for "I Called Them Trees," "Second Dance Poem" and "Your Eyes Have Their Silence."

BELL, Marvin, for "Danger at Funny Junction," "The Growth," "The Perfection of Dentistry" and "The Address to the Parents." "An Afterward to my Father" first appeared in **Poetry** ⓒ 1968 by The Modern Poetry Association and is reprinted by permission of the editor of **Poetry.** "On Returning to Teach" first appeared in **Poetry** ⓒ 1967 by The Modern Poetry Association and is reprinted by permission of the editor of **Poetry.** "Verses Versus Verses" first appeared in **Poetry** ⓒ 1968 by The Modern Poetry Association and is reprinted by permission of the editor of **Poetry.** "The Delicate Bird Who Is Flying Up Our Asses," "The Giving In," "My Hate," "How I Came To Rule The World," "The Israeli Navy," "Things We Dreamt We Died For," and "The 3 Corners of Reality" appeared in **Things We Dreamt We Died For** ⓒ 1966 Marvin Bell, The Stonewall Press, Iowa City, Iowa, reprinted by permission of the author.

BENEDIKT, Michael, for "A Beloved Head," "The European Shoe," "The Eye" and "Joy." "Divine Love" is reprinted from **The Sixties (#10)** by permission of The Sixties Press. "Some Litanies" first appeared in **Poetry** ⓒ 1967 by The Modern Poetry Association and is reprinted by permission of the editor of **Poetry.** The poems will appear in **The Body** ⓒ Michael Benedikt, Wesleyan University Press.

BERKSON, Bill, for "East End," "Out There" and "Sura Baya." "Variation" appeared in **The Paris Review.**

BERRIGAN, Ted, "Tamourine Life" is reprinted from **Mother** by permission of Lewis MacAdams.

BLASING, Randy, for "A Book of Shells," "Dreams of the Accuser," "Oklahoma Plates," and "The Dynasties, The Sky Overhead."

BOND, Harold, for "Dreamside Bestiary," "The Glove," "Him: The Roach," and "The Menagerie." "Foibles I: HP" appeared originally in **North American Review.** "Foibles II: Acquaintances" and "Foibles III: The Game" originally appeared in **Fall River Review,** reprinted by permission of **Fall River Review.** "The Glove" has been accepted for publication by **The New Yorker.**

BROWNSTEIN, Michael for "Diamond" and "The Plains of Abraham." "Against the Grain" is reprinted from **Angel Hair 3** by permission of the editors.

CLARK, Tom, for "Sonnet," which appeared in **The World.** "The Lake: Coda" originally appeared in **Poetry** ⓒ 1967 by The Modern Poetry Association and is reprinted by permission of the editor of **Poetry.** "Stationery Motion" and "You (I)" originally appeared in **The Sand Burg** Copyright ⓒ 1966 by The Ferry Press, 177 Green Lane, London SE9, England.

COOLIDGE, Clark, for "Blue Kinds" and "Scrip Ant." "Styro" is reprinted from **Art and Literature (Number 12),** Paris, France by permission of the publisher.

COTT, Jonathan, for "Angels Adoring," his two "Untitled" poems (There Are Words," and "You are Lighting Yourself"), "He Spends Time in Southern California," "What is Going On Inside His Head," and "Foresaking the Course" is reprinted from **Angel Hair 3** by permission of the editors. "There Are Words" is reprinted from **Angel Hair 1** by permission of the editors.

ELMSLIE, Kenward. "Feathered Dancers" is reprinted from **Angel Hair** by permission of the editors. "Japanese City" first appeared in **The Paris Review.**

FRASER, Kathleen, for "A Child Drowns in the Sea of Its Own Imagining," "Song For A Man In Doubt," "Grass," "Poem In Which My Legs Are Accepted," "Reaching: Out Poem." These poems appeared in **Change of Address** ⓒ 1966 by Kathleen Fraser, Kayak Books, San Francisco, California. "Letters: To Barbara" and "Soundings" are published with the permission of the poet. "Change of Address" first appeared in **The New Yorker.**

GLÜCK, Louise, for "Cottonmouth Country," which originally appeared in **The New American Review #1**, and for "Early December in Croton-on-Hudson," "The Edge" and "The Inlet" which will appear in **Firstborn** published by New American Library. "The Edge" © 1967 by The Atlantic Monthly Company, Boston, Mass. is reprinted by permission. "The Inlet" is reprinted from **Madmoiselle** © 1967 by the Conde Nast Publications, Inc. by permission. To appear in **Firstborn** © 1968 by Louise Glück. Reprinted by permission of New American Library.

HASS, Robert, for "Adhesive: For Earlene," "Black Mountain, Los Altos," and "Letter to a Poet." "Book Buying in the Tenderloin" is reprinted by permission from **The Hudson Review**, Vol. XX, No. 4 (Winter 1967-68), Copyright © 1968 by The Hudson Review, Inc. "On the Coast Near Sausalito" is reprinted by permission from **The Hudson Review**, Vol. XX, No. 1 (Spring 1967), Copyright © 1967 by The Hudson Review, Inc.

HEY, Philip, for "Möbius," "The Poem that Tries to Be a Tree," "Popcorn," "Subject, with Apologies," "Supposition at 2 A.M." and "Window Painted Shut." "Lines Written in Objection, or the Limpopo Express" will be published in the anthology **Midland 2.**

HUNT, William, for "Autumn in the Plains," "The Dead Knock About," "Moving Along," "My Work With Snow," "So that Women Will Talk to Trees," "What You Can Get From the Body," and "Wintering in the Heartlands," "Song From the End of the Earth" appeared in **Big Table** Magazine and is reprinted by permission of Paul Carroll.

JOHNSON, Ronald, for "Three Paintings by Arthur Dove," which appeared in **A Line of Poetry, A Row of Trees** © 1964 by Ronald Johnson, The Nantahala Foundation, Jonathan Williams, publisher; and "Emanations," in **The Book of the Green Man** © 1967 by Ronald Johnson, W. W. Norton & Company, New York. "Letters to Walt Whitman" first appeared in **Poetry** © 1967 by The Modern Poetry Association and is reprinted by permission of the editor of **Poetry.**

KELLY, Robert, for "Thor's Thrush: Spel II, IV, VI, VII" and "Three Organ Rituals for Erik Satie" which appeared in **Twenty Poems of Robert Kelly** © 1967 by Robert Kelly, Matter Books. "Face in the Rock Wall," "The Moon Closes" and "Song XXVI" appeared in **Audit/Poetry.**

KNOTT, William, for "Goodbye," "Sleep," "Poem (After your death)," "Death," "Poem (Alright if I have to be famous)," "Karezzas, Cuntras, Cockturnes, Manshrieks, Carrioncries" "(Sergey) (Yesenin) Speaking (Isadora) (Duncan)," "Poem (When our hands are alone)," "[Untitled Poem]," "Song," "Poem (The beach holds)," "To American Poets," "Prosepoem," "Poem to Poetry," "Poem (I am one man)," "Poem (The only response)," "Poem (My sperm is lyre)," "Nuremburg, USA," "(November) (Light, Short Days) (Dark Fiery Sunsets)," which appeared in **The Naomi Poems, Book One: Corpse and Beans** © 1968 by William Knott, Follett Publishing Company, Chicago; and for "Late August to Early November," "I am the Stars' Bugging-Device," "Survival of the Fittest Groceries," and "Poem (It must be true)."

KOSTENLANEZ, Richard, for "Tribute to Henry Ford I," "Tribute to Henry Ford II" and "Tribute to Henry Ford III."

L'HEUREUX, Rev. John, S.J., for "A Bat in the Monastery," "Celebration," "Encounter," "Landscape" and "Three Awful Picnics." "The Concert" originally appeared in **Rubrics for a Revolution**, © 1967 and is reprinted by permission of The Macmillan Co.

LIPSITZ, Lou, for "For WGF . . ."; and for "The Pipes," "Drunk, Two Afternoons," "Skinny Poem," "I Am Thinking of Chicago," "Already Late," "A Way of Judging Politics," "For Kayak Magazine," "City Summer," "Fantasy for Those Who Hate Their Work," and "Thaw in the City," which appeared in **Cold Water** © 1961, 1963, 1964, 1965, 1966, 1967 by Lou Lipsitz, Wesleyan University Press.

MAC ADAMS, Lewis, for "After G. de Nerval," "The Clock Works," and "Meditation: What is a Stocking in Eternity." "The Ache" and "The Animals" originally appeared in **The World** (No. 4, June 1967) and are reprinted by permission of the publisher. "The Claes Oldenburg Story,"

STRAND, Mark, for "The Marriage" which originally appeared in **Partisan Review,** Vol. XXXV, No. 1 (Winter 1968). "The Dirty Hand" is reprinted from **The New York Review of Books** © 1967 by The New York Review, by permission. "Eating Poetry" is reprinted from **The New York Review of Books,** © 1967 by The New York Review, by permission of the editors. "The Man in Mirror" originally appeared in **The New Yorker** © 1967 and is reprinted by permission. "The Man in Tree" originally appeared in **The New Yorker** Magazine © 1967, and is reprinted by permission. "What to Think Of" originally appeared in **The New Yorker** © 1967 and is reprinted by permission. "Keeping Things Whole" originally appeared under the title "Reason for Moving" in the **Oberlin Quarterly** © Oberlin College, Oberlin, Ohio.

TATE, James, for "Plea Based on a Sentence . . ."; "The Destination," and "The Trust," "Coming Down Cleveland Avenue," "For Mother on Father's Day," "Why I will Not Get Out of Bed," "The Descent," "The Lost Pilot," "Intimations of an Autobiography," "Rescue," "Death on Columbus Day" and "Late Harvest" are reprinted by permission of Yale University Press from **The Lost Pilot** by James Tate, © 1967 by Yale University.

TORREGIAN, Sotère, for "The Age of Gold," "Eulogy for the Vain Hours," "On the Anniversary of the Death of Frank O'Hara," "Is It For This I Live?," "On the Death of Frank O'Hara," "Poem," and "Poem Written During Sleep."

TOWLE, Tony, for "For Irma During April," and "From the Spanish," which appeared in **After dinner we take a drive into the night,** Tibor de Nagy Gallery, New York; and for "Elegy," "14th Street" and "Enchantment."

The estate of VAN BUSKIRK, Alden, for "from Nightletter," "Kitchen," "Lami Poem," New Miles Poem" and "Tales: #14: (Not after but within this poem . . .)," all of which appeared in **LAMI** © 1965 by David Rattray, The Auherhan Society, San Francisco, California.

VAN NEWKIRK, Allen, for the three "Spring" poems from **A Spring for Scorpios** © 1968 Allen Van Newkirk, Island Press.

VINOGRAD, Julia, for "I Saw the Picture," "The Rising" and "Shorthand." "Untitled" is reprinted from **Choice #6** by permission of the editor, John Logan.

WAKOSKI, Diane, for "George Washington Absent from His Country," "Sometimes Even My Knees Smile," and "To Celebrate My Body." "Apparitions Are Not Singular Occurences," "Belly Dancer," "A Child, A Wasp, and an Apricot Tree" and "Follow that Stagecoach" originally appeared in **Discrepancies and Apparitions** © 1966 by Diane Wakoski, Doubleday & Company, Inc.

WALDMAN, Anne, for "About Face," "After Les Fleurs," originally published in **The Ant's Forefoot** © 1968, "For You" and "Sonnet for the Broken Windows."

WARSH, Lewis, for "Up There in Snow" which is reprinted from **Angel Hair 1** by permission of the editors. "Suicide Rates #9" is reprinted from **The Suicide Rates,** © Lewis Warsh, by permission of Toad Press. "Black Boundary" will appear in **Coyote's Journal** to be published by City Lights Books.

WELCH, James, for "Christmas Comes to Moccasin Flat" and "In My First Hard Springtime" which originally appeared in **Poetry Northwest;** and for "Blackfeet, Blood, and Piegan Hunters," "D-Y Bar," "Montana, Nothing Like Boston," "Spring for All Seasons," "Winter Indian," "Wolf Song, the Rain," and "The Wrath of Lester Lame Bull." "D-Y Bar" and "Spring for All Seasons" have been accepted for publication by **The Malahat Review.**

WHITE, R. T., for "Night Letter" and "O Please Read Backwards."

Every effort has been made to trace the owners of copyrighted material in this book. Should any material have been included inadvertently without the permission of the copyright owner acknowledgment will be made in any future edition.